VIRGO IN EXILE

Ave Virgo! G-r-r-r- You swine!
Browning

AUTOSVENOGRAPHY: Volume 2

By the same author

Alfred Wallis: Primitive. 1949. Nicholson and Watson, London.
I am Lazarus: A War Book. 1961. Galley Press, London.
Dark Monarch: A Portrait from Within. 1962. Galley Press, London.
Jonah's Dream: A Meditation on Fishing. 1964. Phoenix House,
Dromengro: Man of the Road. 1971. Collins, London.
    ISBN 0-00-211832-7
Pride of the Peacock: Evolution of an Artist. 1972. Collins, London.
    ISBN 0-00-211675-8
Amergin: Enigma of the Forest. 1978. David and Charles, Newton Abbott.
    ISBN 0-7153-7447-8
The Coat of Many Colours: Autosvenography (Vol. 1). 1994. Redcliffe Press, Bristol.
    ISBN 1-872971-08-3

Acknowledgements

The author and publishers gratefully acknowledge the assistance and contributions from the following. John Sansom *(of Redcliffe Press)* for reading through the entire manuscript and for his editorial advice, leaving all poetic statements alone for the final decision of the author. Vicky Tattle *(British Library)* for her research and other help. Ray Tattle for research and for some of the photographs. David and Tina Wilkinson *(The Book Gallery, St Ives)* for permission to photograph some of their stock and for other assistance. Irving Grose *(Belgrave Gallery, London)* for loan of photographs and other assistance. Toni Carver *(Editor, St. Ives Times Echo)*. Tommy Humfrey *(of Education Interactive, Stevenage)* for all the image digitising and editing. Sandra Santos-Costa *(Finishing Publications)* who typed the manuscript and Jan Anthony *(Pantile Publishing)* who typeset it. All photographs not otherwise marked are by Dopita. Last but not least, Sylvia who was in at the beginning and right at the end.

A.T.K.

SVEN BERLIN
VIRGO IN EXILE

Finishing Publications Limited,
Stevenage, Herts SG1 4BL, UK

First published in 1996
by:
Finishing Publications Limited, Stevenage, Herts SG1 4BL

© Sven Berlin

ISBN 0 904477-15-0

British Library Cataloguing in Publication Data
A catalogue record for this book is available from
the British Library.

All rights reserved. No part of this publication may be reproduced, stored in a retrieval system, or transmitted, in any form or by any means, electronic, mechanical, photocopying, recording or otherwise, without the prior permission of the publishers.

Typeset by:
Pantile Publishing,
Knebworth, Herts SG3 6AH

Printed by Redwood Books, Trowbridge, Wiltshire.

CONTENTS

Dedication vii
Salutation 8
Prophasis 9
Virgo in Luna 12

PART ONE: EXODUS

Outisde the Gates 15
Man of the Road 24
Eden Time 31
Metamorphosis 38

PART TWO: THE FOREST

The White Buck 51
Ghosts in Attendance 59
Ice Queen 70
Prospero: Magician 86
Prospero's Island 93

PART THREE: KINGS AND QUEENS

Dark Monarch 113
Madonna 123
Marriage 130
The Sacrifice 140
Fiery Furnace 144
Inverted World 151
Queen of Heaven 157
Pietá 166

CONTENTS *(Continued)*

PART FOUR: FLOATING WORLD

    The Forest Show 179
    The Creation 189
    The Reluctant Angel 197
    Lone Woman Moor 206
    Kaleidoscope 214
    Merry Tree 223
    Pharoah's Tomb 234
    Circe under the Clock 241

Inscription 256
Index 257
Appendix 1 261
Appendix 2 269

DEDICATION

TO THE ARTISTS OF ALL TIME

Don't exile the painters
Who use the Inner Eye
To find unknown places –
They can never die.

Don't ignore the singers
Who sing from the heart
The agony of love and grief
When man and woman part.

Or the poets, voices calling
From the mountains of the mind –
Do not destroy the poets
Or you kill mankind.

With sculptors and the music men
Who live by ear and eye;
They create our vision –
Art, the sacred lie.

Sven Berlin

Where there is no vision,
the people perish.

Ecclesiastes

Self-portrait. ca 1940 while living on North Cornish Coast

PART ONE

EXODUS

AIE WAS I ERE I SAW EIA
Sven Berlin

I made my way, once more a vagabond. Perhaps I had more than a touch of my distant ancestor whose garment I wore — the Coat of Many Colours — + would take with my children into exile.

SALUTATION

About all those whose names I have mentioned I have written: all those of whom I have not written I have not mentioned. In each case it is with love and not forgetfulness that I have or have not got their names right, and in no case have I dishonoured their memory by omitting them. A book about myself is about everyone by whom I am increased or diminished, and the answer to the equation is largely with the Gods.

In the vast wilderness of old age most things become clear and almost everything is remembered, but only a few emphatic personalities have really shaped the course of my life: of these I have written with deep devotion, unfathomable sadness or both. There are others who formed a moving echelon that protected me through all kinds of experience it was never expected destiny to have in store. And others who have been as pilot fish attending the ocean of my years, swimming in and out of the vast mouth of existence, knowing all the intimacies, ready to guide or clean away waste material, be constantly kind and even, like the remora, clamp on to my under side. They are a need and become close friends, but are equipped with a mechanism that enables them to suddenly abandon their range of knowing and simply vanish after years of trust with no explanation which is the one hurt they commit if they use it, as if it was their purpose to do so. The wound heals, leaving no scar, and when it comes to writing there is nothing to say as though guest and host had never met. Here there is no gap to fill except a vacuum in the heart.

Others finally who are forever unknown because they are lovable for what they are, like Annie Bright, Microcephalic Jacko, Rosie Smith selling snowdrops on a winter's day, and Black Fred searching for a shilling in the grass.

This time, instead of a list of players, I will leave it to the actors themselves: those who have appeared for a short while; those who stayed for a long time then disappeared into silence; those who waited in the wings and drifted across the stage as ghosts, those who cast a net and themselves got caught, or fired an arrow and missed. Those who loved and went away and those who stayed in the excoriating chains of love till death. All are saluted and each knows to whom I am speaking on a revolving stage where the procession has no end, even when the curtain falls.

PROPHASIS

In writing *Virgo* I suddenly found myself up against a wall I could only surmount like a climber, step by step: the implacable face of the future and aloneness where I had to make every inch on my own decision. There was no friendly wainscot to run through or warren to withdraw into: no group to give strength. But that aloneness was an invisible helmet against evil: I knew if I got it wrong I would die: thus turning each day into an equation whose answer would be evening. It was a unique experience.

As I moved away from the blue hills of Zennor Moor over St Ives I found each day's dying was an illumination which was changing me into tomorrow.

I had written about the gypsies before, but not about the deep Forest or not more than a thick red volume marked 'Merlin' and the story of Amergin both of which I had made over the years. These contained the spirit of the Forest: they were a grintern of jewels, from the night heron to the red fox; the piebald field mouse to the golden carp in its lakes. It was an entrance into a strange and beautiful land which I shall share with you and show you how these creatures were part of our lives, and the Forest people with their rough humour, humanity and quick minds were grown out of the trees and knew every deer slot in the mud. I who was vagrant, put on their green jacket of leaves and wore it as mine. I ate with them. I hunted with them. I painted them. All because I knew how to enter a closed community and obey the unwritten law of anonymity. And then, as if by magic, those who were with me or those outside who wanted to be with me, were drawn in also, quietly, through the trees to be with me.

So I met wonderful people, like Vaughan Williams who gave out humility; Mai Zetterling, who gave out light; Robert Graves, who gave out poetry; Henry Williamson, who knew the animals; Grant Watson who gave out wisdom; Augustus John who gave out personal genius and when it came to writing about them, in turn as friends – as though Rembrandt or Homer or Helen of Troy had turned up to tea – I entered a warmer, more universal world where art and literature were woven on a loom that was our lives and an interpretation of our experience at all levels of what we were doing and feeling, searching for – lovingly poured in bronze, formed in paint, caught in words, or sounds, cut in stone and came out of our hands, our eyes, our minds and our being – indeed our loving.

Although tragedy came and went, joy passed, love ended and began, the magic shuttles of our deliberate art were making something like extra-existence of every moment. The destiny of creatures were woven into our own. We were adding to the stature of man from a diadem of light.

So I have written 'Virgo' in this way: the search of one man for total vision containing in one continuum the slowly moving wonder of existence. In that way it is a prayer, through the miracle of the eye.

In every age this has happened. Happen also that I am Virgo: perhaps pointing to a slim layer of innocence the rough tongues have not licked away and which I use as a fragile shield against the hatred that is generated towards works of art and those who go their own way to create them.

'Gr-r-r- you swine! there goes my heart's abhorrence. . . .'

To turn and smile – no longer afraid – knowing truth is all: all is truth. Searching also through poetry, which is a kind of bone observatory fitted in the skull, as though the mind can look out of a quarter-slot door and not only watch the stars but what goes on in the deep nebulae of the psyche, recording a shooting star here over the death of Helen or a new sunrise at the return of Ulysses to Ithaca, and see that in love and war we are the same: that the golden helmet of tears still shields us and the spears defend in ordinary skirmishes with the man at the critic's turnstile or the foibles of a Swedish Ice Queen. Truth remains all. Love does not cease and it might well be that an aggregate of both are gathered by our deliberations into our art.

I am free from the circus ring of art performed for the cognoscenti. I move toward those adventures that are waiting for a man when he becomes invisible, but still at your side without knowing, having added one facet to the great crystal that turns in the universe as a virgin miracle of conscious existence, and is inherent in every moment of our most ordinary daily life.

SVEN BERLIN *DORSET, 1996*

OVER THE BALL OF IT,
PEERING AND PRYING,
HOW I SEE ALL OF IT,
LIFE THERE OUT LYING.
Browning: Pizgah's Sights

The way to study the past is not to confine oneself to mere knowledge but, through application of this knowledge (and experience) to give actuality to the past.
I Ching (Trans: Arthur Waley)

If you have writ your annuals true, 'tis there,
That, like an eagle in a dovecot, I
Flutter'd your Volscians in Corioli:
Alone I did it.
Coriolanus

VIRGO IN LUNA

Out of Virgo I was born, a male
At harvest time in orchards of delight:
Cock and hare and grinterns of magic corn
As love herself lay by me golden and pale —
And I'll never forget the flash of blinding light
As I came out from Paradise that night.
                                    Sven Berlin

Since then, at an uncertain hour,
That agony returns:
And till my ghastly tale is told
The heart within me burns.
                                    Coleridge

$

It is my belief that a man's work is the sun that lights his eye and transmutes its Beauty to our souls, adding a fraction to the stature of Man, and increased intensity to our vision of the universe, making him the antennae of the First Creator, spinning a silver thread unbroken from age to age, without which the human experiment would be extinguished.

It is the unique faculty of man & woman to be able to perform the act of art, and make illumination of the mind possible through poetry, painting and sculpture, which, in their essence are messengers of Creation and a profound need to our existance as useful humans.

I write of the struggle to do this.

SVSVBERLIN

Ralph Vaughan-Williams, OM. Drawn sitting on a chair in a field

Outside The City Gates

Looking across the bay to the blue hills and the houses sleeping below them, extinguishing their lights – St Eia, the Little Bethlehem, the Unholy City where my heart was still caught under a stone – as I made my way once more a vagabond with the poverty and pride that would try to extinguish my voice of oceans, I felt that I had more than a touch of that distant ancestor who broke the gates of ice and morality only to be murdered for his Coat of Many Colours, as I prepared to go into exile with my new wife and children.

I had stepped out of the eye of a historic hurricane as, like the huge planet earth and the universe above, it started to slow down. Now I must get used to each day's travelling and each night's dying under a different hill, covered only by the light of the stars, with no rearguard echelon and no money to hope for.

It was in this situation and state of mind I found myself. My cottage had been burnt out the winter before, as if to cauterise my soul for any sin I might have committed and to purge the soil on which I had stood, because I did not know that to stand for a main truth leaves one no feeling of victory, but an enormous collective guilt which appears as personal sin. The law of the hills that formed the backbone of the Dark Peninsula and exorcised the enemy within its people, had activated upon me. They did not like my new wife and I had to go, because one man threatened to throw her down a disused mineshaft, naming her a witch. From being one of them, I was now an outcast. All but one man they stayed in their houses when we left. It was the same experience as I had know in the milk factory in 1939 for being a pacifist. Ishtar was frightened by the experience, which happened when I was out, but she did not mind being called a witch, rather as Mai Zetterling, who became our friend later on, enjoyed being know as a white witch when she lived in the South of France. Nevertheless I was very distressed. I knew the dangers.

The Art Circle within this set of forces I have called the eye of the hurricane, now that it was formed into a tight society, would not accept a new intrusion from me, although it was going slow enough to take the hand rail and step on, as on a steam roundabout at the Corpus Christi Fair in Penzance, where the horses were painted bright colours and the change was collected later. If you let your animal take you it was not necessary to know how to ride a horse. In the new roundabout at St. Eia it was surprising to know how many changed horses almost over night. It was no longer a question of being sculptor or painter, but are you abstract or old fashioned? Like an advertisement where two women are using different cleaners on the same floor, causing a split, and bedevilled by all those who thought it avant-garde to join the new priesthood, which only those deep in their devotion to their own God or Goddess ignored.

Except among my friends, I was looked upon as a drunken helot and pointed out as an obsolete romantic always getting into fights, cutting huge boulders of stone into the night. Gifted rogue or strutting Samurai? In this way legends are built and become true because others believe them, because they see only the dark side of the moon when the whole planet – light and dark – is the truth. I was searching for a transparent crystal of totality rather than a specialised fragment discovered long ago by the Greeks. As in that crystal, every possible aspect of vision can be included, creating an aggregate of Truth and Beauty, Horror and Desolation.

Having paid allegiance to the Abstract, and indeed Classic, if terms of distinction must cling, through the horrors of being a Forward Observer in France, in the killing machine I had seen that people and things were the immediate keepers of human destiny carrying the onus of Good and Evil, and through them was the way to contribute to the law of creation and help to further evolution into the unknown which, for me anyway, called for my work to be a prayer where nothing else would do and could not be altered by the destructive beaks of my dissenters.

As I stood there in the lessening light I knew that the magic of St. Eia was paid for at the cost of every cobblestone being a monument to a broken spirit, every rock the shipwreck of a life. I knew also the inner law of the landscape and its people whom it protected, upon which the flying disc caused by a disturbance had now settled and overlapped, but not entirely obscured its secret life or blocked up its fogous. The starcrossed rocks of cromlech and quoit, so ancient and beautiful against the moon, would in time crack away this covering like plaster. The great institution to be built later smelt of ice – like the Titanic it would lose its magic and sink, slither into the sea unless it opened its beautiful structure to receive the widest and highest aspects of human vision and become a monument to the triumph of all great art of our time.

OUTSIDE THE CITY GATES

In my inmost centre there was a flame still burning which told me that my own link with the people of menhir and cromlech was not extinguished, and that I had to pay penance in exile: our love would endure.

'He is a Bohemian!' people would say, which I thought meant a man from Bohemia. But it was originally the name applied to gypsies when they first appeared in western Europe, in the belief that they were denizens of Bohemia or because they arrived in France by way of Bohemia in 1472 on their journey from northern India.

When they presented themselves at the gates of Paris they were not allowed to enter the city, but lodged at La Chapelle St. Denis as cagoux: unsociables, thieves, vagrants, gypsies.

There would not be any point in telling this were it not that I was now in exactly that position, outside the walls of society, shut out by the city gates. With it I experienced a new kind of loneliness, with my woman, my children, dog and my great horse, Atlas, who carried our world on his shoulders.

In some ways the lone artist who makes the complete break to achieve his way, which you had to in those days, always shares this 'mystique' with the gypsies, as my brother once called it. Because artists break down social orders which prohibit freedom, as they have done, the gates are closed against them, at least historically speaking. Today it is an art-orientated society and everyone is an artist, but you have to go with the masses controlled by the faceless Establishment who have the keys to the gates and still use them.

In the thirteenth century the gypsies could not get into the city and so the artists, like Jacques Callot and others, went out to draw and paint them, copy their dress, use their vitality and, as Lorca called it, the *Duende*, a Romany word which meant the Spirit of Life that rose up through the soles of their feet in their dance. And of course their music from which the great musicians have drawn.

These influences have continued in the cafés of Paris and Soho and in the artists' communities ever since, and come into our own day through English writers like George Borrow and Walter Starkie, painters like Augustus John, composers like Vaughan Williams. Each to his age. Picasso and Dali.

Workmanlike clothes are best when dealing with paint and stone because they are workmanlike occupations and their substances stain. A red handkerchief is only what the old workmen carried their lunch in, but put on a seaman's hat with them and you are a raging giant hurling stones at Odysseus.

Thus I found myself outside the watery gates of the bay looking back at the unforgettable and much loved place of which I had so lately been the centre, feeling for the first time what it was like to be an exile and the haunting vacuum in the heart it gave. Although I was born in England of an English mother, I can now say: 'I have been a stranger in a strange land', because I did not know before that once the gates were closed against you there is a sheath of silence which surrounds you and within this you live apart from others.

I called this my Exodus because in a way it was a calling forth, but there was no pillar of cloud by day or pillar of fire by night – only the sunset and the light burning under the heart: nor Promised Land before us. We were cut off to walk the face of the earth in which direction we chose – with no rights and no money.

In today's society this might seem incomprehensible, with the many sources of help from Government grants and State pensions: they did not apply. Nor friends nor men of mercy: simply the stars in their courses and the alternation of day and night. But once faced and understood, fear gave up its tenancy and, like the inverse light in a negative, we were free in a curious way that brings its own delight.

This is quite different to playing at gypsies and all the claptrap that goes with it. I had a few pound notes from the sale of my 1924 Morris motor car or was it the sale of a mermaid? I cannot remember.

Most of this has been written about in my book: *Dromengro: Man of the Road*. It would be pointless to repeat in depth, but to follow the new experience of being outside society will be of interest, because this book is about the evolution of an artist. To an artist every new event is a new experience, he finally is the interpreter of the spirit of that experience: and it should be important for everyone. When I found that being on the road was such a consuming occupation that it was not possible to paint or cut stone, I was thankful for my habit of writing which had been a secret devotion all my life.

I was standing on Hayle Towans opposite St. Eia, with its sand dunes and couch grass and a few wooden huts, sweeping round the shore to Gwithian where the Red River emptied itself into the bay, from the golden valley in which I had first drawn dragonflies by taking them by hand from the air while their great wings and huge motor muscles thundered in my ears; my image recorded in thousand-lensed eyes. I stooped to pick up a smooth transparent scapula of a rabbit while I was thinking about this: the sand was full of them, with skeletons of fish and a few fossils reminding me that each individual life had added to the shape and order that evolved into the next, down aeons of time. With a few naked trees it might have been the place where the coelocanth had returned to the sea after rejecting a short experiment on land. Or where the archaeopteryx had left the sea to become a kind of lizard and grown feathers the colours of a sunset because that is the first thing it saw, and started to climb trees with its articulating hand at the end of the ulnar and radius, just like my own – and then to fly. How miraculous that must always be! If only the lumbering Sunderland flying boat I saw land in the Isles of Scilly with John Wells could have been seen by Da Vinci or Daedalus!

Such thoughts had not been possible in the busy roundabout of St. Eia, where the pubs took so much of our time and the girls beguiled us. The rest was art: art was something else. I didn't know what it was till much later, because there it was a collective psyche that floated between us and ideas were not altogether our own, and if a new vision came uppermost it was sucked dry by the others and became the property of whoever got it down first and showed the incestuous creation as their own. I escaped from this by drawing a dolphin's skull, a fish skeleton, a rock formation, an insect or frog or wave formation, which was nothing to do with the quarrelling communities, particularly in winter, who talked a strange language of the intellect and who were often ambitious, ruthless and unkind. The light as it faded was kind: they were unkind. But out here the universe was vast and wise and beautiful as though I was in the presence of a friend, and as a great green grasshopper leaped on to my hand, my loneliness began to go away.

The children had gone to bed early after a long and exciting day. Ishtar was seeing to the horses, that they were tethered safely and had water, near a good patch of grazing at the back of the Towans. The sea rushed in to the mouth of the Hayle river, where the difficult ferryman held his dominion of tides and would not accept anybody he did not like on his boat, which he rowed in a curve from one side to the other.

A friend told me recently of this man. He had a seal which he trained to swim with his boat to and fro across the estuary. One day a man with a gun crossed to shoot rabbits on Hayle Towans. He shot the seal. The old man rose up in a great rage and struck him with his oar splitting his head open. 'E killed 'en, said my friend.

'Did he get away with it?'

'Yes no-one knew. Let 'em float out to sea on the tide.'

Then he went to the pub, which, strangely, I no longer had any wish to do. I got down under the waggon and like a wild creature made my form in the sand and fell asleep, watching the moon rise over the vast savannah of the Atlantic ocean.

Had I known about my ancestor, David Abraham Brody, at that time it might have been thought I was imitating him when he fled from Germany in 1771, through Schleswig Holstein with a white ass and crossed at Helsinger from Denmark to Halsingborg in south Sweden, where the channel is frozen over in winter. He must have rested thus by his animal, perhaps in straw from a shore-side cattle shed with his Talmud and a flask of wine, not knowing his destiny: the first illegal Jewish immigrant into Sweden, who converted to Christianity and named himself Johan Christian Berlin and married a Swedish woman, so giving himself her nationality.

There are many similarities between the gypsies and the Jews, which finally led many thousands of each race to the horrors of Auschwitz when the Satanic Prince of Evil, Hitler, was in power. Although I had the Brody stamp, left also on his progeny who became Christian pastors, deans, archbishops, soldiers, explorers, professors, engineers for 200 years, I am neither Jew nor gypsy but I have an affinity with both races, and carry the persecution of both. Augustus John said one day, when he was painting the gypsy Cliff Lee, 'There are only two lives worth living: that of a gypsy or that of a gentleman, and I don't know which I am!' Well, what does it matter. He was an artist, which is classless. The last of the great portrait painters. The best draughtsman of his time. There was no artist called Berlin till I came along.

I had met Augustus in Mousehole through the painter Adrian Ryan. His magic remained with me and was one reason I was going to the New Forest. Another reason was that I had passed through the Forest as a young man on my way walking to Bournemouth to see a girl, who ditched me when I got there, so I walked back to London. But in the Forest I saw a gypsy girl who haunted my dreams. The Dark Anima, The Black Madonna who counter-balanced my soul with the Ice Queen, whom I was also to know. Perhaps the first was Ishtar: who can tell!

Juanita, whom I called Ishtar had become my second wife as soon as I was free to remarry, in spite of opposition from her foster parents, who lived in Bournemouth, where she wanted to return. She claimed to be a gypsy and looked like one: even the gypsies thought that. I don't know if she was a gypsy: I never thought so. What made it difficult to tell was that she had been educated at a school in Lymington and spoke like a lady most of the time, but changed her voice when she was with gypsies or swore appallingly when she chose. She dressed like a gypsy and had long Prussian Blue hair like an Indian woman. I called her Ishtar because she was like the Cretan goddess of that name whom she much admired. She most likely had Indian blood. I don't think she was sired by a Spanish bullfighter and an Irish tinker woman brought up by a Saanan goat, which was the biographical material she gave Donald Zec when he wrote an article on her in Cornwall for one of the colour magazines of that time.

I had nothing against this. It was like an actress who thinks she is Ophelia and drowns herself: simply a fixation. But it was embarrassing and I refused to be in the article. I once asked her family solicitor many years later, because we had a beautiful and gifted son between us and I wanted to know. 'She says she is a gypsy. Is that true?'

The solicitor said: 'Best not to know, Sven. I should leave it alone!'

So I did. After all, it does not matter, except to our son. All we know of Homer is that he was born by a river called the Meles, in Boeotia to a natural mother — the rest is mystery which 3000 years has not lifted. If there is knowledge of this perhaps she prefers to keep it to herself. That is her privilege: if not, her sadness.

The threat to her safety scared us, just as the same threat scared me, and must have scared D.H. Lawrence and Frieda, during the First War. The Cornish are still primitive and very direct people: this ancient law is their protection. They do not ask if they can activate. If you press the trigger it will activate itself: in this case possibly by sexual jealousy on their part, that came out in her horsemanship, which was both attractive and brilliant. She also knew about horses. They came to her, they fell in love with her. I found it unique but difficult to be jealous of a horse. There was no way of dealing with that except to try and become one yourself, which I endeavoured to do by being a good horseman, but I was too afraid because they know more than we do. Perhaps this taught me how to draw them and is the reason why Ishtar could draw them so much better. She *was* a horse.

OUTSIDE THE CITY GATES

Like a king I was given a white horse I called Virgo and rode him full stretch gallop along the Wharf at St. Ives trying to catch Ishtar who rode her high-stepper Giorgio like the wind up Island Road out of sight. On one occasion we rode across the peninsula to Sennen to see Denys and Jess Val Baker and stay the night talking and drinking, and rode back the next day, the AA man holding up the traffic at Penzance to let us gallop through. This was all part of the life of the hills, which cannot be relived or found again anywhere. The place of granite where a man of stone can find his own fogou and cut his way into his own destiny. When you cut elsewhere you cut out of your skull: when you cut there you cut out of the caves of the universe. This is what I let go.

The family solicitor, whom I was to consult a decade later, was sent down at this point when they heard Ishtar was living with me and, after he had reported back, the old man came down: a rude, difficult and very ill person. He refused my hand so I went out and played with Paul, son from my first marriage, who was over for his weekly visit, until the old father climbed into his Daimler and was driven away. He had delivered an ultimatum. Either Ishtar left me and came back to Bournemouth with him or he would cut her out of his will. Half a million pounds. I said that I did not want that kind of money and would leave myself at once.

'There is no need,' she said 'I am here, aren't I?' I took this as a sign of trust. She, like myself, had decided to stay outside.

Ishtar had bought the cottage in the hills at Cripplesease when we moved from the tower on the Island at St. Ives and for the first time ever I felt safe in that I had a mooring which no one could take away. I had turned the cowshed into a workshop with the help of a poet who had a builder's licence, named Keith Baines, who seemed to live on black coffee and very little else. Together we dug out the old dung which was breast high and put on a new roof, fixed a bench and doors. With a yard outside there could be no better place to work. There was a small granite quarry at the bottom of the village where I got a stone, and a blacksmith, Bill Wright, halfway there, who tempered my chisels. To complete my need, John Craze, my one-eyed friend from St. Ives who had shown me how to drill and cut granite by hand, came up and directed me in shaping a stone to contain a mother and child. More like Charon, more like a God, tough and green in his old age.

Then one night when we were out the cottage was burnt down.

OUTSIDE THE CITY GATES

My stepson was in there and was rescued by a friend. I was in time to rescue the goldfish, waist-high in water. There was an enquiry because the boy was alone which was wrong, but there was no further trouble. We rebuilt but the spirit of life had gone and we too had to leave. With our last money we bought a waggon and a horse and I became *Dromengro: Man of the Road* – outside the city gates.

Man of the Road

By arrangement with my first wife, Helga, who remained in Cornwall, my son Paul and my daughter Janet, were with us: both beautiful and sensitive creatures who were very excited by the adventure on which they had asked to come, but who stayed within their secret cocoon of privacy as a protection. I had been away at war for the first part of their childhood and since then had separated from my wife, so they did not know me that well. Ishtar was good with them but also new. Jasper, like a holy child, was asleep in the waggon most of the time.

There was a boxer dog, hideous like Caliban. The great horse Atlas was cast on the first day by the beautiful tantrums of highstepper, Giorgio, being used as trace horse – to which job he was alien – and started rearing on his hind legs, making Atlas back and jack-knife the waggon and fall on Gwithian Hill. Probably he was also showing off to Ishtar with whom he was in love. My main concern was to rescue Jasper from inside the waggon in case it went over. I handed him to Ishtar and then gently climbed up the heap of the fallen monster who waited with patience and trust; held down by the harness and waggon he was immovable. He seemed to be under the spell of my low chanting as I did this: 'Careful, my darling! Stay quiet, my beautiful! Don't be afraid! I will set 'ee free!' until I got to the strap holding the collar and harness. It was then that I blessed the power of a sculptor's hand and the balance of a dancer's body. With one hard effort I pulled the strap against the horse's weight of two tons. It did not break but unlatched as I had hoped. As the harness fell away I shouted to Atlas: 'Hup, my beauty!' He reared to his feet with only a gash on his knee, as I leapt away.

We had spent the summer getting ready for the journey: painting the waggon, having the harness made by Mr Nichols of Penzance, fixing a toolbox underneath and a vice on the footboard in front to use as a work bench; a ship's stove inside and bunks for sleeping. Everything was in top condition. Only one thing was missing. I had no experience of horses in harness, except from working on the fields fifteen years before. This one incident made me realise how vulnerable I was and how an emergency could take place like a flash of lightning. I was relieved that I had dealt with it successfully by spontaneous laws, while Ishtar looked on, holding Jasper and the rein of a restless Giorgio. The two children sat in a trap driving the flea-bitten pony called Sixpence. It had not made me into Dromengro: not for a long time would it do so.

The incident also prevented us from going a greater distance. We had started early and taken the back road under Trencrom having to leave the goats, an old English Billy and a Saanan nanny, with a friendly neighbour, at Halsetown as we passed, saying we would send for them later. Then Lelant, where we had a minor repair by the blacksmith, round Hayle Causeway on to the Towans where we stopped the night, mostly in meditation, and had hoped to get to Redruth or even Truro by the next evening, but were forced to stop. A man named Mr Manchester, who I never saw again, towed the waggon to the top of Gwithian Hill beyond Hell's Mouth to the moorland where we settled for the night still within view of the blue hills of St. Ives. A country very familiar to me. I had lived there and worked on the fields before the war. It was there I started my great quest of learning to draw. Here, down the road, Helga and I had gone five days without food in a snow blizzard. Here I had been kidded to jump into a pit of lime, nearly losing my eyesight and lungs. Here I saw a man burn out a horse by putting a flaming gorse bush under his belly. From here I had had my first one-man show at Camborne in 1939.

It was as though a stone wall of history had been suddenly built across my way: something I had not expected. I knew if we went this way to avoid Camborne Hill and the town, we would have to pass the cottage, but had hoped to be far away by evening, had not things gone wrong.

To the right were the same fields on which I had worked, running back to Tehidy Woods and the home of the Lords of Bassett; to the left and north the great arc of the Atlantic Ocean; between the two the strip of moorland, some of which had been reclaimed, running to the cliff edge and a 300ft drop, where the horses were tethered quietly grazing.

I don't know what happened to me. My stomach and bowels were burning, my head on fire. The horses started to get restless and it was as though something terrible was about to happen, as though my presence had awoken lost souls from the lower circles of Hell's Mouth.

MAN OF THE ROAD

At this point a young man appeared whom I recognised as the son of the Cornishman and his wife, Mabel, who were my great friends: now grown up and named Bert like his father.

'Mother an feyther want 'ee to come down 'ome tonight for a bite!' he said as though I had never left. I said I would but did not know what to do, and asked if the same farmer was still there. 'Ayse – would 'ee like to see 'en?'

'No I don't think so, I'll be down later!' I said, and he went.

As evening came on the horses became more restless and I more distressed – beginning to vomit.

This was the land of the Cornish peasant as I had known and worked with him, using horse-drawn plough, steam thresher, horse drawn cornbinder, hand scythe, horse rake, dung skating by hand and Cornish spade. I knew them in the heart like a root mangold in the same earth; shared their hardship while drawing their faces; men, women and creatures working together. We knew and trusted one another, because there was no need to pretend about things, put on a front: they knew instinctively what I was like and took me as I was: even then, surprised, I stood up to the hard life. There was no room for fraud or evil people: they would go over the cliff. Through them I knew the fishing community and later did my research on Alfred Wallis who was of them, though a Devonian. I fought in France as one of them. It was in this way – working on the fields for 21 shillings a week for a 13 hour day, both here and on the moors over St. Ives, I got to know the Cornish people of cromlech and quoit in their centuries' old battle to survive. I learned also to know of a profound presence in those dark moors, ancient rocks, tall cliffs facing the ocean like primitive sculptures. It was the soul of place, and of the people in that place, behind the facade of art that had been superimposed. It was that presence I feared I had awakened.

The sudden impact of these conflicting emotions was affecting the horses more. They were charging to the end of their tethers and stopping suddenly. It was like being of one psyche of which I was the conscious point. I called to Ishtar who was in the waggon preparing a meal, saying the horses were upset. 'They'll be all right!' was all she said.

'Anyway you won't want that meal, whatever it is. The've asked us to eat down the road!'

'Oh, you go. They're your friends. I'll stay here. Someone has to look to the horses. You can't, you don't know enough!' She looked at me.

'You all right?'

'Yes why?' 'You look awful!' She went on with the meal. 'Paul was saying he felt queasy. Perhaps you've picked up something. Probably the stew last night. I've given the rest to the dog. If you take my advice I should get your head down. We've a tough day tomorrow.'

I turned on the steps of the waggon as I heard neighing. The great battlehorse, Atlas, was charging towards the sea. I ran towards him at an angle. When he saw me he seemed to be aware of danger and turned, rearing against the sky like an early Chirico painting of Horses by the Sea.

After this, Ishtar came out and the creatures became quiet, almost as though she was activating them. Giorgio, who was jealous of the giant Atlas because Ishtar had stroked and talked to him after he had been cast, had kicked the bigger horse in the chest like another man and Atlas had broken tether. They settled.

'You'd better go to bed!' she said to me, 'or we won't be able to leave tomorrow. Look, I've packed a small bottle of brandy in the tool box under the waggon just in case. Have a swig and get your head down.' I obeyed like a small boy.

It was not that I was ill, but that the soul of the place held a force which I activated − I don't know whether good or evil − and I was helpless to control it. As I let go consciousness it awakened all sorts of deeper terrors.

Since being here last I had been to war as forward observer. It was my job to go forward in front of the infantry between two great armies with three others in a small carrier with tracks. Our journeys took us through minefields, sniper and shellfire. I suppose because now I was travelling through wild country where I had suffered great hardship, my defences fell away and let the nightmare out of her stable. My head was on fire and I saw the young labourer put the flaming bush under the belly of the farm horse to force it out of the mud, screaming as it reared up in the shafts, until I struck the man; but I was myself caught in coils of barbed wire in a shellburst area, struggling upside-down to be free. Finally I woke, Ishtar leaning over me. 'You all right?'

'Yes, I must have been dreaming!'

'The horses are restless again. I've just quietened them − we nearly lost the big horse over the cliff. I don't like this place. Let's get away early.'

'What's the time?' I asked. 'About four, it will be first light in an hour.'

I slept for that hour realising I had not been to see my friends who would have been waiting. Probably made pasties and all.

There was something about this happening I did not understand.

Did I really want to go into that world, even for a moment, where I had found the most true people I had ever met, and live again in the stark austerity of their history and present myself as a traveller with a gypsy wife who spoke with a Girton accent? Would they have accepted me or felt the same if I seemed to be dishonest? They knew my son Paul, but the history in between they did not know: except that communities like this have a better network of information than ours. The crack was in the pitcher of my soul – not theirs. I had let them down and even now, after 40 years, I still feel the disgrace of it.

When you are a travelling man there is no time for anything else. From the moment of getting up, lighting a fire and cooking a meal after seeing to the creatures; carrying water, cleaning and fitting harness, packing the waggon, seeing that the brakes and shoe work properly; gear on the rack roped down, toolbox, buckets, corn bags safe under the waggon; site left clean, fires out, kids OK; pony and trap in good order. It's a long job. Everything must be there and work well or, like going forward in war, it might cost a life.

We tied Giorgio to the back of the waggon and the children followed in the trap. I usually joined them later, leaving Ishtar to handle the big horse in front, giving safety watch and overall control from both ends; especially at the back, because cars were constantly swinging in between the trap and the waggon when they couldn't get past it, not caring it was living creatures they were endangering.

Starting a cortège like this was a momentous thing. To see the great horse lean forward in his harness to take the strain on the shoulders inside the collar, the chains and traces tighten as his huge back muscles and legs pressed his whole weight forward, directing his power into the morning. Everything seemed suspended for a moment before the horse and waggon moved forward and momentum was gained with gathering velocity. Once this had happened there must be no stopping. Ishtar held Atlas by the bridle and I stood on the foot-board holding the reins. We moved over the rough moorland to the road toward the cottage where I once lived and nearly died. Mabel had heard us and was standing at the door of her cottage with shining red face and strong arms, trying to talk to us. 'Can't stop, Mabel!' I shouted. 'I was ill last night, where's Bert?'

'He's gone to work – we waited for you!' 'Yes, I'm sorry, I'll write and tell you what happened.'

She looked perplexed and distressed when I did not stop, but it would have been very difficult with a slope on the metalled road. As we moved slowly forward and our voices ceased to carry – I waved, but she stood with her arm lifted and her other hand holding her black hair back in complete disappointment. I wrote later to explain. The letter was returned: 'Not known'. Some things happen for which we can never forgive ourselves. This was one of them, for which I carry my shame for all time. Ishtar was not affected: she did not know them. The children did not understand.

I don't think I realised what was happening – that as I was entering exile, I was exiling myself as well as being exiled.

This was my last link with the Cornish people and it was broken at the exact place where I had come in 1938 to work on the land and link up with Arthur Hambly to learn to draw at Redruth and to attend Dr. Turk's lectures on philosophy, psychology, biology, oriental art, literature and the English poets.

The blue hills of Zennor – as they receded a little after each day's journey – and the lights of St. Ives reminded me of my journey into art and the strange new Priesthood of Abstract Painting and Construction which overtook me so surprisingly, but which I passed through with some ease and delight – as when a child, I passed through the wonder of the Crystal Palace and the excitement of drawing great cantilever bridges at the School of Engineering where I passed out as a mechanical draughtsman. Most of all, and much closer, those hills recalled that almost anonymous little magician who was of the people of the fields and fishing boats: about him I had written my first book, *Alfred Wallis* and the great adventure of the second world war, like going to some historic opera that lasted four years, and then, by some enantiodromic process I could not understand, turned into the hurricane of creative activity at the centre of which I found myself in St. Ives.

All this was quite a definite process, but whether pre-ordained I could not tell. I begin to think that destiny is conditioned by what we do as much as by our doing things because they must happen. It is a two-way system like the wheels in a clock engaging before the point of strike and the knack of getting it right is very much the spontaneous instinct of timing. If the cuckoo appears at the right moment: that is the creative act. Whether or not, this moment spelt my name on the way to an unknown answer.

I did not know if my art had failed and I would be extinguished by the forces I had set in motion. I did not care. What concerned me was getting this waggon from one point to another like part of an ancient caravan journeying to old Cathay.

MAN OF THE ROAD

In this, if things are hereditary — and it seems they might be — I was doing the same as my Swedish cousin, Sven Hedin, hero of my childhood, who by crossing the Gobi Desert gave me the idea that if I could not be an explorer like him, I could at least explore the hidden deserts of the mind — and that is one of the things I have perhaps done best — as well as those vast savannahs of the eye seen by a dragonfly and the haunting caverns where the last mermaid lives, with the Muraena eel.

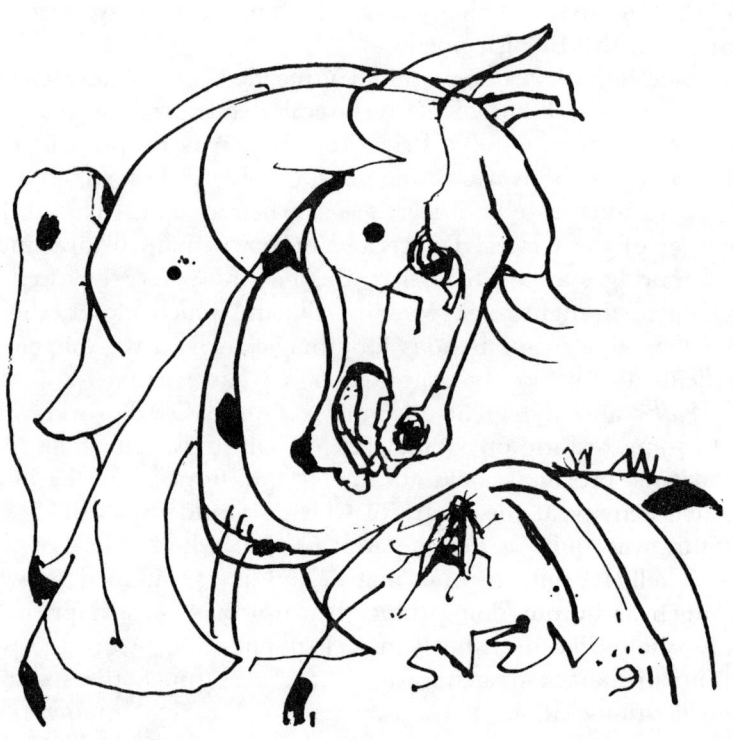

Eden Time

Travelling by horse and waggon is a matter of living at four miles an hour and the whole structure of life is changed. The first thing is that you can look into the hedges and fields as though they are under a microscope. You see what is happening and the creatures living their secret lives, for in the hedges there still lived a civilisation several millions of years old, now fighting a rearguard action against machines used to trim the hedges and make them look tidy by snatching out the branches with steel fingers – often destroying the living creature at the same time – and another machine that, like a preying mantis, tears out the whole hedge as though it were a butterfly and kills the rest.

My journey was in time to see hedges with their castles, minarets, domes and citadels still intact; the worst shock being perhaps a badger, like a huge brown stone, that had been hit by a passing car in the night and crawled to safety, only to die of its injuries; or a hare with its back ripped open showing the great vertebrae by which it leaps; perhaps a human fragment thrown from Bacon's abattoir truck, for art is also the vision of death.

It also strikes the mind how masterful the spider is with its conning tower of eyes and jenny in its belly to spin silken ropes and swing like a mountaineer from pinnacle to ridge and build a mandala in the sky as beautiful as the Clifton Bridge: hold a butterfly, like a lost soul tumbling the fields, till a swallow takes the spider and lets beauty free. The corn still held its minute harvest mice in their golden turrets and grasshoppers leapt across the rim of the sun, burning with fire. My eye held each image to emerge years later from my sleeping hand.

All this was a great comfort. I had found familiar friends still living out their lives as they had done down the ages and in the quiet lanes of childhood where one could still hear the orchestras of insects playing their symphonies beyond the sprays of death. The Delius curlew in the fields at dusk played the cor anglais and copulating doves in the wood a duet on the French horn. Here there was no evil – and better bread.

In the estuaries we saw the heron with his glistening feathers stalking the maverick bass in gullies of muddy water between reed and couch grass. A cormorant, like a Japanese diver, almost choked trying to swallow backward a flat Picasso-eyed flounder that forced his fin-spines into the lining of his throat until his assassin had no choice but to let him go.

Other things on the road disturbed us quite a lot and we had to stop. The carcass of a dog fox without its brush: cut off by the driver that killed him. There is no sign you see:

> A FOX IS PASSING:
> HERE WALKS THE HEDGEHOG – TAKE
> CARE STOP. NATTERJACK TOAD
> CROSSING. BADGER – RIGHT OF WAY.
> THEY CONSTITUTE THE INSPIRATION
> OF THE FIRST CREATOR. DON'T KILL
> THEM.

Either way they constitute my history so much that this hand that writes is wing-claw to a pterodactyl as he flies in the first sunset; this brain that defends him is the nomad jellyfish floating in the seas of prehistory; this eye that sees is God the Octopus.

As the days passed the whole world opened up for us with its beautiful performance, behind the age of man, still continuing. We watched the swans on their Pegasus wings whispering over the fields, avoiding the electric pylons in their flight-path, and how their long necks complete their headless meal-times, working with violet skin-diver's feet. We knew the swan carried an image of death in the Swans of Tuonela, with the haunting music of Sibelius and the grace of Pavlova. We knew that a God had changed into a swan to sire Helen and let fall her beauty on our eyes. Always beside physical truth there is also poetic truth which sees into the human psyche and helps us to understand the total meaning of life. When invisibility is conquered they will be seen as one. Eden Time is for evolution to catch up.

So it was that our journey showed us the secret lives of the creatures who had not yet learnt to talk or create beyond their own image: who live in their private cities keeping our histories alive – and the mind became sanctuary to greater excellence.

The thing it did for me was to confirm the structure of all life. When it came to drawing I knew where I was going because they carry the same life-force. When my imagination sparked, it created out of this foundation within the crucible of the original material of which I was an evolutionary speck.

It was the same with the heavens which I wore like a planetarium on my head, almost hearing the Holstian silence. I found that I could see the constellations as though I was a Greek sailor steering his ship by the stars – even though I carried an oar inland. The vastness of it all seemed to be at last the same as the human and non-human mind, in which I was conceived and understood. A man walking through the universe from nowhere to nowhere but, like a glow-worm, carried a tiny point of light.

I no longer needed a Priesthood of Art, which seemed to be beautiful in a cold, pitiless manner. Nor to wear the vestments of the priest who made it, but who disconnected from the original fountainhead, excluding the great female spirit in the act of creation and depending on the intellectual, negative, homosexual process which was dry and void of mystery. And with this realisation it was possible to go on alone outside the spinning disc I had left behind, hovering over St. Eia, which was already beginning to wobble.

There was a good deal of difficulty and excitement each day, such as meeting two dealers whom we knew and were following our progress to get Giorgio, which they finally achieved by chopping him for a proper trace horse, or one which was said to be, while the beautiful high stepper went off into a stranger's care. But the new horse, a very primitive, Celtic grey animal with a long back, was no good either as a tracer. I had to give my whole manhood to master him on a hill to avoid tragedy. I called him Satan. It was not till Bodmin moor on my birthday that the dealer with half an ear missing, and his mate turned up in the rain with a gentle piebald mare, a map of India on her thigh: perfect in every way at tracing and later pulling the ralli. Great! But with a secret love for all God's creatures I watched Satan go on his ugly way, carrying the evil of his previous owners. We called the new horse Asia and she stayed with us. My book *Dromengro* tells more. So enough! 'What's so tedious as a twice told tale?' as Homer put it so succinctly. I give you the smell of a horse reeking in the rain and the sight of her breath in the lights of the dealer's car. That is all.

We got to Charmouth, a little beyond the tunnel, and found grazing at the top of the hill. Leaving the waggon on the wide verge we descended on foot into the little town, on to the beach, where the cliffs were built of laminations of blue lias, holding a great library of stone books carrying fossils of past history and the beaches were equally exciting with their museum show cases. As the incoming tide covered the stone slabs carrying fossils of birds, fish, ammonites and plants, seen through the water as through clear glass, we wondered at the mystery of it all. We could look along the coast to Lyme Regis hanging on the cliffs like a cluster of molluscs in a westerly direction and to the east, Portland, like a great golden eagle hovering over the ocean. It was a magical place and the children were ecstatic gathering their treasures straight from God's great hand.

I did not then know – for fate had only dealt me this card once before – that this place was to become a special magnet in my life. I had come here when I was a young man in pursuit of a young dancer. She was staying with her brother who was a wing commander in the Royal Air Force, but when I saw her in the sunshine standing against the ocean I walked away. I struck a rock and found an ammonite, complete with the original enamel from its shell. It was beautiful, unique. I did not know what to do.

'Supposing it had been a portrait of yourself, what then?' she said, smiling with her blue eyes. I knew I could not draw a portrait of myself and felt awkward.

'I could not do that!'

'Then you should, an artist must be able to draw everything.'

'I will do that!' I said quite seriously. 'I will draw the whole of creation!'

After that I did not want to stay, go to her brother's place, be in a party. I had no money and the clothes I wore all I had. There was a burning need to go away and be with her equally. I turned and walked home.

'See you in London?' she called, I turned and waved sadly, then did not look round in case she saw that I was crying.

Here I was now at the same spot where I had not been since then, twenty years before. How could I have even guessed about the future, nearly twenty years ahead? But it was here – held in the rock as surely as the beautiful enamelled ammonite had been – that another young woman of the same age, a direct relation of Mary Anning who found the first ichthyosaurus, and a direct descendant of Alfred Wallis's wife from Beer near Seaton on the other side of Lyme, would be my third wife.

As this extraordinary pattern began to click into place I said nothing to Ishtar, who was with me now.

I had married the young dancer when I got back to London and she later became Janet and Paul's mother who came with me and went through the appalling hardships on the North Cliffs when I was trying to become a painter and working on the fields.

'I wish I could break a stone and find a fish,' I shouted.

'I found one once,' Ishtar shouted back, 'but they are rare! Think of that old country woman finding the first one. Have you seen it? It's huge. It's in the Natural History Museum in London. Gavin de Beer looks after it. 'MY FISH' he calls it. But it isn't: it's Mary Anning's fish!'

I knew Gavin because he used to come to Cornwall often and bought small carvings and drawings from me. A dynamic little man with a red face and white hair who loved to drink with the artists. His wife was a gentle lady who looked just like the Queen Mother and used to paint quite courageous pictures. The threads were beginning to show, even to tighten at this point. It was Gavin who told me not to forget to go to Lyme or Charmouth to look for fossils if we got that far on our journey. Here we were between the two.

As the long afternoon dissolved into the September evening and the sun started to move towards the ocean, we collected our trowels and hammer and fossils together, feeling tired and burnt, looking like any human group of an early tribe walking along the long beach, Ishtar carrying Jasper, until we got to the stone steps at the base of the sea wall. I climbed it first and looked up near the top to find Helga, the children's mother, standing above me: arms akimbo, her dancer's feet turned outwards.

It was a shock, but I felt no anger. Nor had she come in anger. I had made proper arrangements for the children when they had asked to come with me. I was perhaps surprised that she agreed, but when she did, I did not question it. It had proved a right decision. They were loving it as a unique experience in childhood. Her face was set. I knew she had come to take them back.

'You've come to take the children?'

'Yes.' I agreed at once because she had custody and anyway it is wrong to quarrel about children, especially when they are present. I told them. 'Your mother wants to take you back to Cornwall!' They were both silent. I could only suppose that friends of hers had unsettled her after they had left. 'Fancy letting them go like that and him with that gypsy woman. Nothing but a witch if you ask me. You won't see them again and that's for sure!'

I heard that sort of conversation in my head because Helga was a woman of her word and I could not understand it. But I have learnt since that she was under pressure for not returning them to school. It was September time and I had thought they would be with me till we got to the Forest, and then go back as arranged. There was nothing vindictive in her mission, but there was an urgency because she had taken a taxi all the way from Cornwall. They climbed into the back seat without any fuss, their dear little faces started to cry as they were driven away, waving sadly through the window.

When they had gone I turned away and spewed my gralloch into the sea.

Ishtar was quiet and it was that quietness I needed to climb the hill in Charmouth to the waggon. There was an old man who was doing a cut-and-lay job on the hedge, whom we had called the Natterjack Toad because of the warts on his face.

'They stopped and went in!' he said, as if he knew what had happened, and nodding to the waggon. 'The boy that was!' – then went on packing up his tools and said good night. Inside the waggon Paul had left the money he had saved, with a note to say that was all he had. It was about thirty shillings.

We slept a little and got the horses from the field early, paid the farmer, and after hitching-up, made our way slowly down Charmouth Hill and the long climb over the next hill which was Chideock towards Bridport. It was only perhaps five miles but it was so difficult that it took us all day till nearly dark, when we swung off up a lane to the right that took us to Eype, where we were able to make camp.

I could not speak for a long time, as though I had been kicked in the throat. Thankfully Jasper, who was Ishtar's child, was still with us, asleep in the waggon.

We tethered the horses on the hill above us, had an early meal and got our heads down, emotionally and physically spent. But that night a gang of local country boys came with their guns and long dogs to go lamping. To do this two of them had car batteries on their backs with headlamps fixed over their heads. When they switched on, the whole area was lit up on the rabbits and hares grazing. The long dogs went in and slaughtered them while those that got away to the perimeter were shot by the guns as they ran to safety.

This of course frightened the horses. They reared, broke tether, thundered down the hill, past us, on to the main road into the night traffic, running full stretch gallop back towards Cornwall.

To catch them needed both of us, which meant leaving Jasper alone. Not to catch meant being immobile, in certain trouble with the police and perhaps a horse being killed. The decision was instant. Out on the road we could see them threading in and out of the traffic as in a dream, but it was not till we got to the top of Chideock that we saw them quite close, huddled in a field gateway looking frightened.

'Come, my Beauty! come my Lover!' Ishtar slipped a halter over the head of each and we took them gently with mind and hand into custody and they came quietly, thankful to be under control, and led them back through the traffic unharmed. I stayed under the waggon all night on watch.

Realising I had no money when I woke, I got out my tools and by using the footboard on the waggon as a bench, where I had thought of fixing a vice before we left, I was able to set myself to carve an ivory tusk, from a bag slung under the waggon containing small pieces of wood and stone also. It was a mother and child, which I had been commissioned to do by a lady in Cornwall during the summer. I would post it to her. But first I took off the front wheels of the waggon after jacking it up safely, so that the police could not move us on for a few days. Legitimate breakdown!

Ishtar had a beautiful silk shawl with coloured flowers embroidered on it, which she took round the houses, begging from door to door, and came back with some money. I finished the little carving and posted it to Cornwall with a message to send the £15 on to the *Poste Restante* at Lyndhurst in the New Forest. We went shopping and a gust of wind snatched our last £1 note away: we sat in the trap watching it go. Thus we moved on the last leg of our journey and arrived in the Forest penniless.

Metamorphosis

The whole journey was filled with incident, sudden emotion, grief at an unexpected happening, or joy at suddenly seeing one's children as part of evolution, so that the mind was jarred and shuddered as a result, until it became part of human change and – it was seen as such – a metamorphosis into something else, as Chuang Tzu put it after dreaming he was a butterfly.

The shape of the journey and the performance of it were not haphazard, nor were they calculated, but they were controlled by an homologous law of inner and outer worlds that caused progress in the same way as the nymph changes into a dragonfly in the heat of the sun. I felt that if any one thing was changed by reason the performance would not have come off.

It is difficult to make clear what I mean by this, because I have had to use the book I wrote twenty years ago as a map, pinning certain incidents on it in order to explain my exile and how it altered me, rather than repeat what happened to me. But to show as an evolving insect how I was changed inside my Man. This also causes shunting of events to other sidings.

I remember Lawrence Durrell telling me how difficult it was to write about things over again in the *Alexandrian Quartet*: how difficult it was to describe the same oasis of palm trees four times. His was an invented story which probably gave him greater freedom: mine is the recurrence of an episode, as though I wrote the book before I made the journey. But since the journey started with my exile I am bound to follow it, even if no Angel of Fire has appeared to direct.

My book, now thrown away like a stone tablet that described that part of my life, can tell how I changed into a dragonfly – no longer living at the nymph stage on the riverbed and being ambushed by the vicious lesser life around me. But feeling my back crack open as I push the early casing away, the hot blood pumping into the exo-arteries of my wings, as they dry and go hard ready to take my first solo flight, watched by the golden coaches of the sun.

At a village called Bridestowe, just a little way this side the Tamar into Devon, I found a letter waiting from a man I had met in Cornwall. Grant Watson had written many books, the best being on transformation, and was living near – Barnstaple – I was just below

Okehampton. He wanted me to alter course and head north to join him. He had field and accommodation at Ox's Cross, Georgeham. He was eager. His neighbour was Henry Williamson, whom I admired from *Tarka The Otter*, and would have given much to meet him.

One thing about being a Travelling Man is that you are also a lonely man and when you do meet up with others of vagrant choice, it is good to talk and drink. But in the end they too are outside the city gates and like yourself are outcasts which, joined to one's loneliness, is a deep sense of inferiority, of being a creature lower than Quasimodo, to be kicked around and persecuted one way or another, even though it might be only in the court of one's own soul, where judge and jury sit in implacable judgement, and pass sentence. This is very harmful and difficult to deal with, for the sentence is often a kick in the heart.

The other side of this feeling of complete spiritual and intellectual isolation, to balance the scales of the psyche exactly and stop going mad, was to find a way of filling the need to talk to a man of vision. I went to a place alone and sat on a stone, recalling conversations with Adrian Stokes who told me stories of D.H. Lawrence and how he suddenly died at St. Paul de Vence. Norman Douglas, the novelist, had taken him some peaches when he was in bed and started to put them in an empty bowl on the side for Lawrence to take from. Lawrence sat up in bed very disturbed:

'No, don't do that Norman. If you put them there Frieda will come in the room and see them. She will take one and bite it with her beautiful white teeth and I shall fall back dead.'

'Nonsense, Lorenzo!' As Norman Douglas said this Frieda came into the room, saw the peaches and exclaimed. "Ah Lorenzo, what lovely great peaches." She took one and bit it with her beautiful white teeth and Lawrence fell back dead.'

When Adrian had finished this tale, he went on painting my portrait with that curious smile that was part of his charm and natural elegance, and I asked him if it was true.

'As far as I know it is, Sven. Norman Douglas told me the story because I had sent him to find Lawrence and see how he was and then come back to tell me in Italy. Which he did. Mind you he was a terrible liar, most novelists are, but he came and that is what he said.' 'Anyway,' he added after a pause, 'it's very symbolic, even if it isn't true!'

I thought of this unusual and elegant story about the death of a great writer, who was a son of a drunken miner, as a natural compensation to my need, being as I was dressed in rough clothes, an overgrown vagabond penniless and down at heel, and was uplifted.

When I am faced with an important request that will change my life, yet is made to please someone else, I get down into myself and wait till the water is clear and still and I can see the answer written on the surface, or spoken in the silence by my reflection. This time the answer was NO, in spite of my need to see men of culture and it caused great disappointment to my friends, Grant Watson and Henry Williamson though the latter I had not met. I was to do so later through Denys Val Baker.

The current practice is to write books by committee and even make personal decisions in groups, or opinions about those books, which are never properly read. It takes the full man to go to a place of stone and decide what to do with his own life according to the inner voice which knows, one step ahead, what destiny intends. Long ago he has broken the fear barrier: he knows what to do. There is nothing more the Establishment can take, for he has nothing to give but his own integrity in this matter, which is unique. The call in this case was from friends who had already worked out their lives: I had not, and I thought it would deflect me from my purpose in getting to the Forest, where both Ishtar and I had need to go. When two people are together, they are a syzygy for that time. As in Cornwall, when I said 'No!' at the Tower door and another friend came to give me help, I now said 'No!' to my friends at Georgeham, even though it caused us to pass through many frightening experiences, such as my son, Jasper, coming near to death from advanced enteritis when we reached the Forest and were cut off by snow that winter.

This was one of the most terrible things I had experienced, far worse than war, because this enemy was invisible and had advanced when we were working the horses without our knowing and it was impossible to tell how far. I got a doctor by cutting through brambles in a snow-drift, but he passed it off as 'flu, saying to get his partner if matters got any worse. This gave me a feeling of root uncertainty as night came on and I knew I must face it without flinching. I had a strange pain down the centre of my back and felt again as though the splitting of the hard chitinous casing of youth that still held me from manhood has cracked open in the heat of the moment and I must save my son. I could not contemplate his death as sacrifice for progress or for not changing my direction – even for not going with the crowd in Eia in the first place:

AIE WAS I ERE I SAW EIA

My first children had been snatched as an osprey takes a fish before me, back to the dark Peninsula: was it now that my other son was to be taken?

I went into the wood and dug under the snow till my fingers bled for turpentine wedges of pinewood left by the axeman and filled a hessian sack, feeling a great white presence round me in the silence of the trees – except for Ishtar keening over her child and giving him salt in the waggon, which stood like a wooden horse with one eye alight in the Forest, watching the distant flare-off at Fawley Refinery.

I was alone, but I knew I was being watched by the gypsies who are the shadow life of the Forest whom no one sees. I walked to the main road north of our wood to see a man who sold coal and carried a hundredweight sack two miles, watched by the gypsies who lit a fire at the bus stop waiting for the bus that would not come, warming their hands and talking about the giant on the horizon against the winter sky, carrying coal. As I fought through brambled snowdrift, as I wept alone, as I scattered the deer and wild ponies in my track, as I reached the waggon and the door opened – a man in a lounge suit appeared: a live magician in the Forest. It was a young doctor whose name was Baird for whom I had phoned at the coalman's house before I left. He had responded like Ariel to Prospero and come at once.

'It's all right' he said. 'Your son will live. The balance of the salt has corrected itself in the body! He should have gone to hospital but it was too difficult and cold to move him. His mother has done it for us. He's a bit thin, but he will be OK!'

Ishtar had sat with her son for two days and nights giving salt and water every two minutes and singing her gypsy song to him: this saved his life. I went in to see for myself and Jasper, with his little coat of skin hanging loose about him, smiled at me.

I felt like Jarius when he thought his daughter had died and another young magician had made her rise from the dead. This had meaning for me. The threads had been true and the direction of my journey had been right, even to paying the coalman with the money waiting at *Poste Restante*, Lyndhurst, in payment for the Little Madonna in ivory carved in the Dorset hills and sent back to Cornwall two weeks before.

The gypsies called me *Dromengro: Man of the Road*. I wore a tall black hat given me by Luvvie Cooper, and an old fashioned green cord coat bought at a second-hand shop in Southampton for a few shillings. I wore it as I wore the Forest, like a jacket, and it fitted exactly as though the trees had put their green arms about me after the initiation by death. I looked more like a gypsy than the gypsies themselves, but they did not mind. They accepted Ishtar as one of themselves, but me because I was a friend of *Sir Gustus* and would do no harm. And I started to paint them.

When I was in Southampton searching for the jacket and some leather jackboots, I came upon an art shop in the Northam Road run by Alan Musselwhite and a young painter named Peter Jackson. When I told them my name they knew me from earlier St. Ives days when my work would have travelled as part of the Arts Council exhibitions. This in itself was a relief for the obscure traveller. I told them I was broke but they gave me credit for paints and brushes until I was on my feet, which proved to be quicker than I thought, but no one knew that. They became friends. Such events, more than anything else, made it possible to reconstruct my life within, which was to be so different from the past. I was to learn to take the image before me and transmute it direct into the created image of the mind, no matter how excoriating it was to do so. For this I chose the gypsies.

This was my new life, in a green cathedral of trees, out of which the dark inhabitants would appear at my side like ghosts. Ishtar decorated the gypsy waggons with horses and I fitted windows and stoves, for a few pounds, refusing the occasional favours of some, in lieu, when they were attractive but *lubanie*,[*] which was not always an easy decision, and one I have always preferred not to take, in any walk of life: a personal rule. And I painted their portraits in the flowing underlight of liquid verdigris moving in the Forest, sorting *roozlums*,[*] and sitting by their open fires which linked their centuries.

We hunted together, kept vigil with their dead, and defended them live when the keepers and police intruded. A lost legion which

---

[*] *Lubanie*: Romany word for prostitute. *Roozlums*: Romany word for flowers.

had somehow slipped through the net of the law that trawled the years, and remained themselves: the first Asian immigrants to Britain in the thirteenth century: vagabonds and magicians of the human race, who preferred not to be told what to do; said to be thieves and liars who had one word that made me understand them: The word is *tacho*, which means *true*. If you were *tacho*, they would die for you: at least not let you starve. But staying alive was your problem; as for them it was theirs.

During this time we did a television programme with Brian Vesey-Fitzgerald, a very knowledgeable countryman who had written *The Gypsies of Britain*. But the programme had been produced from Swansea because it was about Welsh gypsies and Augustus John, being Welsh, was supposed to be there too, but forgot and went to London instead. The point is we had to go there and stay the night and when we went into the lodgings arranged there was a tall man with a dark face, a clean white collar and suit and black hair with a cast in his left eye.

'BBC?' I said hesitantly.

'No', he replied in a North of England accent, 'Cliff Lee!'

He was with an older man, who was Manfri Wood of the famous Gypsy Wood family who first came to England in the fourteenth-century and from whom John Samson had garnered the rich language for his great Romany Dictionary.

'I saw you in my dream!' said Manfri when we met and shook hands. I gave him a small bottle of brandy. His face lit up as he slipped it in his pocket 'Tatto pani!'* he said smiling. 'Kushti!'

That is how I got to know Cliff Lee, who was a friend of Augustus and was painted by him on two occasions when he stayed in the fields round Fryern Court each summer. Where once I took Mai Zetterling, and her husband David to spend an evening round Clifford's fire. Another gypsy, of the Locke family upset a swarm of bees and ran round the field screaming until the whisky overcame him and he fell in a hedge and slept the rest of the evening. Cliff was also visited by Dominic and Beshlie, another two travellers, but Augustus wrote a note to say he was unable to come down as other friends were calling at the house at the same time. Later on, when Augustus died, Cliff and his family came to stay with me. As a result of one of those miraculous happenings that do occur in this life if

---

* *Tatto Pani*: Romany word for Spirit Water: in this case brandy.

you leave things alone and let them work themselves, I had suddenly changed from a Man of the Road to a Man of Substance, and we became fast friends, for, with a gypsy as with an artist, there is no class; Cliff was as proud of his roots going back into the Wood family as I was of mine in Sweden and England. When the Forest gypsies first saw him in the pub they were over-awed, for he had a certain nobility and grace with his long Indian and strongly cut head.

'I am the Blood Royal!' he used to say when they asked who he was, and were honoured to drink with him. And somehow for me this was true aristocracy, even as he went off each morning to go knifegrinding and 'totting'* in Southampton. I painted him and his son Ken many times, before Ken passed through Liverpool University with honours. I only regret I did not extend this and paint Greta and Angela, Cliff's daughters and Sheila from Ireland, his devoted and long-serving wife, with tawny hair and blue eyes, but not related to the Irish travellers. From outside it seemed she submitted to his Eastern domination but knew enough craft through womanhood and through love and patience, to get her way. They were a devoted couple.

When Cliff died, Sheila phoned me from Liverpool and I sent *Roses for a Wild Man*, which she placed at the head of the coffin when they kept vigil after he was brought home before burial.

She wrote:

Sven. I think you more than anyone would like to know the details. If a man could have arranged his own funeral, Clifford's every wish was granted. He *was* buried under a hedge and is in a lovely small churchyard, not in the main one, which he says is water-logged in winter, dressed in his best suit with a pure silk handkerchief on his neck, horse-handled stick in his hand and the magnificent wide-brimmed hat Ken brought him from Australia (meant to wear at Appleby Fair). Our musical granddaughter composed the music they played in the church. He would have been proud of that!! . . . we shared some lovely places to live, including your field at Emery Downs, and now I have got a beautiful place to rest when I join him. What more can a partner want!

---

* Totting: collecting rags and scrap.

METAMORPHOSIS

PS. Don't think I'm being morbid, Sven, but the 'wild man' bit brought my mind back to the time you and Clifford visited the RAI'S* resting place, and you were both disappointed.

When I wrote recently to ask Sheila permission to quote from this letter she wrote back. 'Although they took Cliff's 'body' out of this house, I feel he is close by us telling us what to do. The answer is yes Sven, we are pleased.'

After this, Cliff and Sheila with the two girls came every year, to stay with me, Ken the son bringing with him his school pal named, I think, Owen. I gave the two boys a painting to share: I have often wondered who has it now, Ken living in Australia as a university lecturer. They came to my daughter's wedding and, a year later, to my wedding with Julie in 1963 when she was only 19 and I 52. So I had all the families from both sides spreading over Devon, Yorkshire, Wales, Ireland and Sweden as well as the wandering tribe from India to bless us and bind us together. That was a jewel in the lotus and it worked.

Sheila, in referring to the Rai's resting place was remembering the day I drove Cliff to Fordingbridge to look for Augustus's grave – for we both loved him. Cliff always called him the Rai which means Gypsy Gentleman, or Great Lord in the Romany language which John himself could speak fluently. 'Better than we can!' Cliff used to say. We went to several churches and searched their leafy graveyards, but found him finally in a field, a kind of allotment for the dead, among councillors and shopkeepers as though he had never been a Prince among Men. Cliff was electrified as he stood holding a rose he had torn from the hedge:

'This is the first time I have seen you take a back seat, Old Rai!' he said talking to Augustus as though he was there and tears falling down his long dark gypsy face: 'Here's a wild rose from a wild man!' He threw the rose on the grave and turned away. Later that day I wrote this:

> I would care to see
> A tall chestnut tree
> Over thy grave and thee.
> I would desire
> A consuming autumn fire

---

* Rai: Romany word for Gypsy Gentleman, in this case Augustus John.

METAMORPHOSIS

Burn over thy quiet grave, Sire:

With candles pink and white
And green fishbone leaves unite
To shed a more gentle light
Than this bleak place,
This mediocre space
Where no tree shades thy frail face.

I would choose to see a tall tree
As monument to thee touching the sky.

The field at Emery Down, mentioned by Sheila Lee in her letter, was part of a property I was to own, after being vagrant for so long: which proved, if nothing else, that within the calyx of every plant exists the flower and fruit and seed of the future.

After we had first arrived in the Forest and Jasper was so ill, we stayed in the deep forest, till the following year, living a perfectly balanced life of simplicity that yielded a stillness of soul, harmony and equilibrium I have not equalled, taking our water from silent puddles at dawn and gathering wood as the nightjar made his ghostly purr and flew soundlessly away at our approach. I was a crack shot: I killed to live. Within the very strict law of the creatures' world we made our bargain with life, having faced the white tiger and seen him turn away.

But for some reason that I could never divine, Ishtar sent for the goats we had left in Cornwall, instead of arranging to sell them or give them away, which I wanted. She insisted: the bit was between her teeth; they came by train and were tethered in the Forest. The reaction was immediate. We had orders to go from the Forestry Commission, even though they had tolerated me defending the gypsies. They knew Augustus came to see me, and as a weapon I mentioned Lord Radnor, who was Head of the Forest, and a friend of Augustus. 'Goats – No!' They would bark the trees, as indeed they had started already to do. I had read somewhere that the Sahara was at one time fertile forest that was barked by the goats until it eroded. If this was true there was a deep racial fear of this happening here, perhaps, even though deer barked the trees in winter. Nothing would shift them, and it was after all, a good legal weapon to hoick us out of it. They refused to renew our permit and after a week had passed, in which the yawning void of homelessness opened before us, they sent a Keeper with a strong-arm man to tell us to go. They were tough countrymen: I did not resist, nor wished to, though I wanted to stay. I asked for another week and they agreed. Then we must be gone.

During this time there was a dealer named Brixy Veal who had helped us in various ways, who wanted to keep us about because he was after the horses, but it was a man named Stan Peckham — the first man we had talked to when we entered the Forest — who found the answer. Through him we found a field belonging to a kind countrywoman; she was called Edie Gailor and ran a smallholding on her own, and here we rented a field for 10 shillings a week, where we moved the waggon and horses. This was a great relief because only the week before the horses had broken tether and run north as far as Downton and we had a long walk. Some gypsies returned them eventually and I gave them my last money.

In this field we gradually put up huts and a tent round the waggon until in the course of time, with the help of Benny Wells the gypsy, we had built a tiny city of our own, with apple blossom, rhododendron, cherry blossom each in their time to garland our days. And here I set up a tarpaulin over the ralli and started to paint from drawings I had made in the Forest and among the gypsies at Shave Green. Here also was the beginning of having a stable home. Friends started to call — among them Augustus John, with a present of Canadian whisky, Vaughan Williams with a crate of Tollemache beer, Sir Gavin de Beer with a bottle of rum, Bryan Wynter, Vesey-Fitzgerald, Guido Morris, Val Baker with his wife Jess, Froshaug and many others. Robert Graves sent his son, Juan to recover from an eye operation and my children joined us again from Cornwall. It was here that Guido Morris met his son for the first time and gave him a Hebrew Dictionary.

We had found the place where the magic stone was hidden. But it wasn't all by chance. One day I had a card from Anthony Brode who was working on the *Southern Echo*. Could he come up with a photographer and do an article. I wrote back 'Great! this is my last stop to eternity!' They came in an Aston car with long overcoats and trilby hats, looking like thirties gangsters. Graham Finlayson took photos and Tony Brode asked the questions. There was a great friendliness and when they had gone, I felt that after my expulsion from Paradise, I had been given my place as a living artist in the consciousness of society. My magic returned, as with Ishtar, and I am sure that is why so many people of rare grace started to call, for, whatever the detractors say, there is a steady flow of Beautiful People who are a little taller, with a magic touch, who are magicians and create a thin golden thread that goes from age to age and because of them is unbroken. Should this not be so I believe the human experiment would gradually come to an end.

One morning, after we had been in the Green City for two years, Ishtar came running up the field, her Prussian Blue hair like a mare's mane in the wind and a letter in her hand. 'I'm rich! I'm rich!' she shouted. 'My uncle has died and left me some money!' For me it was like a death knell.

For a week we were completely stunned and went on with our primitive life, fearing, I suppose, the news would take away what we had so secretly found. Then we bought an old Morris van and ordered a chalet which I set up on a foundation of bricks I laid myself – a 30 foot long job with a verandah. When it was finished I lit the Courtier stove I had installed and there was an explosion. Red coals thrown all over the wooden interior: pine at that. We reacted at once and each took a shovel and I lifted each separate coal outside without combustion taking place: a miracle complete. Edie's well was over a hundred yards away. How or why it happened I can't tell. A nodule of dynamite from the coal mine? Or from a Cornish tin mine among my things? Was it sabotage? Or simply the ghost of the field who thought we had gone too far? I shall never know.

The field became a Little Paradise. I continued to sleep outside, listening to a society of fourteen nightingales in the wood, interspersed with a cuckoo with a cracked voice, dreaming perhaps of ancient times no different to now as we spun round the universe in the same way. The long painful metamorphosis was complete.

PART TWO

THE FOREST

This is the forest primeval.
Longfellow

Do you know what I wanted to
chisel into the back face of the stone?
"Cri de Merlin!" For what the stone
expressed reminded me of Merlin's
life in the forest after he had
vanished from the world. Men still
hear his cries but cannot understand
or interpret them.

Carl Jung

Vain Merlin
Lonely Stone
Sven Berlin.

W.S. Graham

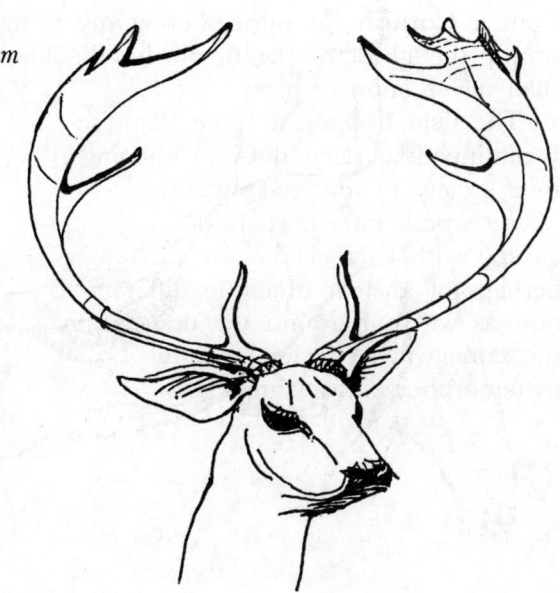

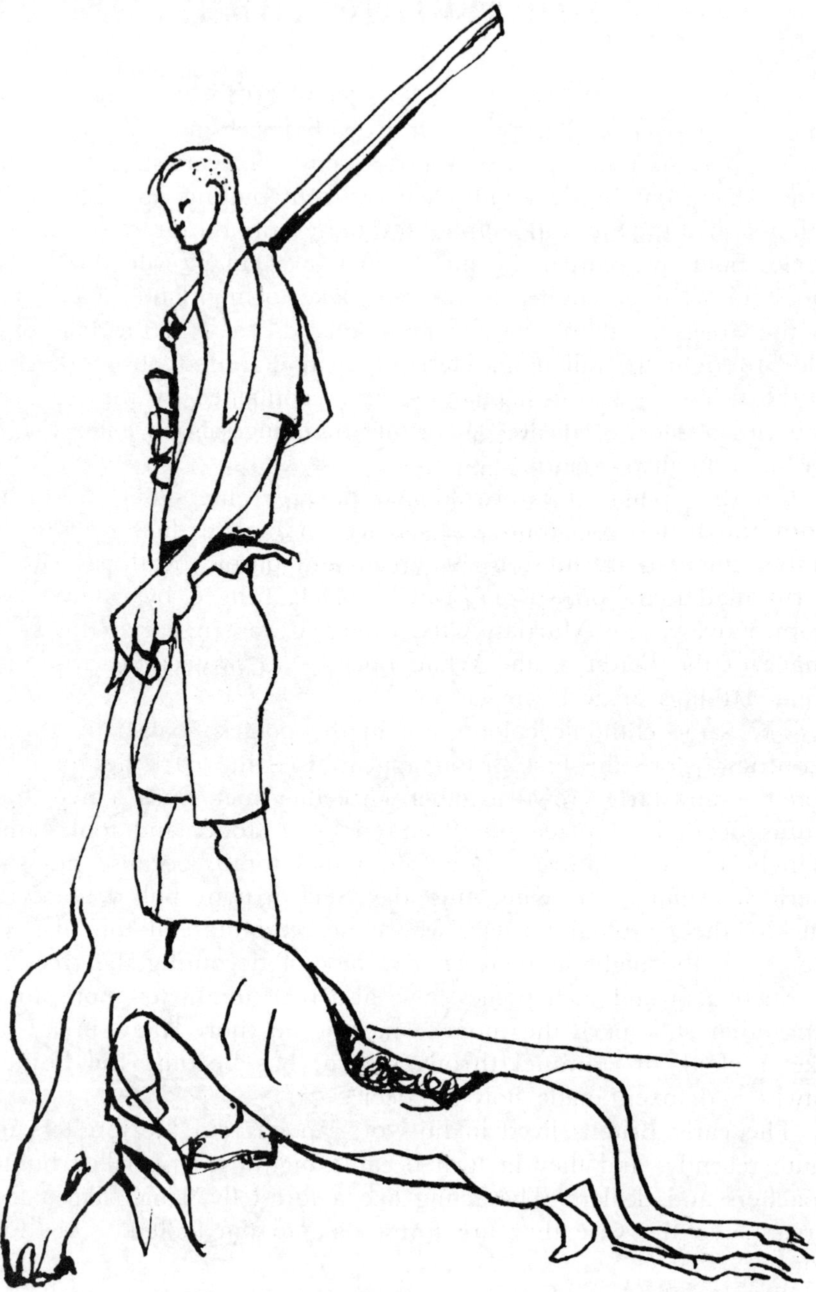

The White Buck

The Forest does not sleep: life and death never quite catch up with each other, so there is everywhere a sense of everlastingness. There is a silence that remains unbroken by trout putting up circles in the still waters; time casting circles of bones on remote moors; stone circles built by man in the mind's first awakening; wild duck scissor the spiral silences, cutting curves from lake to moorland and fly south to the Solent — almost itself a great inland sea with the hills of the Isle of Wight to wall it in. Here many rivers empty from the heart of the forest, as in the Camargue; are recontained by the sea at the estuaries of life and death, where the migrating salmon enter England for their mighty orgasm.

On the open moor the oldness of earth enters one, as distinct from the feeling of stone and its demanding hardness, gentle and umber intervals intrude on the green and purple heath: at autumn, burnt mad mare brown and Devil's black, fringed by catalyst flares from Fawley, the Martian City where I was to carve the sacred image of the Forest — the White Buck — to protect the wisdom of created things against science.

The same chthonic colours are in the ponies, soaked up through centuries before the first Briton appeared — the dark hunter of the Forest — and have grown together since they met. Such a man found Rufus dead, in a place now marked by a stone, and took him to Winchester to be buried in an unnamed tomb, because he was a sacrificial killing. The King must die! Such a pony pulled the cart of Purkiss the charcoal burner, whose descendants still toil like glow worms in the night at their endless task of devouring the trees.

Such men and such ponies have also built tombs for more ancient kings that still mark the moor, which is no more than spread land like a cloak of stammel thrown down; has become the home of hawks and foxes, made holy by deer.

The early Britons lived in huts of clam, as did the foresters until quite recently, and they in turn became highwaymen, skilled hunters, poachers and dealers. They sting like a forest fly, laugh like a forest stream. To the wise they are forest oak: to the fool they are forest bog.

The north of the Forest is a strange desolation Nomansland, still holding a few potteries, which is about all the use the Romans had for it.

The west grows grander for poet or painter over Fritham Moor where I watched the emerald horses and red deer grazing on time's long hill in dark parks of thunder: a stallion neck of land sweeping back to Fordingbridge and the ghost of Augustus John.

South awaits the ghost of Nelson visiting Bucklers Hard to see his ships built of Forest oak. East, King Rufus at Malwood, and north again beyond the desolation, the ghost of Constable staying at Wellow to paint the Grey Lady — Salisbury Cathedral.

These are the cardinal poetic points of the Forest, whether we seek them in words or stone, or less successfully in paint: best and most difficult, direct in ink, a Forest boy riding bareback on his Forest pony in absolute harmony with natural laws — far more beautiful than the awkward performances of the nouveaux riches.

Wild apple tossing like snow in May is another poem; moonlight spilling in branches of mercury; the white buck leading his herd across Marrowbone Moor — each are of poetic instance.

Benny Wells, the last gypsy, dancing for his beer; the secret channels where the sea trout pass to the gravel beds; the soil where fallow deer come to drink to an oration of owls, badger grunt, vixen bark — all these things are the soul of the Forest and help to compose the collective ghost; even the spirit of Merlin caught in the thorn bush sounding his cry; all are an overtone, an extra-sensory Presence, awakened first in the slime of primeval bogs where it still drags its saurian tail.

The Forest is an archive of evolution, a place of natural sacrifice in which we know the forces that control the anatomy of existence are preserved: most valuable, the machinery of life and death in its original condition, working perfectly if left alone. Those who are sacrificed later hold the knife.

The extra-head of our time is as dangerous to natural survival as was the long tooth of the sabre-toothed tiger. It will kill the Forest. How do we know that the Spirit has not already turned away with the last gypsy?

> The fool sees not the same tree
> As the wise man sees.

On a misty dawn the deer drift like the swimming reindeer of

Lascaux and it is only a tick of time that an inter-glacial memory clicks back the woolly rhinoceros, the mammoth with his domed head and the great elk: even the original tapir and wild boar. Another click back and the pterodactyl would come to poach the king perch, the Sargasso eel, the Goliath frog, instead of the monastic heron doing so. At dawn the sun roots the trees as fierce as a golden pig, and a wolf trots home with a young fawn in his jaw, over the lawns of peace in summer, and the frozen lake in winter. Nothing breaks the silences until Spring with a nightful of nightingales and a cracked cuckoo bell.

One click forward – death by concrete and bull-dozer and pyloned flight-paths of electrocution.

As a man of earth, as a man of stone, as a man of poetic compulsion, I would have it said that as long as there is Time and Vision, the Forest shall open its green eyes in May: winds shall toss its green hair in summer: fling wild cherry and apple toward winter. Even the cuckoo, late on the north wind, shall speak his poem – more esoteric every Spring; the white stag roar on his raft of sex at autumn to defy his black challenger; the lakes stay clear and still for the golden carp, so beautiful we dare scarcely breathe; the eagle-footed oaks tug at England, shipwrecked only by sunsets.

After a short feeling of delight and relief at our release from poverty I became deeply depressed and walked the Forest like a tree moving in the green light. I looked into the lake where, among trees, the fish swam through my head. I was able to feel peace by doing this and when I saw the white buck grazing with his herd I felt better. But peace for a troubled mind is not a cure. It seemed also in the Forest there was a green hunger that devoured men, shredding them like suet with its crab-like claws. I found myself without love. The shadow of a darker magic had taken over my life, about which I did not know.

I walked to the beech wood where I had first drawn the waggon in and my son had nearly died in the snow: cooking fat soaked into a holly tree where I had spilt it, a rusty nail where I had put up a shelter for my greyhound, bought from a gypsy, where he had been gored by a stag and had to rest.

Enough! Too much!

The past is not nostalgia: it is a hieroglyphic that explains the future. I felt better when I got back to our City in a field.

One of the important things I did almost at once was to find a disused wheelwright's shed, behind a butcher's shop in Lyndhurst, complete with forge. I rented it for a few shillings. We were trying for a smallholding not far from where we were, but it would take time; things started to move with my work, which was the real life force I needed. So we lived on in the chalet for a time, grateful for the improved conditions of life after having spent six weeks on our bellies in a tiny tent, cooking from a Primus at its mouth because of an incessant downpour. At another time sleeping in straw in 14 degrees of frost. A perfect condition to show how the romantic situation is also one of the toughest reality. Don Quixote on a windmill.

I worked from the forge, getting alabaster sent from Staffordshire, and started to carve. It was good to use tools. More so to be working in the third dimension, which all craftsmen do – the others live a Picasso-faced existence with a flat-fish vision.

It was at this time a Catholic priest made friends and asked me to carve a Madonna for his church. Although I was never a Catholic I had, as I have always had for all religions, a total respect for his, and was very excited at the idea. I got a 6ft block sent from the Hixon Mines and with the help of Brixy Veal and Benny Wells set it up on a brick pedestal I had built. It glowed like a gentle column of candle-light. I told the priest 'I have the stone for your Madonna, Father. It came yesterday!'

He looked at me for a long time, then poured me a sherry. After taking a sip and setting his glass down on the crimson velvet table cloth he said: 'I don't think I really meant that about the Madonna. I was very lonely and wanted someone to talk to. Perhaps I should not have said it!'

I was devastated. I went to London. Adrian Ryan lent me his flat in Tite Street, where he gave me permission to hang work on his walls in place of his own and get the dealers in. The Leicester Galleries took some and Tooth's took small carvings. That was a relief. Then Peter Jackson came one Sunday, helped me clean up and leave the flat tidy before we drove home, but first went to the Old Kent Road to his relations in Gas Street, for a meal and to watch television for the first time ever: a memorable day. I wore flat commando boots without soles, bought through an advertisement when I was broke. Thus friends became jewels in a paper crown.

THE WHITE BUCK

Tooth's sold my smaller carvings and I was in their annual show, 'Important Contemporaries', for three or four years, with Frink and Epstein. This started to make my name, or remake it, independently of St. Ives. For although I had become established as a contemporary painter at my show at Lefevre in 1946, thanks to the help of the Elmhirsts of Dartington, Bernard Leach and Ben Nicholson, all status was confiscated when I left St. Ives. Shadowy sanctions crippled me. This was a new beginning.

I had a show in The Fox and Hounds in Lyndhurst which was a local success, and money began to get easier, as it always does when the need is not so great. Augustus John came to this show and bought a painting. The dignified old landlord, once Major Domo to the Duke of Porchester, laid on Mâcon at room temperature, and when Augustus arrived, looking like a pirate in a straw hat Amaryllis Fleming has painted black for him, he was bowed in with true grace, which Augustus took with gentle humour and humility. He loved my paintings and the one he bought was of Luvvie Cooper, who used to cut Bennets ('Bennets' – tall grasses used for basket and beehive-making. Probably gypsy slang: Bend it!) in the Forest when I lived within its depths. I was proud when later I saw it at Fryern Court, hanging with Matthew Smith and Renoir.

During the period of this show a man in a suit, with a lively, intelligent face and thinning hair, stood me a drink and told me his name was Donald Bennet. He then asked me if I would be interested in carving a sculpture for a factory he was building at Fawley. He spoke with some insight and sensitivity, and I was surprised when he said his factory was to take the waste products from Fawley Refinery and convert them into blocks of synthetic rubber. I said that I could not find anything exciting in the proposal because I had an allergy to rubber. Unless he could accept an image from outside.

'That's what I want!' he said. Something from the Forest!' I was at once excited.

'What about the White Stag – the sacred image of the forest?'

'Fine if you can do it!'

'Of course I can. I'll get some drawings out for you right away if you like!'

There were so many details to work out, which took a good deal of time, and of course I lost out because I didn't know what to charge, did the drawings for nothing and finally quoted only £500 plus expenses. I got the job.

THE WHITE BUCK

At first it was to be done in Beer stone and I went down there with someone from the contractors, Marshall Hall, which, apart from the business, was a stirring experience for me, because we drove down the same route I had taken with the waggon and every foot was a moment in my recent life – especially at Charmouth.

We finally wound down the hill to Beer Quarry, but not into the little village where Alfred Wallis's wife, Susan, was born. Even then I did not know I was touching the roots of my future life, which will be clear later. We were met by two directors, Mr C. Lister-Kaye and Mr Bill Evans and taken to a country restaurant at the Three Horses. From there, we went on under the quarry which was cut into the side of a hill like a drift mine or a Pharoah's Tomb. The piece I wanted was 15ft × 7ft × 1ft thick. They were apprehensive, but when I told them the Duke of Edinburgh was likely to open the factory where it was going, they took the order for the stone.

I understood later that they got the piece out in spite of geological fissures and faults, but being a soft stone it broke its back when being lifted onto the low-loader. This happened twice. I had to withdraw and send to Italy for Carrara marble and got a block cut out of the mountain frame sawed to size and shipped over to the site for £450. Beer wanted £1,000. Not being a businessman, it never struck me I could have made a profit here but thought it was the right thing to let the contractors save the money. Voila!

The huge piece of stone, weighing 7½ tons, arrived in Southampton Water, at Hythe near the site of the factory and was moved into place by a tall yellow crane. A platform and scaffold was built for me and I was boarded in as I asked, to work alone.

The worst part was the beginning because I knew I must draw the great image onto the marble face and get it right first time or the thing would be wrong all the way through. I trusted my drawing, but at that size – 7ft × 11ft – I was very nervous. I got there at five in the morning with my tools and working drawings. I stood like a man before an invisible opponent and went into it with a brush and red paint. It took four hours: then I walked out. When I came the next day I saw it was right.

Then I did something new for me. I brought with me a small Black and Decker drill with a carborundum grinding wheel in it. I always said I would not use such a tool unless I had learnt to draw with it. This was my first lesson. I did a second drawing, cutting into the stone through the red paint, then washed the paint away, leaving the ghost of the white stag floating, it seemed, in front of the white marble. On the third day I came with my hammer and chisel and started to cut the image out in low relief. not allowing more than ½ inch depth at any point. It took six months to finish.

At one point I got stuck on a leg that looked horse-like – probably from my long journey leading horses. Ishtar spent an entire Sunday morning, with me drawing and re-drawing under her direction. I would not have taken it from anyone else, but she knew about horses and I knew about deer. After a terrible and most ruthless conflict it was suddenly a stag's leg, not that of a horse. Only to think stag, be stag, makes stag!

One other thing worth recording is that I had to pass the Lyndhurst Bull Centre for Artificial Insemination on my way to work every morning. Over the doorway they had a sculpture of a creature with no testicles – which made it a steer. When I got to Hythe I was resolved to balance the image by giving my stag a beautiful pair of balls, but had not noticed that the office girls had cut a sight hole in the hardboard partition between me and the makeshift office, until I heard them laughing excitedly as I worked.

It was a great job. The gypsies worked on the site as labourers, bobbing up from ditches and waving as I passed. And when the directors wanted to come in and see me at work, I wrote on the door in red paint:

NO ENTRANCE. NOT EVEN FOR BRASS HATS.

Donald Bennett did not mind this: he conceded to all my needs because he knew my first concern was to do a good job - and I did. Although only half an inch deep, the great stag had antlers lifted in space 4ft apart at the royal tines. My drawing had been correct. The illusion complete.

By co-operation with Anthony Brode, the *Southern Echo* gave me wide publicity in his column 'Tom Bargate', which helped enormously in building my new thresholds when I was at a blank wall. Once the inner citadel starts to disintegrate it is almost impossible to reconstruct. Taking that long journey and carving the White Stag, sacred image of the Forest, did just that.

It was after completing this sculpture that the time was right, and we were able to purchase the smallholding at Emery Down, leaving dear Edie Gailor who had been so kind to us even though I stole

THE WHITE BUCK

her body board to paint on one day when I had nothing else. I hope she forgave me. I shall remember her for her twenty cats, her Tamworth Gloria boar, her chickens with spectacles and her dog Sam who hated me; but above all for the way she blushed to her arms when one evening, walking up the field with her she said:

'What a lovely evening, Mister Berlin. Look, there's the moon laying on her back!'

'Best place for a Lady to be, my dear!'

'Really, Mister Berlin, you are awful!' She *was* slightly embarrassed.

We moved to Home Farm in 1956 after I had had a show with Ishtar at the Bladon Gallery, Hurstbourne Tarrant, organised by Doris Bladon-Hawton, opened by Augustus John and Lord Moyne*. We blocked the Newbury to Andover Road, and entertained the AA and the police with wine.

We moved everything. The hut in which I slept with bronchitis in 14 degrees of frost became a chicken house and the chalet was put up at the end of our paddock and turned into a paint shop where I was to paint my Creation Cycle of Paintings – as important to me as the White Buck.

---

* An account of this is in *Wanderers in the New Forest*, by Juliette de Baraclai Levy and in my own *Dromengro: Man of the Road*.

Ghosts In Attendance

Home Farm was at the north end of the village. In a thatched cottage at the top of the lane, lived two sisters – Annie and Lily Bright; they who had been so kind to me the day my son was dying in the snow – 'the day Mr Buckle was found frozen to death in his shepherds hut,' they always said. – when I walked to Lyndhurst to collect the money for the Little Madonna. They were completely from another century, lived on the parish and paid a peppercorn rent at the Great Lord's House before it was pulled down. They had both lost their men in the First World War: had said goodbye under the faggot tree at the end of Silver Street and never saw them again, nor did either marry. Annie had a barrow on bike wheels with which she used to collect scrap and swill from the shops in town, old bits of bacon and stale bread and cake from the bins of the restaurant and gave us a basketful each week soon after we were settled. At Christmas she gave me half a pig's face: 'that's for Feyther!' she'd say, 'Special!' They lived on the edge of poverty but were never poor; at the frontiers of starvation, but never starved; at the entrances of love, but never married.

Opposite them was an idiot boy who used to throw his pyjamas on the telegraph wires every day and roar with laughter. There was a charming colonel who walked on whisky as Christ walked on water, looking as though he was stepping over invisible cobwebs. A vicar who was blind, whom I called Blind Dick because he was like Tiresias. A gunner who thought I was the best OP/ACK in the British Army after he had read *I am Lazarus*. And an attractive Jewish lady from London who ran the pub.

But above all, the country people who were the meat inside the pastry: Charl' Penny, Brixy Veal, Jimmy Biddlecombe, Ammer, Charcoal John, Jack Whitehorn and Rig. They were the life-force who kept going by dealing, farming, poaching, work of casual kind, gardening, hunting or even drinking all hours – with humour, some grace and even love. Behind them, the gypsies in the trees and their Green City, selling flowers. Behind them again the animals – the deer, fishes, insects, foxes – woven into a human comedy of pain and laughter, and the miracle of being alive.

This was the background into which, after a little while, we fitted, but we had not long been in residence and sleeping in a house for the first time in three years, when the property adjacent fell vacant and the asking price was so small that it could not be ignored. We thus acquired it with a cottage and outhouses. The main attraction was for Ishtar; a complete run of stables which she filled with horses – and the fields – Appaloosa's, Palominos and Arabs, to help in original research, and made her quickly known in the horse world, even to having the Queen's horse, Zaman, a royal gift from Kruschev and Bulganin, to board in her stables. As with my complete commitment, so was hers. It should have worked but neither of us understood money. She took on staff and an Irish groom who, since her eccentricities had grown rather than the reverse, was made to lead her sitting on the back of a fully harnessed Grevy's Zebra, through the village for her morning ride, creating an entirely new image in the Forest. It was a beautiful but strong smelling animal with a primitive fierceness about it of which I was cautious and gave me the same feeling as Satan the Celtic blue horse we had on the road. It finally tried to savage Ishtar during a TV interview with Martin Muncaster. She seemingly had no fear of it and was concerned only in finding out where it fitted into the evolutionary scheme of things, after the tapir, which also was striped when born. Like all primitive creatures it was not evil: only the victim of being displaced. The vet finally was called and dispatched him with a captive bolt. The skin was cured and used to cover the couch in the front room, but it still smelt of the wild savannahs of Africa, where it should still have been, and stirred the tiger grass in my soul.

There was a Dutch barn which I converted into a workshop, with proper lifting gear for stone and a forge, furnaces and equipment for casting bronze. It was one of the most exciting but certainly most difficult things I have done, and it was a mistake: I did not realise that metal, far more than stone, had its own ideas about what it should be, and it took at least two generations of craftsmanship behind you to have any real success. You could do the whole thing right and get it wrong, and the whole thing wrong and get it right without ever knowing why. The processes were exciting and I found, with Cellini, a certain madness when working with it. But my engineer's training helped.

The best thing I did was completely wrong, full of blow holes, finning, and other irregularities which made it no more than an industrial reject. But I was not looking for perfection or smoothness. This casting was of a forest stag beetle many times its real size. It looked like a maquette for a prehistoric creature thrown aside by a fiery hand half melted back before it cooled – a creature never seen on land or sea. A new image to meet in the Forest, which is a mysterious place getting dark. It was a work of art.

Without any money you are far safer, and like the wild creatures, come through the ordeals with far less trouble and a good deal more peace and happiness than when you have it. I had been so many years without it that I was bewildered. Banks, taxman, health and pensions, rates, insurance. Cars, materials, apprentices, housekeeper, stable girls, Irish groom. School fees, solicitors, telephone and that deadly Second Coming, television.

Immediately some of the money was made over by deed of gift, I notified Cornwall, paid all my debts, took the family off help from the Artists General Benevolent Institution (AGBI) which, since I lived in the Tower after I returned from France, had supported and paid for the children's education. I could now take over. The children at once asked again to come to me, which healed a gash in my soul. First Paul and then Janet: Jasper was with me. Ishtar as central Wha, as they called her: there was also the stepson Willie. I made payments to Helga till her death.

Once more I was aware of the outside forces taking over and setting the wheels of destiny at work. The children had returned. Perhaps after all I was being redeemed as Merlin was unredeemed. Was that the voice I heard in the Forest when I was alone? Do we after all have the onus of other men's souls upon us? Is this the meaning of life's ethic: that we must use our whole selves to turn the wheel and so give what we have to give even if we have nothing with which to give it?

My friend Grant Watson turned up at Home Farm, moved from Ox Cross at Georgeham, though I believe Henry Williamson was still there. He lived now at Petersfield, near Mai Zetterling who also came to stay. The richness of life I so missed when I thought of Frieda Lawrence eating the peaches and killing her beloved Lorenzo, as I sat on the edge of the road in Devon a penniless vagabond, was now flowing towards me of its own volition.

Denys Val Baker came also, earlier when we had been at Edie Gailor's place and stayed a few days in the area trying to buy a boat at Lymington. They also asked us to stay with them in London, which we did. It is memorable for one thing. Denys said to me: 'Would you like to meet Henry Williamson?' See how the patterns work once they start moving? They stayed in a Georgian house in Drayton Gardens – rather, I imagine, like the ones in which Francis Bacon used paint – where the Society of Authors is housed, with huge rooms and high ceilings. They wanted Ishtar to paint a horse in the large space over the fireplace. I don't know if it was their wall but the painting was done with extraordinary speed and fluency leaving an image of remarkable vitality floating over us. Adrian Ryan called, I think with Polly Walker, and a man named Johnson with a marvellous tenor voice was there and we talked of our destinies ahead, and of magical days in Cornwall where we all knew one another.

How Henry Williamson was to emerge I don't know, and even then I expected to be driven into the country to meet him. But no, I was taken to a nightclub between Piccadilly and Regent Street, in Swallow Street, where we had to buy a bottle of gin to get in and descend some stairs. At the bottom of the stairs was a tall man with white hair and a moustache, blue eyes and weathered skin. Seeing my huge form descend he greeted me as Falstaff: 'Here a Windsor stag; the fattest in the Forest, I think! Send me a cool rut-time Jove, or who can blame me if I piss my tallow!' shouting in a loud voice, shaking my hand with a firm hold; with my own sculptor's grip, it was strong enough for me to notice.

'Sven Berlin!' said Val Baker, himself a handsome Welshman, who made a splendid Cicerone, rather than a noisy performer. 'This is Henry Williamson.'

I can't remember if Jess and Ishtar were there. It seemed to have been a stag party until we reached his table where he had been drinking beer with two pretty girls to their gin.

I had wanted to talk to him about Devon, Lawrence of Arabia and 'Tarka', but he launched into praise of Hitler and Fascism, which I found difficult having emerged from a war against them and almost overrun Belsen. I could not understand why he was like that. Val Baker was interested in the girls, but he also had that novelist's trick of switching-on as host and listening. Perhaps he pressed the wrong switch. I could not get a word in about T.E. Lawrence so, lighting a fag, I said: 'What about 'Tarka', Henry?' He stopped dead and looked at me with those blue eyes in which his real genius was alight.

The Author at work on "Pieta". Photo: C. Graham.

The Author's Wedding to Julie.

"Pieta" – 1968 size 6 ft × 4 ft × 2 ft, weight 1½ tons approx.
in Staffordshire Alabaster colouration in amber and red. *Photo: G. Finlayson.*

The Author and Julie

The Author in Black Stardi (1954)

Harry (Julie's Father)

Cutting Stone.

At the casting furnace (1958).

"Lovers". *Photo: R. Francis*

'I can't get back there!' he said at last.

'You mean you have bombed your own city?' 'Yes I suppose I have!'

The lights were dimmed by now and couples were dancing slowly to soft music like an opium dream with the cigarette smoke curling round them. Silent waiters were darting about with extra-sensory bills and collecting invisible tips. It was time to go.

Henry Williamson came out with us to say goodbye in Regent Street. We climbed into the old London taxi Val Baker used as a private car. It was midnight. I asked him about Grant Watson. 'I don't know,' he said. 'He just feels he's left on the shelf, I suppose!'

As we drove off he lifted his tweed hat, lurched smiling and waved to us against an unlikely background for a great countryman.

I saw him once more, perhaps ten years later, on the Ringwood to Christchurch Road by the great River Avon, which is how I wish to remember him. He was standing near a deserted bus stop, with his blue eyes still shining – though by now a much older man, they seemed to enter into my car like water.

I was with my third wife, Julie: 'Wasn't that Henry Williamson?' she asked. 'I've seen him on telly.'

'Yes. I think it was.'

'You should have offered him a lift.'

'I suppose I should!' But there was an inhibition in doing so. I don't know why. Perhaps because I have always hated bearding famous people and he might not have remembered me. I could not stop.

Then he died and the pattern drifted away by the severance of a thread until quite recently. The writer and bookseller friend of mine, Austin Wormleighton, had been to visit Henry Williamson's hut in Devon where he wrote *Tarka the Otter*.

Austin writes: '. . . the hut is actually a frozen moment in time; genuinely just as he left it, the windows covered in dirt and cobwebs which he encouraged to keep out prying eyes and the light of distraction.'

'On the shelves around his desk were Williamson's day-to-day reference books on wild life and the countryside. I heard someone say: "That's a good one!" As I turned round I saw a finger on the spine of the hardback edition of *Jonah's Dream*!'

This last link with Williamson was the one I wanted and of most value to me; that my *Jonah's Dream*, published ten years after meeting him in that nightclub, where he seemed like an Amhurst pheasant caught by chance, was on the shelf of his working books. A writer's real reward. It showed me that what I had searched for in him and not found – whether he remembered meeting me or not – had returned like a ghost in attendance and he had accepted it.'

Austin also writes: '. . . his son Richard told me in Norfolk this year that Henry Williamson had no real idea about painting and music and gave Tunnicliffe, the man who illustrated many of his books, a dreadful time bullying and browbeating him into submission.'

I think you would have had a pretty explosive relationship with Williamson had your friendship developed any further than it did. I recall you telling me Williamson once suggested you set up your studio beside him in Devon.

This last sentence, of course, refers to the time when Grant Watson wrote to try and divert my journey north from Bridestowe to stay at Ox Cross with him and Henry Williamson. Austin Wormleighton was probably right. I am a solitary man at heart and cannot endure any interference with my work for long, unless it is clean technical advice – which I take but don't use.

E.L. Grant Watson, whom I knew simply as 'Peter', was a biologist, psychiatrist and author of some 40 books: a poet also. He was my Wise Old Man for a decade until he died in 1970. Since then I have learned to be my own Magician, which is the next step in self knowledge and integration, because there is no one else to ask in the wilderness of old age. Thus the fashion to let the old die because it helps the economy is the destruction of wisdom by the half-grown young and a sin against humanity. He was not a good poet in the sense of writing from the 'aggregate of poetic instances', or from mining his own gold, and possibly too intellectually mystical (if that is possible) for me to understand. I was already influenced by the seaspray straight from God's house of fierce salt. It was in his writing about animals and insects I found his spark active, his sudden spurts of starlight, and I illustrated one of his books for that reason.

He turned up at Home Farm one summer with an elderly girlfriend of ninety named Ida Baker, a gentle, birdlike creature, sitting on the couch in the front room beside his frail figure. I had not seen him for a long time and almost at once he asked me if I knew the Chinese Book of Changes – the *I Ching*. I had recently purchased a copy and had read Jung's brilliant introduction, but had not so far learned to cast it. My friend said he had no yarrow sticks with him, which was the real and more difficult way to use the text, but proceeded to show me how to do it with copper coins, so we used penny pieces. Very simply the *I Ching* is a book of ancient wisdom from which can be foretold the immediate future from the existing situation of the present based on the law of Chance. I had that strange feeling of destiny again as though I had heard the deep sound of a timpani, while Grant Watson marked down the Chinese symbols as I cast the coins, and finally looked them up in the chart and turned to the reading I had obtained of my own destiny:

THE DARKENING OF THE LIGHT

What followed has just been indicated as present in my past pages, but it was this chance visit of my friend that had made me conscious of it, and I was filled with an almost cosmic sense of distress. The only comfort was in the last sentence of the chapter which I kept by me until it was over, with the feeling of an innocent creature eating a leaf and suddenly realising he was being swallowed by a snake.

> 'The dark power at first held so high a place that it could wound all who were on the side of good and of the light. But in the end it perishes of its own darkness, for evil must itself fall at the very moment when it has wholly overcome the good, and consumed the energy to which it owes its duration.'

It was as though Peter Grant Watson had known and had come over with this one mission, to make me aware of what was happening. He left soon after, and before he went I gave him a copy of my war book, *I Am Lazarus* and signed it, 'From one ghost to another?' because he had told me on our first meeting in Cornwall, that he had been very ill and was now living a posthumous life. My title had come from T.S. Eliot:

> I am Lazarus come from the dead.
> Come back to tell you all, I shall tell you all!

GHOSTS IN ATTENDANCE

It was always on this frontier land I knew him. Although we were poles apart in so many ways, less visible things seemed to dovetail.

During this period there were times when my energy seemed to be suddenly drawn from me till I thought I would die. The Chinese say that if you do not know how to save the vital-energy the body will die. That did not seem to matter because I had been to war and been near death so many times that I was not afraid: I had made death a friend. But death of the spirit is another matter – more terrifying – and this is probably the real meaning of mortality.

I felt this to be more so when I had convulsions by the farm gate which threw me on my back as would an epileptic fit – of which I had no history – only blackouts when I first came home from war. I came to with Ishtar leaning over me.

'You all right?' she asked.

'Yes. A blackout I think. Must have been over-working.'

My doctor, Willis, came and after taking blood tests established later that I had breathed in chemicals while colouring a bronze figure I had cast and upset the haemoglobin balance of my blood. A few days later it happened again and I went to my room and rested, telling the women not to disturb me. Later the phone rang. My daughter called up the stairs. 'It's Grant Watson, Dad!'

I went down and talked to him. He knew something was wrong and asked me to come over and see him. I went to Petersfield in my Humber Hawk, which I called the White Goddess, driving like a drunken man.

The psyche between us was always connected in this way, though neither of us pretended to have any extra-sensory gift: on the contrary. But it was at such times he was a valuable friend and I poured my agony out to him.

He gave me the unsolicited advice that, if there was a force present other than might be compatible with the doctor's diagnosis, the one answer to it was White Magic and suggested, both as an antidote and a prophylactic, chanting all lines beginning with 'I AM' in the gospel of St. John.

I AM the light	which I will	I AM a wave of the sea
I AM the way	compare with the	I AM a tear of the sun
I AM the bread	first poetry of	I AM a hill of poetry
I AM the vine	Ireland 1268 B.C.	I AM a stag with seven tines.
	Song of Amergin.	

GHOSTS IN ATTENDANCE

I don't suppose Grant Watson would have thought of these parallels, which occur to me as I write, and are equally rewarding if they are chanted against the force of darkness.

Peter's wife, Katherine, was a tall sensitive woman who had a hurt look which had been there since childhood, or anyway her youth, when she must have been very beautiful. Her portrait by Ben Nicholson's father, Sir William Nicholson, hanging on their sitting room wall, showed her as a fine young woman with the same look. For some reason they had cut the hands out of the main portrait and put them in a different frame a little way off, which always gave me an uneasy feeling – the rest of the painting was destroyed. They gave me the original frame to use on one of my own paintings. It was an unexpected background for a Victorian painting to be hanging in a semi-detached house in Petersfield, where I went to talk about Blake and Jung and pour out my troubles if I had any: they in turn using my insight and experience to solve some of their own problems. The Old Man was a good listener, but would flare up at some trivial thing, like my drinking too much brandy. Katherine was always patient and kind. It was the catharsis I needed more than anything. 'But you must look after Brother-Body, Sven,' he would say.

Peter had partly followed the voyage of the *Beagle* as a young man of science, but he was also turned toward a mystical answer to life, and it gave a brittleness to his scientific mind, which seemed confounded on these shores, with the result that the motor muscles of art – imagination and invention – were impaired. Perhaps that is why his novels and poems were less powerful than his writings on the works of nature; and why he seemed to couch himself in the arms of Jung, Wilhelm and Blake rather than stand on the perilous rock of his own vision as though he was too fragile to stand it. A man who was not soiled enough by the world but smoothed enough by the tide to become of good intention and high purpose. A man whose blackbird friend in the garden he called the Holy Ghost, and an elderly girlfriend who spoke to him after she died from behind the veil of invisibility.

He knew Conrad, George Moore and Henry James, so linking me with the past and certain wisdom. Our conversations were always on the invisible frontiers where I believe evolution will make its next stand.

With unbelievable gallantry, his wife Katherine had brought him together with his mistress Ida, after a break in which he had gone abroad and unsuccessfully tried to shoot Ida's husband, who was Governor of Madras, because he could not live without her, and had an orgasm without an emission when the attempt failed. Yet there was a spite in the house when Ida was there. I once called when this was much in evidence. He had the women in separate rooms: Ida in the study, Katherine in the kitchen, and I was in the front sitting room, where the Holy Ghost came to the window and took bread and drank clear water from a saucer.

He enjoyed this. 'Both women behaving magnificently!' he said when he returned to talk to me. But it was like being inside a Victorian novel where any wrong word or movement could trigger death.

My visits during the Darkening of the Light were helpful, but I was glad when things got too difficult, and from his support, I learned to step over to my own throne and stand by my own self, often taking a devil or two home on my sleeve from his legion – which was the least I could do in return.

He went on writing his books.

'They never seem to take on,' he said sadly when he was dying. 'I'm only alive because I want to finish my last book,' he added in his piping voice. 'My doctor says there is nothing wrong with me. I am simply worn out. You can arrange to stay alive, you know, if you want to!'

He lay on his couch with his spirit hovering over him like one of those engravings by William Blake, and talked of death quite easily with no fear. Although I can't remember what he said, I know I now have a deeper knowledge of these areas than before. Then he did something I had not known him do before. He asked Katherine for a large whisky which he drank neat – and then another – as though abstinence had never been; and because they did not understand drinking, they were enormous tots.

After that he asked me to lift him over to the table to eat his lunch which Katherine had set for us. I took him up in my arms - this old man of over six feet weighing nothing, like a bird dried up and wasted under his suit of feathers – and put him down where he asked on a wicker chair.

After the meal he seemed to revive and insisted on coming out to the car when it was time to go. He stood under the pollarded poplar trees with his pink suburban house in the background holding both my hands. His eyes were alight with something that was reflected back from the frontier between life and death, and as he spoke I knew I would not see him again:

> Men must endure their going hence, as
> their coming hither: ripeness is all!

He said this as an exact quotation at a right moment and then ecstatically added: 'Come to my funeral, won't you?' I promised.

I watched him walk slowly down the path and with some difficulty climb into the black front door, looking this time exactly like Blake's engraving of the old man entering death's door.

He did not look round and I drove away.

He gave out the hard blue light of genius which he so gently let go. He was less violent than his friend, Henry Williamson. Both were ghosts in attendance who influenced the shape and colour of my life, and what they have achieved is seen now at a distance like starlight in a house of glass.

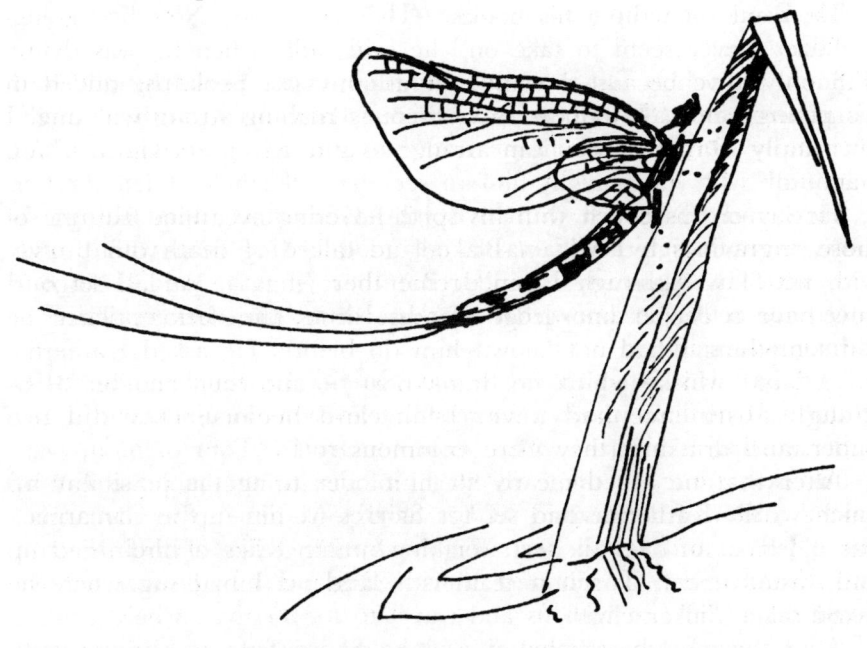

The Life of man if like that of the mayfly !

Ice Queen

I suppose the most charismatic and attractive woman I have ever met was Mai Zetterling. She not only gave out that light of the Goddess, but fitted exactly the niche in my soul cut by time for the Ice Queen: racial because of our Swedish origins. Only Ekland was her equal.

She had been about to marry Tyrone Power. He had either died or changed his mind and she married a friend of mine, David Hughes, whom I had met through Anthony Brode: Hughes was another writer interested in a book I was writing, or had written, and I wanted to get in touch with him.

I sent Tony a note: 'Do you know where David is?'

He answered at once: 'He's chasing Mai Zetterling across Europe!'

'Fuck Mai Zetterling!' I replied. 'Tell him to come home. I need to see him!'

But Brode had the master stroke: 'He's done that. Now he's going to marry her!'

Such parochial wit was not in good taste, perhaps, but had spontaneity and allowed us to earn our daily bread with a laugh. Eventually David came home and brought the mermaid he had caught or who had caught him to see me. Of course I fell for her at once and could not think why the Gods had timed things so badly, even though David was a tall good-looking man with brown eyes, and I was already married. But there it was. We all set our fences correctly, became great friends, Ishtar, the dark opposite – nothing was said.

The patterns fitted in every way. Michael Croucher, the BBC producer, who had made a successful television documentary of me earlier casting a bronze, with a commentary by Tom Salmon, was, at this exact time, in the early stages of discussing the possibility of making a film of the Gypsies at Les Saintes Maries in the Camargue, where Ishtar and I had been for the Spring Rites of their Patron Saint, Santa Sara. To connect it with England I had suggested we should take Cliff Lee with us and travel to the Festival, where gypsies from all over Europe gathered to take Santa Sara to the sea and wash away their sins, escorted by Les Gardiens de la Camargue.

It was in the midst of this that Mai appeared – the complete opposite to the black-faced Sara – and my Patron Saint, so I thought. But I did not know that at this time she had put aside acting, to make and direct films, having grown tired of being a film star for which the world loved her; for that was her true genius and her womanhood. She had just been to Sweden with David to travel in the far North, where my mother had married, beyond the Arctic Circle, and filmed the Lapps living in their tents and tending their reindeer on the tundra. And now at our first meeting sitting by the fire in my front room, this all came out.

'But you are not old, Mai. You are still beautiful!' I said, watching her face in the firelight. 'Don't they offer you films any more?'

'O yes, Schwen, zay offer me films, but where before I played ze young girl in ze Vild Duck, zey now offer me ze part of ze old mother, which I turned down.'

'What is your next documentary then?' I asked her.

'I vant to make a film about ze zjypsies. Do you know anysing about them?'

And when she turned and smiled at me it was as though the room lit up. I could not quite believe it. It was as though I was myself in the centre of a fairy tale she was perhaps making. She knew she could do this and later when I was accustomed to being completely liquidated, and realised she used it, I called it the Zetters Magic: I think that was her own name for it as well.

'But this is uncanny,' I said. 'I am negotiating at this very moment to make such a film.' I told her of my plan – everything that I had already discussed with my friend. She was very excited and wanted to know more.

John Boorman was my near neighbour in the Forest at that time. He had also made a splendid one-hour documentary of my life and work more recently called *A Portrait in Time*. He was about a lot and asked me if he could meet Mai when she came. I arranged this in my studio one day but she did not take to him and was almost rudely silent. He was not interested in the gypsy film but had wanted to do one of me casting the *Rise of Lazarus*, which had to be dropped because of extra expense. Not long after he went to Hollywood and wrote a card from New York to say he had seen a self-portrait by Rembrandt in the Museum of Modern Art which looked just like me, then was silent for some years until recently. We remained like good wine, mature friends, silent but worth tasting now and again.

I was pleased when Michael Croucher and John Boorman had

both made films of my work. It helped to wedge me back in the moving puzzle of the art world, but I did not want to get into films and be deflected from sculpture or painting in this way. Already I began to realise there was another person walking about whom people stopped in the street and addressed by my name, which is not what I was after, and I became reticent and wary.

Over the next few weeks Mai often visited my home, even staying overnight in the chalet with her old father and David. Her father was a keen fisherman, as I was. I was writing *Jonah's Dream*.

'To wish you luck!' I shouted one morning at breakfast, and fixed a huge salmon fly on its hook into the lapel of his jacket, not realising until afterwards that he was wearing a new suit. He could not get the hook out. But he was kind and quiet. He did not mind and smiled over the eggs and bacon – this man who fathered Mai as a love-child, she told me – but she seldom spoke of her mother, and then not with affection.

A young horse dealer and his wife who had slept in their horse box overnight were over-awed to find themselves having breakfast with a film star.

'Is it?' the man said, looking at Mai. She nodded and smiled, looking pleased. The atmosphere was happy and illuminated by her presence. It helped to balance things also, because the tough world of dealers was Ishtar's side, with the gypsies also, which fitted in with my sculpture and painting, but now there was the link with writing and films: I was working on *Jonah's Dream, A Meditation on Fishing* and also planning a book on the gypsies which was not to come till much later, yet here began to germinate.

Next time she visited, by some change of policy at BBC Headquarters, the idea of the gypsy film had been switched to London and the contract to make it given to Mai Zetterling: she was in charge. How this mistake worked I never knew. Ishtar and I were taken on in an advisory capacity. Croucher was left out.

One night a peacock from the small zoo I was running, was killed by a fox, but not mutilated: probably Reynard was frightened off before he could sling it over his shoulder with its neck in his mouth to carry it away. Touch a peacock's neck and he is dead – that was enough.

I was drinking tea early the next morning outside, as was my custom, when Ishtar walked up the drive with this beautiful creature in her arms like an offering. A natural but rare occurrence, an event in nature which carries a visual and emotional shock is exactly what happens when a painting is triggered in the mind. This tragedy was also an archetypal image. I took him from her and walked down to my paint shop in the lower farm which was a converted barn, and there started right away to do some drawings and watch the extraordinary sequence of colours in his tail as he lay there in the sunlight on a long table. A six foot canvas had to be stretched and colour notes made, drawing in the main long, rhythmic lines of the body. I worked all through the week transmuting him into paint, which took all the experience I had and all the knowledge I did not have, to invent a language more beautiful than a thousand sunsets, till finally I had a painting.

When Mai saw it she was wildly excited – 'It is so beautiful, Schwen!' – and immediately wanted to buy it. I agreed, we settled a price of £100 and I delivered it when we went over to stay with her the next week at Berry Grove, her house near Petersfield, where she had the tomb of an invading Viking king under an oak tree in her garden. It was quite near where Grant Watson lived, but he hated her:

'Oh, you mean that awful film star of about sixty who lives round here. I can't stand the woman. Quite hideous.' I never found out why Grant Watson made this quite fierce attack, unless he had crossed rapiers with her at some parochial meeting I did not know about or was it simply jealousy, which is usually the case in these matters – especially as his girlfriend was 90 and Mai was only 35 and more beautiful than Helen of Troy.

Mai's house was a splendid Georgian building where I took my sacrificial offering of a dead peacock, which she hung lovingly in a long space she had made for it on the wall of her sitting room. Over the fireplace she had a nude drawing by Epstein and I remember on the stairs a masterly drawing of the Albert Hall by John Minton, whom I had met in Cornwall with W.S. Graham. There was a small Lowry and a few things by Lawrence Durrell which I did not like.

Mai was about me all the time like a spirit inside me as well as outside and at one point sat at my feet chewing some reindeer boots she had given me. She said that in Lapland, 'zee women chew ze boots when they are sewn, to soften zem for zee men.' I don't know how well this pair had been cured but they hatched out larvae later in the summer when I had them at home.

She had also a Lapp hat and looked beautiful when she put it on, with her blue eyes laughing. 'It is a man's hat you see, Schven.' With a toss of her head she flicked the huge bobble of red wool to the rear. 'When zey are young and zey are not interested zey wear it at the back. When zey are at work they wear it at ze side. But when zey are grown up men and are interested zey flick it to zee front. Zere! like ze stallion's crest!' I was enchanted.

Then she got up and put it on my head. 'It suits you. You should vear one like it!' And flicked the bobble to the front.

'You mean it is mine? You have given it to me?'

'No. – No I cannot do zat!'

'But you *must* – it fits so well!' She shook her head again. 'No, Schven.'

'Look,' I said, getting eager. 'If you give it to me I will paint myself in it and you can have the painting!' She hesitated, standing there in her little Swedish skirt with flowers on it.

'You promise?'

'I promise!' The deal was made. Later I kept my promise.

We went into the garden to the mound under the oak tree, under which she said there was buried an invading Viking king. This, though, stirred something very deep in me, as my painting of the dead peacock had in her, but it was impossible to tell what it was. Nor can we ever tell when man and woman become involved with each other, how it comes about.

>He crossed the sea at one oar's stroke
>When truth was but an arrowhead,
>This giant that sleeps beneath the oak
>The roots his bones, the leaves his bed.
>
>Force him not to climb the towers
>Of years from which his ghost might fall
>Nor trouble his great sleep with vows
>His deaf ears cannot hear you call.
>
>Queen of the Ice leave him there
>Where love cannot wound his heart
>With dreams lockt in the sockets bare
>Beyond the chemistry of your art.

Mai's children were about, both by her first husband, Tutti Lemco, the ballet dancer: free self-contained people, Christopher and Ethel. I got the girl's name wrong at first and called her Etienne, which stuck. My stepson, Willie, fell for her.

'Your influence is complete, Schven. Look at all the coloured glass things I have in ze vindows against ze light. Just like you 'ave at 'Ome Farm. I 'ave even ordered a car – ze same 'Umber 'Awk but dark blue instead of vite'.

I took my father on one visit because of his being Swedish and made it quite a family affair. David's father was also there. He was headmaster of a famous school whose name I have forgotten, but well used to people of all ages and an extraordinary talker which enabled him to articulate each of us into his right place with complete charm – so much so that, like a good actor, he forgot to play himself, or only as Cicerone of high order who held the company together until Mai took us into the garden outside to cook steak on a charcoal fire with Mozart on the record player dissolving his timeless sounds into the sunset with the strong opiates of red wine and Swedish aquavit.

Mai seemed to enter right into our lives, becoming a rare and memorable person to know by somehow submitting to everything we said and thought. I found that I loved her. Ishtar didn't mind in the least and used to talk about 'when you marry Mai' as a kind of obvious conclusion to our knowing her. There was no rearing of the green serpent behind her words – though I did not know anything then of Ishtar's own secret life in the stables, and wish I never had. Never mind. I was very happy at this time because the poles of my being were axled by this new experience of the Dark Goddess Ishtar and the Ice Queen Mai, coming together in my life and making a totality.

I wrote a poem to myself.

LOVE'S COUNTERPARTS

> You of the double-ghost,
> How fare you now?
> Does a dark queen of Nineveh
> Or the fairest Northern flower
> Lean at your throne's post?
> How do you resolve your heart
> With Love's twin counterpart?

ICE QUEEN

'Love's counterparts are three,
Dear poet of the open wound:
The dark queen of Nineveh
And the Northern flower, I've found,
Both lean at my throne's post.
I am the third ghost:
Love's counterparts are three!'

You find your resolution then
In the dark flower and the Ice Queen:
What is the final image, Sven?
'To make all women I have seen
Transform the heart
And my own soul, by my throne's post,
Resolve into a single ghost!
This I can only do through art!'

And what if she, the Arctic flower,
And she whose sundrenched image burns,
Come as one within the hour
We breathe, each merging as she turns
Into a marvellous final ghost?
'Then would I ask to give up art
And leaning against my throne's post,
Merge with my uncrown'd counterpart.'

I even took Mai to Charmouth where, so many years ago, my children had been taken from me. The wound it had left moved for a moment like a fish under a rock: then with a sudden sharp pain, it was gone. A perfect cure. I said nothing. We all searched for fossils of prehistory. I found a perfect fish and gave it to her. It was another sunset fix into ecstasy. Mai enjoyed being recognised on the beach coming back. She was very famous in those days.

She had asked me several times to take her fishing for salmon, but the trip never came off. Had we done so and caught a great salmon, the fish of life, anything could have happened. But nothing irreversible of a nature that occurs on timeless shores or incomprehensible rivers of experience – a happening that could not unhappen – did happen.

What came about after long planning, was that we set off for the Camargue and the Gypsy Festival at Les Saintes Maries, in the first half of May of that year. I was very excited, having had a final conference with the cameraman in my orchard.

David and Mai had to go to Munich first, and by arrangement met us at Chartres, in order that I could see the tall Giacometti-like Gothic sculptures of saints on the cathedral and the great rose window on which to centralize my soul. The next day we drove south to Perigueux and from there I took Mai to see the Hall of Bulls at Lascaux, with which I had imprinted my mind the year before. When a man with a woman sees these paintings, he and she are locked into the caves of the beginning and from then on, they move toward their Everest by the light of animal oil burning in the deep heart under a low hill. For me at that moment Mai was that woman, though she would not have known. When we came out into the warm furry air that stroked our faces she was silent, as she was later when I took her to a bullfight in Mejanes in the Camargue a week later and all emotion was used up like a spent candle flame.

At Perigueux, David, who had perfect French, asked me if I thought the money I got for my traveller's cheque was all right. I told him I didn't really know and after a calculation he said: 'No it certainly is not all right. They have just tried to do us.'

We went back into the bank and a huge man in a glass case like a sacred carp listened to David and then, without arguing, gave him more money which was passed to me. I took it in dismay saying: 'What happened? Whose fault was it?' The Great Fish moved a fin, pointing to himself. 'C'est moi! C'est moi ! m'sieur!'

'Christ, David,' I said as we went out. 'That was lucky. Thanks.' 'Yes, Sven, he must be doing it all the time. Lucky I was about, you mean. Crafty old devil.'

There was a diversion here. I took them to dinner after we had settled in an enchanted caravan site with magic ferries over a river and coloured lights. The next day they went to Bordeaux to deliver a translation David had done of another writer. We missed them at the meeting point under the spires of the medieval city of Carcasonne, and found them a day later already in Saintes Maries waiting anxiously for us, which dispelled any idea that they were trying to shake us off. That would be silly, I thought. They were anxious because they were in the middle of a campsite in the square surrounded by Spanish and Italian gypsies, who were very suspicious of northern *gorqio** people being among them. When we arrived the same gypsies came out to meet us: partly because Ishtar looked like a gypsy and partly because I in my tall *stardi** and green jacket, was treated as a Rai — a true Gypsy Gentleman. Even if a gypsy passed in a crowd in London, on the other side of the street and saw me, he would lift his hand and smile in recognition. It was something in me they recognised and told them I was an *aficionado*, and *tacho** therefore. This same unconscious magnetism drew gypsies from Spain, Italy, France and Russia on this occasion. Mai and David were therefore included from then on, when we had explained who we were, and they were able to settle down. Ishtar helped me put up the huge army tent we had brought with us on top of the Humber. I think they had been frightened.

The one thing very noticeable to me was that Mai was changing. No longer was she the charismatic woman casting her magic spell around all who were near her. She was becoming remote and silent in her attitude.

At supper one evening she started to cry when I talked to the cameraman, with whom I got on, excitedly about the war — a subject that always gets me going. I was bewildered to turn and find the tears running down Mai's cheeks. Should war have upset her, I wondered? Then thought perhaps she was frightened because the young gypsy men who swaggered about in black hats wearing cummerbunds and knives were quite dangerous and she would have to go amongst them. I was concerned for her safety.

That day we had met Lawrence Durrell and his wife Claude drinking rosé and eating telline at Le Café de La Mer with some Brazilian poets. It was midday, but I had driven Mai at 5.30 that morning to Marseilles to meet the cameraman. A long journey through Cézanne country en Provence. The plane was on time and we started back with Mai in the back of the car talking concentratedly to the new arrival about the film, and we were left in silence till we got back to the Café where Lawrence Durrell was by that time holding court with great energy, smiling, in shirt sleeves, short, a little truculent perhaps, but giving out light from his amazingly blue eyes, which were how I imagined William Blake's to have been. It was just after the publication of the *Alexandrian Quartet* and he was enjoying his fame. Durrell was one who had starved with

---

* gorqio: non-gypsy. * stardi: hat. * tacho: truthful.

a stone for a loaf till his soul was a dry parchment and still wrote books and poems. He deserved what rightfully had come to him. I enjoyed meeting him and wanted to talk and drink rosé and eat millions of telline. But Mai was actually hurrying us up and cut my order of rosé down to a demi-bouteille, which I immediately reversed. Suddenly Durrell, who had met Mai before, said: 'Do you always get the whip out with your workers like this, Mai?' 'Yes, I get zer vip out!' retorted Mai with her eyes flashing and marched off with a dominating stride with David and the cameraman, looking ridiculous in her tight trousers with head lifted, leaving me bewildered. I stayed with Durrell and his friends talking and drinking my bottle of rosé, which under my contract of £2 a day for us both, Ishtar and I thought only reasonable. But underneath I felt quite painfully torn and connected it in some obscure way with Grant Watson and the darkening of the light when he had come like Tiresias and foretold the future. In the brilliant sun of the Camargue this was a troubling experience. This was the point of change: the postern gate of my exit. I did not know what was going to happen.

Looking back, I realised that Mai had changed from being a famous actress and a most beautiful personal friend of archetypal presence, to become an aggressive film director, learning a most difficult job among quite hostile and dangerous people, like a man. I should have been helpful, considerate and submissive as the others – the cameraman, David and even Ishtar, who had become neutral and acted like a hand-maiden to the Goddess, which I suppose is what happened. There was also something in common that Mai had with Ishtar – both being partly illegitimate? as far as was known! I had been advising Mai for weeks and with Ishtar's knowledge, it was quite a considerable contribution. I lent her Walter Starkie's book, *In Sara's Tents*, on which she finally based her film, besides cautioning her when we went among the gypsies, who were friendly, but still very suspicious and uncertain. Unlike the English gypsies they had not been tamed and their wildness was apparent. I told Mai to pay them, which she did not. One night when I was not there, a band of young men started goose-necking her and threatened to smash up the cameras, which had frightened her, though I believe she was very brave. But I did not know – was I her minder who should follow her about and protect her – at which, in any case, we took turns? But then it was my night off from being there and paying for supper.

When we had first got to the Camargue we drove about the salt lakes taking shots of that strange delta with so many waters, though Le Grand Rhône and Le Petit Rhône were the main rivers running into it. To do this we based ourselves on the ranch of M. Denis Colomb, who bred herds of fighting bulls and white Camargue horses used by Les Gardiens. He laid on a *ferrade* – a branding of young bull calves – and the chasing and throwing of the animal from horseback was exciting, but Mai thought it was too realistic for an English audience and did not make the best of it, which was a pity. One Gardien, unbeknown to Mai, held a red-hot brand to her backside while she was leaning over examining a calf for the amusement of his mates.

M'sieur le Patron, Denis Colomb, was a kind of medieval Lord of the Delta whom everyone respected and a man of great courtesy. He himself had made a classic film called *Crin Blanc* in 1953 which was a moving and powerful achievement but not liked in England. Other film stars were working there – Eddie Constantine was one I remember – and when Mai was among them she was very much her own actress self whom we all loved. I too felt at home in a familiar atmosphere from having been on the professional stage as a travelling performer for a whole decade. But when we returned to making our own film, the difficulties continued.

Mai's husband, David, was a silent and patient friend and was used to people falling for his wife, and I heard that she nearly drove the cameraman mad in Sweden when she was making the Lapp film, so he was accustomed also to those situations – the man had to leave in the end, I believe – so when he took me for a walk on the seafront one night with the great stars of the southern constellation looking down on us, I realised it was an act of friendly arbitration, as he started to give me a fatherly pep talk on the difficulties of the job and the obtuse nature of the creative mind. Having served my apprenticeship in this field with the One-Eyed Woman who always says No, and being an expert in my own field, I listened patiently realising he had a right to try and to preserve our growing friendship. But I did not see it as he did.

After that Mai and David locked themselves in their waggon writing the script. Ishtar was allowed in to do the washing-up and on May 24th, Mai's 36th birthday, in the early morning I was allowed to go to present her at the door with a beautiful plate from Arles, with a fish on it. But all remained austere and negative; she remained locked in. I went off drawing a good deal among the gypsies, only entering a situation while they were filming if it got dangerous.

ICE QUEEN

Mai had one of the first Polaroid cameras, which the gypsies thought was magic because it produced a picture almost at once instead of taking their image off in a black box. Even then I was apprehensive when she took a knife away from a Spanish gypsy who was cleaning a chicken, because it did not fit in with the shot she was about to take. For a moment it was tense. This time it was all right, but I was always vigilant in case it flared up.

I was told not to send photographs back to Tony Brode for the *Southern Echo* as he had asked, and as he was also David's friend I was acquicscent. But this added to the feeling of being cut off and squeezed out, by not allowing me to contribute to a record of these wild people about whom I knew a great deal. I was very distressed and just did not know how to handle the situation, so I decided to leave, after having waited a week for Ishtar to complete any work that might be needed, by standing in as an English gypsy because Cliff Lee had been unable to come.

Cliff did the trip later for the *National Geographical Magazine*, travelling from London to the Camargue, then on through routes taken by his ancestors to India where all gypsies originally came from. A beautiful book emerged.

I was sorry to go for other reasons. Durrell had the writer Henry Miller coming down, and had invited me over to La Somière to meet him, which I had wanted to do ever since I did a dust jacket for his book *Sunday after the War*, published by Tambimuttu in 1945, for Poetry London.

Just after I had loaded the car ready to leave I was driving along an unmade road by the sea looking for Ishtar, when my wheels went down to the hubs in loose sand with the engine screaming. At that exact moment – not knowing I was there – Mai who had been learning to ride a Camargue horse, suddenly mastered it, galloped from the shore and appeared towering over me on a sand dune sitting her white stallion – triumphant as it reared on its hind legs and neighed. This was a powerful woman whom the Gods only were allowed to love: this was the birth of Venus from the sea. I have since remembered how she brought the hero in *The Master Builder*, hurtling to his death at her feet.

That was her genius. She was a greater actress than a maker of films. The film about the gypsies was well photographed, but being so intense about writing the script, yet lacking experience or knowledge of the subject, it had been made on the wrong day. There are two processions every year: the one held by and for the Romanichals and gypsies from all Europe when they take their Patron Saint Santa Sara to the sea, is on the 24th May, Mai's birthday. The next day there is another procession, but only with Jacobe and Salome for the Church and the priests of the Church and the People, although the gypsies are there. It was on this second day that Mai filmed the procession for the documentary she made of the gypsies, *The Lords of Little Egypt*, which title I suggested.

This was because, on the actual day, Mai hired a boat for the cameraman to take the ritual on the beach from the sea, but they were too far out to reach it and found cameramen of all nations had waded into the shallows and were dancing to get shots between them and the ritual. When I saw them out there from the beach I realised they had also missed the real Gypsy Procession and would have to take the people's procession the next day. In my opinion this did not properly present the gypsy race at their devotions to their Black Saint Sara.

On their own day (the 24th) the gypsies take their Santa Sara from the great Saracen fortress church, out from the crypt where she lives all year by a Mithraic altar, into the upper church to be blessed, and from there carry her out chanting into the blinding sunlight as if the black guillotine of the shadow of the great doors had been lifted from them, chanting Ave Maria – the outcasts, the wandering tribes of India. She of the Silver Face, the Black Madonna in whom all their dreams had been woven and whose soul goes back to the beginning of time when God made the light and saw that it was good. They were the shadow of that light.

I was in this procession with Ishtar, helping to pull on the ropes of the catafalque carrying the image of Sara to the sea, with the Gardiens of the Camargue on their horses, their hooves plunging in the waves, just missing my feet and head as I, by sheer life-force, was impelled forward and submerged in the sea close to the image of the saint Sara herself. A fierce and primitive religious rite never to be forgotten. But the one Mai Zetterling directed was not the Procession of the Romanichals, although they were there, but of the people led by Père Fleury of Poitiers and his Priests chanting:

Viva Jacobé!
Viva Salomé!

ICE QUEEN

I realised now I had been displaced. I had fallen in love with Mai the Ice Queen, probably encouraged by her, to get her film made. It was the knife she used. And all that is left is the Lapp Hat which still hangs in my workshop over my desk. Not the Black Madonna, but my Northern Anima to whom I made an irreversible transference by projecting it on to her. David told me she still had my painting of the Dead Peacock and the self-portrait in her home in the South of France where she retired, probably after making many more films and driving many men to the delta of desolation. Enigmatic as the Arctic moon. I still grieve that we never went to the great river to hunt down the fish of life. It could have been so beautiful – and we would have got it right. She preferred to play out her life as a white witch in obscurity after she retired near Avignon.

When something beautiful yet tragic happens to a man it is a happening for all time even though by it he is extinguished. The day someone I love very much said to me years later: 'Mai Zetterling is dead!', it was a kick in the heart which I could scarcely contain. Later I wrote this:

MAJ ZETTERLING

'Switch on the Zetters magic, Mai!'
That's what I used to say.
And you diffused your arctic light
Across the sky of my day.
Then, fierce as a wild Swedish lynx
You could scratch
A sunset across my face
Quicker than a man thinks.
With shining gaff poised, pierce
The dorsal spine – unlace line,
Unlatch to catch attention
Without intervention or fear,
But with tragic grace,
Kill the fish of love with a single tear.

Now the *Daily Mirror* says you are dead,
Magical Mai Zetterling,

ICE QUEEN

I bring you roses as I hear the angels sing,
For you who loved a Warrior King
Laid under an English oak:
Felled a Master Builder with a single stroke.
How grandeur at your feet dies!
You stroked a painted peacock with your blue eyes
More lonely than a wild duck
And brought my Viking despair
To invoke your beauty and your power:
Hear that distant snowbell struck
Across a vast silence of icebound prayer
To lay before you my last frozen flower.

Ice more beautiful than a northern sky,
Power that held you in many coloured air
For only a little while,
Content to be there, dear Mai,
With only your smile and your golden hair:
Ice Queen on her throne.
Yet somehow you were always alone —
And I didn't know you could die.
No one could be your King:
No one from the far north
Beyond you could father forth,
Strike miracle and not cry
At being excluded from your arctic ring:
THAT was a terrible thing!

If you listen you will hear men say:
'Speak only with care, such special secret care!'
O, careful care not to hurt or start
The wound bleeding that is always there
From someone who was a silver strand
Woven in the ruthless robe of art
So that they could not stand ever alone and bear
The thought of such a one without that care,
Such secret care, terrible care from the heart.
How could death take such beauty unaware,
When she was weak and could not turn her head
In time to meet her majestic lover's stare

ICE QUEEN

Bending over to cover her till she was dead
And not snap her brittle spine of ice in air?

L'ENVOI

Dear, beautiful terrible Mai Zetterling,
Natural child of the snow,
As your midnight sun, like a golden butterfly
Thaws the fjords of Time, ice angels go caring
That the Enchantress, only I dared defy,
Is always remembered by me wearing
Your love orientated Lapp Hat
Painting myself as I die;
And your flashing sword of magic
That cut a sleeping King from your sky,
Faster than I have seen
Quicker than the heart shrinks:
I courted the Ice Queen
But was caught by a wild lynx.

Prospero: Magician

To be welcomed into my own home by someone I had never met was the strange experience of meeting Robert Graves: as though I had projected a thought as I walked up the path to my seventeenth century cottage of red brick covered with ivy: amid the japonica the front door opened and he was there: a tall grey haired distinguished man with a Greek nose and pale blue eyes confronted me. He smiled and took my hand.

'Hallo, Sven,' he greeted. 'My name is Robert Graves. Do come in!'

The house girl, Myrtle had admitted him when I was out and I had no idea that he was coming or how long he had been there.

I had recently returned from France, where I discovered a small zoo near Biarritz. It gave me the idea on my return of starting a zoo for children in my paddock, to open to the public. There were already peacocks, a llama, macaws, and an armadillo added to the Appaloosa horses and a Vietnam pig. To look after these there was a staff of two attractive Forest girls and the Irish groom called Fergus. As well I had my hands full in the workshops and studio. It was to be expected to have unusual creatures attracted to Home Farm, since the psyche was orientated thus. Who better than the Ice Queen herself, followed by Prospero from his Island?

At that time Robert Graves held the Chair of Poetry at Oxford University and had been there to give his annual lecture. With a curious kind of snobbery I did not expect of him, he was annoyed because Charlie Chaplin had been there to receive an Honorary D.Litt. Robert had given his lecture in Latin, which Charlie had not understood: whether Charlie had replied in broad Cockney and put in a comic remark is not known, but Robert was disgusted at his being there and Chaplin who was a latter-day philosopher after being the world's greatest comic was probably hurt by this.

'We can do without people like that!' said Robert.

'But he is a great comic!' I ventured. 'Out of the gutter with no education. Like most Cockney boys he had a great chip on his shoulder about that. So have I, so I know how difficult it is!' Robert looked at me and grunted.

'You don't think universities are any good then?' Robert asked, turning round. I was looking at his son standing beside him in front of the fireplace, William, who was shorter than Robert, wearing a Spanish hunting hat of brown fur: a sharp lively young man – then back at Robert.

'I don't know,' I said, a little nervously. 'I've never been to one!'

'But look at US, Sven!' Robert answered proudly.

'That's what I am doing!' He laughed immediately. This humour was a test of each other, like sounding a glass.

My little front room with its coloured glass against the light, which Mai had loved so much, the small stone sculptures and prints of horses, one or two small paintings, was once more alive with the presence of an unusual visitor, as if a magician – indeed Prospero himself with his Spirit Ariel – had appeared.

One of the Forest girls brought in a tray of cheese with new bread which we ate with whisky, talking all the time. Most people who have just met talk avidly, but people like this talk because they are vitally interested in one thing – life, its mystery and its interpretation – in a word, *being alive*, and when they talk they carry lightning that flashes from mind to mind. In a pause I asked Robert if he would like to step across the hallway to look at my writer's room.

'I've already been there,' he replied. 'You have all the right things for a writer's study!'

I was astonished. But perhaps it was his writer's curiosity, I thought. 'Was it?' I said out loud.

'What, my writer's curiosity? Yes, of course. But it's all right. Fine,' he said, 'especially the *Oxford English Dictionary*'.

I paused before my answer: 'I always say, 13 volumes of the *Oxford English Dictionary*, 13 volumes of Frazer's *Golden Bough* and a copy of the *White Goddess* are all you need to get through.' It was significant because I was writing the *Dark Monarch* which changed my whole life.

Robert was delighted with my answer.

Beryl was there, but said little. She sat quietly in the armchair eating and was probably fed up with hearing Robert saying over again the same things every writer's wife has to listen to as part of her devotion and quiet hatred. A quiet Queen living behind her King perhaps, but with a watchful eye, behind all the noise and glamour. Anyway we were all too rude to give her the chance to say anything. At this point Ishtar came in and Robert bent her back to kiss her so that her black hair nearly touched the carpet.

'Fergus is all right!' he announced when he had finished. 'He took me round and showed me everything. I've seen it all. Fergus is all right!'

PROSPERO: MAGICIAN

I was perplexed by this sudden statement, but it confirmed what I had believed, that she had known Robert before, in her first marriage when she lived on a Brixham trawler in the harbour at Palma Majorca. And had now asked him to come and vet Fergus, the Irish groom she had recently employed.

I had driven past Fergus the day he arrived, approaching the village with a haversack and no hat, and a red beard and knew he was heading for Home Farm and that he was to change my life, but I said nothing. The reference from Robert disturbed me because I was not supposed to understand it. But instead it sparked the same awareness in me and finally sent me on a torturous journey to Deya the following Spring – almost with loss of life. It was this kind of magic Robert carried with him and at once made me feel the magnetism of his personality – even the pre-Christian magic expressed in *I Claudius*. This was the 'Darkening of the Light' which Grant Watson had made me aware of: and the cymbal crash of my distant ancestor travelling down the centuries.

But Ishtar showed no sign of being disturbed and I remained outwardly calm as we saw our visitors down the long pathway to the car. Robert's tall figure in a camelhair coat with a wide-brimmed black hat on slightly overlong hair made the archetype of the magician which the ancient Forest could only evoke with Merlin, whose cry I thought I heard. Nothing untrue about him. A poet, if he is good is also unique. As he himself wrote: 'There is no gold but gold!'

I led him past the heavily scented musk roses, which were a cutting from my Aunt Slade's garden in Brighton, where I first smelt them as a boy and saw Augustus John drawings in her house. Augustus was only ten miles away at this moment, but as far as Robert was concerned that was as far as he would get, for he hated the great painter who tried to copulate with his mother.

'Need we be so silly, Mister John?' she had said when he was chasing her round the table, and he had stopped.

Augustus, who was a fan of Robert's, had asked me in a letter to help him make contact with Robert so that he could paint his portrait; he even sent a telegram at one point. But here I was with the man only held for a moment by the smell of musk roses and could do nothing.

Robert anyway was declaring he must catch the plane at Lydd which was a long way, drive through France to Barcelona across the Pyrenees, then fly to Majorca. He did not drive: Beryl and William had to do it: a long journey with winter approaching.

'I see you have VD, Robert?' said Ishtar, casually teasing him about his number plate on the Land Rover, at which he smiled and made some retort, at which exact moment I realised she had known him well and even more, as we laughed and waved them goodbye down the long lane and they were gone.

In the vacuum after friends have left we said nothing but went off to our various tasks that normally held us late in the day, both feeling conscious perhaps that a situation was emerging that would be even more difficult than we thought, though Ishtar had a way of submerging her emotions and carrying on, whereas I could not. She was more skilled than I – or knew more or simply didn't think it mattered.

I sat in my writing room as the place I had naturally gyrated to after another writer, so unassuming and yet so renowned, had been to see us. I looked at the Lapp hat on a nail over the books and a voice from inside: 'What about Mai, Sven?' Well – what about her? It was still painful.

But it did not occur to me that my earlier obsession with Mai Zetterling might have anything to do with Ishtar wanting Robert to vet Fergus – and get his approval. Shall I buy this horse? Is it all right? Will it go wrong if I do? It could well have been so. But I did not think Ishtar ever needed an excuse for anything she decided to do, simply because that is how she saw life and she reserved her right to live it direct. I had been so open about Mai and she had not hidden her interest. It was like sunlight through the window and we all accepted it. Ishtar even spoke of me going with Mai, and to me that seemed a natural sequence of events until she changed so dramatically and I became a whimpering Quasimodo. I had felt for some time that Ishtar wanted to be unlatched from our marriage. I am curiously Edwardian in that I never betrayed my woman unless marriage had been insulted from her side. When that taboo was broken it was a different matter. Although Mai had played the final polarity I needed to feel complete. When she went I was even more deeply concerned to hold the polarity that remained. Ishtar had the bit in her teeth and wanted freedom. In this way she had come from her first husband to my Tower and taken me, arriving like a young filly backing in the wind with her blue mane flowing. There it was – the same pattern: I could not hold her.

Looking across the starlit distance it does not seem strange that I met Robert Graves at this time of personal anguish, that he should have confirmed his cause and later helped to staunch the wound with his advice and wisdom.

The damage Mai had done was not healed but covered over. If Ishtar went, north and south of my soul would be a vortex. I did not know how to handle the situation. I had fallen into the bear-trap of loving two women and could say with Goethe: 'Alas two souls are housed within this breast!'

I got neither – from one a kick in the heart magnetic north: from the other a horse bite southerly. I had not been unfaithful to either, and David who was my friend I did not betray. The damage was done in silence. Was I saint or sinner? I ask myself – or just a prize cunt?

The rest of the winter was taken up with the difficulties of casting bronze, and because I had not enough experience I could not divine the ways of metal more than to tear one image out of the fire now and again that had the imprint of creation rather than technological perfection. I had a young painter to help me, whose pregnant wife worked in the kitchen and they both lived in the chalet. My commitment was absolute and I was about at all hours because the furnaces had to be brought to right temperatures and held till every drop of wax was melted from the mould before the metal could be melted and poured at 1100° Centigrade for the fierce transfusion to take place.

To keep awake I sometimes walked to the edge of the Forest lake, below my fields, to watch the fish move in the moonlight; perhaps take my small fibre-glass rod and cast for a golden carp, watch it take the float in a wide circle and move under like a submerging submarine; tighten the line by moving back slightly, pressing the tiny golden hook into his gutta percha mouth; see him break surface and fight; smash to moon like a glass of aquavit; bring him slowly in, obediently following the thin silver line that pointed at him like a finger between his ruby eyes; slip him into the gentle net and expertly remove the hook without harm or disturbing his slime coat that armoured him against fungus and death by burning, as my hot hand touched his cold body, and watched him move like a ghost back into the caves of his own mystery.

Then again the lake became the still centre which held together all I most cared for in life, with its tree roots reflected in the sky and a meteor shooting into its silent depths. Yet I could not clear myself of the feeling of uncertainty and heard the voice of Robert telling me the truth; it was also the voice of the poet and of magic, though he knew nothing of how I felt. When I asked Ishtar she only smiled. The people who worked for me closed ranks, even my own family – partly in defence, partly fear and partly not wishing to hurt me further.

With brown beard, happy face, decayed teeth, the otherwise handsome Fergus was about all day seeming to work, shouting as he pruned the roses: 'Up the IRA!' and as he mucked out the stables: 'Down with the British!' which seemed like a personal opinion so I did not interfere. He often got very drunk but it was some time before I realised he was an alcoholic: it only made him more genial and evasive with, always behind his beard, the enigma, the humour, even the taunting, sometimes deceiving remarks that might suddenly slash open the truth and blow up in my face. But I stayed silent. The tragedy is, I thought, that someone broke the thigh of Ireland so that it never grew straight, made it into a Man with a Limp, who gave us great poetry from Yeats; great painting from his brother, Jack; heavenly song from O'Hara, immortal books from Joyce, trenchant scholarship from Stephan MacKenna, plays from Wilde, and a box of bombs.

But what the young groom wanted I could not find out. He got death. One night after I had been pouring bronze I was about to go to bed for the first time in thirty six hours, when the young painter came to me to ask help his wife was in labour. I got out the car and took her to the Fenwick Cottage Hospital quite near. On the way I stopped at the stables to tell Ishtar, who was on watch for a foal to be born, but my daughter, pale and frightened, was on watch instead. I had walked into a situation where shadows and silence coming from the groom's living quarters spoke the truth.

I continued my journey to the hospital without saying anything. Later a son was born to Roger and Paddy – they called him Iwan.

When I returned there was no one in the cottage except Jasper asleep upstairs. I went to my study feeling the disturbance in me threatened my life and knew indeed this was the darkening of the light Grant Watson had cast from the *I Ching*. The force seemed to have turned inward against me and there was no one to talk to. I wrote on a piece of paper a note to myself:

> My life is breaking up. I am still sane
> and believe I am being betrayed. I feel
> suicidal, but hold on to life because I
> believe I can and must continue.

I then hid the note in a secret drawer in my desk, so that in a quiet moment I could confirm my experience to be true. Yet there was that awful element of uncertainty with which jealousy, when it is awakened

– the green serpent – injects the mind, as if some dark unseen Iago of the shadows was telling me that Desdemona was 'making the beast with two backs'! This was the terrible reality that the attraction between man and woman awakens in the mind of the third person. A thought that leads to rage and is death – suicide and murder, if the taboo is broken. And yet it was I who knew that the solution to life is polarity and therefore the love of two women. Simply because men are polygamous creatures and women, once they have their man, are usually monogamous. But no generalisation will solve this paradox or ameliorate the agony.

I thought of flying to Majorca to ask Robert Graves. He was the one who would know for certain and would speak because he was a man of truth, though I did not know if, like Prospero, it was he who had raised the tempest. And I hardly knew him. How could I ask? I was afraid.

The next morning I got at my young painter friend to tell me what he knew, but he was silent. I held him against the bench but he would not tell if he did know. I was very angry and could kill. He remained rigid and white, would not speak: courage linked hands with fear and locked his jaw. He went away to see his wife in hospital, maintaining his loyalties.

The metal I had poured the night before had now cooled and I broke the mould away gently to see if it had held. To my surprise it had, and when I cut away the bronze vents and runners the image was revealed, which I ground and polished and finally stood at the end of the day on a small pedestal: a tall Queen looked sadly down at me, Goddess of all my desires, for whom I would die. A poet's destiny. Art has no other orgasm.

Prospero's Island

Coming out of winter into spring the devils have their last fling and I was careful to protect myself against them, by reciting the chants Grant Watson had given me and some from other ancient books.

One morning a chicken's foot was left on the seat of my car; another morning a puma's foot was lying outside my workshop. Then there was that moment when I had convulsions by the farm gate and woke to find Ishtar leaning over me, all my life force spent. It was after that I went to see Peter and Katherine at Petersfield, but although I was able to tell them of my fears and the strange things that were happening, there was no solution – or only to practise white magic against the darkness, which I did.

Finally I made a decision to travel south. Though I wanted to go alone, the others wanted to come too, so I took Ishtar and my daughter Janet now about 18, my son Jasper, aged 8. Paul and my stepson, Willie, stayed at home with the staff and had a good time as far as I can tell. We drove first to Chartres for regeneration as before; next to Lascaux for the source energies of life, down through the Pyrenees where I saw a Bonelli's eagle on a telegraph pole and a society of vultures on a table of land on the way to Barcelona. We left the waggon at the Laughing Whale Camping Site and flew to visit Prospero on his Island which, Ishtar remarked, as we glided down towards it from above, was shaped like the head of a he-goat.

Soon we were being driven away from the town and its busy beaches through quiet villages, with dull red houses and orange trees in dusty squares, up the steep roads into the mountains until we reached Deya: it was no more than a group of houses on the mountainside with terraces of olive trees thousands of years old, twisted like serpents towards one another. We could not find Graves' place at first and the driver had to ask a local peasant who was at first mystified then suddenly it flashed on him.

'Ah si, Senor. Roberto Gravez! Si Senor!' he said smiling and pointing up the road. In a little while we were swung into the drive of a square Spanish house called Cannellun, with lawns and shrubs, lemon and oranges trees, where Robert and Beryl Graves greeted us with great friendliness. The heat, the silence, the beautiful light and scented air from the sea and Africa made my mind clean and it seemed the emotions I had felt all the way from England and made me morose, had gone. Kindness is a threat to every enemy.

Beryl had been scratched by her Abyssinian cat and was in some pain after having the wound dressed. As we came in another man was leaving. 'This is Anthony West,' said Robert, 'son of Rebecca West by H. G. Wells!' which was the strangest introduction I had ever had, but now seems normal since it happened in exactly the same way thirty years later – in fact recently in Dorset the phone rang and a voice said: 'You won't know me, but my name is Kitty West, wife of Anthony West who is son of Rebecca West by H. G. Wells!' Anyway a significant peg in history, worth recording because that's how it works. I never took up either introduction so I don't know what was in destiny's store.

I sat and talked to Beryl about her hand and other things. She seemed to be a kind and sympathetic person, but I said nothing about my immediate trouble and did not know how much she knew – unless she was Ariel in this:

> Sit then and talk with her, she is thine own.
> What Ariel! Industrious servant Ariel!

Robert took me off to his study: a small square room with windows looking out to sea and books all round, as with most writers, those used mostly for reference – but the sea, always the ancient sea in attendance, which is what I missed so much at home. In this case the sea of the Greeks, Phoenicians, Romans and Arabs. Somehow the atmosphere was charged with history, and if Robert had said the white flash of foam I saw was Icarus falling into the sea, I would have believed him and he would have smiled. He showed me some sculptures, all symbols of the White Goddess and some quite early. I gave him a small bronze I had cast of a standing woman holding a child, which he put among the others saying:

> Another White Goddess, Sven. Another White
> Goddess!

I talked to him about the book that had penetrated deeply into the heart of most western poets and how it affected my sculpture in Cornwall when it was first published ten years before. He told me how the books of reference he needed to write it had come on their own as if by magic and the whole thing seemed to go by itself once he was started.

'The White Goddess wrote itself!' he stated quite suddenly, as if to be emphatic was of paramount importance.

He seemed to be more free and natural than when, in England, he had invited me into my own house. His hair seemed more silvery, his skin more sunburnt, his clothes light and casual; a cotton shirt with a pair of ridiculous Bermuda shorts and a wide-brimmed Spanish straw hat when he went out. No colour. But outside and inside were quite different here, because they were more fluid than I was accustomed to, so I was only aware of being in one place as on a live line which might itself move at any moment.

In this room I was unable to talk as I wanted, about private matters. The things he talked about were of first interest to me and the underground stream was lost sight of till it came up in the garden where his Tiberian profile was stamped on the Mediterranean like the prow of a ship on a Roman coin. His mind was lively and humour (thank God) quick. I was not surprised to know he had Spike Milligan staying. As with others I found no incongruity of talking to a great man in a local situation, as though Homer had dropped in for a glass of wine. It was all so natural and real. The build-up was on the outside in the world, and nothing to do with this private meeting of two men interested in the same thing — poetry. At one moment I was discussing poetry and at another following an argument between him and Beryl about getting his hair cut before going to America at the end of the week on a lecture tour.

'It looks all right to me!' I said.

'But Beryl thinks I look too much like a poet!'

'Well it IS rather long, Robert!' 'I tell you what,' he said, brightening up. 'I'll get it done at Brussels when I change planes. There is sure to be a good barber at the airport. Do you know if there is, Sven?'

'Yes, I think there is!' I replied, but as I had not been to Brussels Airport since 1944 when I was coming home on a stretcher, I thought I had better say no more. I don't know if Beryl was convinced, but it seemed to settle the matter.

I can't remember the sequence of events, or only like toothpaste coming out of a tube, during those few days because, behind the experience of staying with the Graves, was the central darkness that dominated me and I could not be unbearable as I was on the journey down through France and Spain, but there was fear and inner tension as before a battle, knowing there must be a breakthrough. Talking to Robert about books, Beryl about Majorca, children and England I was already beginning to win and put the trouble away when it came up in an unexpected manner, as if on its own.

'Let's go the the sea!' said Robert suddenly. And we got up and went there. In England it would have meant walking down some side street to a crowded pebble beach. Here we walked through orange and olive groves, where a young girl came out and talked, standing with long hair and brown skin, bare feet, skirt of cotton or silk, as Robert paused in his large straw hat to talk to her – imposing, beautiful and courteous like a noble stallion, making us all a little less worthy of life, except Jasper and Robert's son Tomas in their Cyclopian childhood, shouting and laughing as they came to the cliff edge, up to which they ran, throwing huge stones over the edge, stopping just before they were in danger of going over themselves – awakening in me the terror of watching my horses on the North Cliffs in Cornwall, charging the Atlantic Ocean. Down below, the sea churned as though it was being whipped up by Prospero himself, opening its throat as if to swallow us. The tempest inside me seemed to break and I wanted to leap in.

'Hell is empty and all the devils are here!' I shouted. Ishtar followed quietly without even a smile as though she had done it before, while Robert led us down a narrow path past rocky enclaves like those in Blake's drawings of Hell, and every now and then we had to leap across crevasses that loosened stones and sent them hurtling down to the boiling sea. But for my dancer's balance and obedient feet I am sure I would have fallen. I was shaking all over. But Robert sauntered on chewing a grass with indifference.

'What do you think of it?' he asked over his shoulder.

'Terrifying. It's like one of Blake's drawings of Hell!'

'Why are you terrified?'

'The height, the loose ground, the track, the mad sea below. It is Hell! Do you expect me to be enjoying it? YOU are doing it. I'm sure you are!

He smiled to himself and walked on.

I was relieved to get into the cool orange grove where the young woman came out and talked to us again. I felt there were more young women hidden everywhere on the mountain, this side of which he seemed to own: handmaidens of the White Goddess to whom his dedication was complete. It was a further relief to get back to the cool garden and a cooler drink. Robert brought out some manuscript poems for me to see and on which he was still working. They were some of the finest later love poems at which he so excelled in their intimacy and insight, taking you into and out of the experience or just leaving you to contemplate it, without the craggy difficulties of other contemporary poets, leaving a thankful and kind, if sad lyricism, instead of a bleeding mind. He said, simply:

'The one theme of poetry is, properly, the relation between man and woman!' That is still so for me, since the same postern gate encloses our vision.

It took the last of my vital energy to read them but in return I was recharged at source by what they contained. While we talked about them afterwards, he walked round me, bending over to snatch at the grass on which I was sitting. I don't know if he was weeding or grazing or just exercising a primitive habit of medication, listening to every word I said and snatching again as he answered. In this way the invisible thread of poetic instance passed between us.

At this point another poet, who had helped me in Cornwall to change a cowshed into a sculptor's workshop at Cripplesease, appeared. His name was Keith Baines, a wild Russian-looking fellow who showed me more poems, but I was quite near mental exhaustion and could not give them full concentration. Years later, when I found the same poems in a shop in Salisbury dedicated to Robert (which secretly I don't think he wanted) I was able to give more to them. The point here is that Keith's appearance made me realise that he was one of many artists living in the village who gathered round the Master, who was generous and kind to them. When we had been there a little while longer they came one by one, and, with free entrance to the house, went in and helped themselves to whatever drink they wanted from a cupboard and drifted away again, perhaps saying a few words especially if they knew me, like Cheeko the Bum from St. Ives days.

As the afternoon wore on I found myself at the front of the house with my daughter, Janet. Instead of being sunburnt and pleased with a book Robert had just given her, she was pale and distressed. We sat on a plinth talking until Beryl came out from what seemed to be the kitchen just inside the front door, carrying a bowl of nuts. She gave us each a hammer and asked us to shell them. As we gave each shell a sharp tap a brown nut fell on to the sunlit stone. It was a dreamlike situation which made me realise it was a moment in which I could speak: and I knew that Jan knew. Once a thing is said its force increases and can be understood. I heard my own voice speak.

'I must *know!* If you tell me I am right I can go to Robert: otherwise I can't. I am going mad. *I must know!*'

Between each sentence a nut was cracked, emphasising the urgency of my need for the truth to fall out. Jan had stopped working. Her beautiful blue eyes were filled with tears.

'Am I right. Is it Fergus?'

'Yes, Dad, it is him!' she said quietly. This is a moment for which I will always thank her. I put down my hammer and went to Robert in his study.

'You busy, Robert?' I asked gently pushing the half-open door.

'No. It's all right. I'm not doing anything, Sven. Come in.'

'Can I see those small sculptures again?'

'Of course!'

He started to show me the Goddess sculptures from Babylonia, Rome, Greece, Crete, Cyprus, among which was my own little bronze of a Mother and Child I had given him, looking strangely familiar among the others. He picked it up.

'That is the fulcrum!' he said. 'Once there is a child, domesticity ensues, which is suicide to the Goddess! You have to choose.'

'Fergus!' I exclaimed suddenly. It worked like magic.

Robert was not surprised or uneasy. I think he expected it and, because he thought I knew about it, he talked freely. We listened to one another because we both had a natural understanding in these matters which cut across the arrogance in each of us. For me it was a relief because of the fragmentation in my life caused by a sexual device being placed in its centre ready to go off. Now it was much easier. And Robert was in no way new to such situations. In fact I think he handled them quite frequently. But he was on the side of the Goddess and I had so far failed to give absolute allegiance to her by failing to conquer Mai. The breaking down of marriage shattered the dome of many coloured glass I was trying to build. I had not yet seen that Truth is All.

'Christ!' I exclaimed. 'It's like being under fire in France again!'

'But it's worse, Sven. Far worse!' he said. Coming from one who was given up for dead on the Somme, this was a powerful reply. And he meant it.

I returned his gaze. He knew the comparison but was not sorry for me. If anything I was hurting myself. I tried to counteract it by being practical. 'I can't go back while he is there,' I said. 'I shall have to kill him!'

'No, you must not kill him, Sven,' said Robert calmly, leaning back. 'Don't do that. Don't kill him. Simply send a message and say he must be off the premises before you return. In that way you won't see him again. But you mustn't kill him.'

I followed Robert's hard common sense and sent a cable later from the Correrro Central in Palma, instead of flying straight home to kill him.

'Fergus isn't important you see, Sven. He is only an instrument being used to lever you out of the way. *STAY FIRM.*'

'Yes, but it makes me suicidal as well. Don't you understand? I swing from one to the other and the emotion is so violent it is too deep to understand. I am afraid it will break the bridges of the mind!'

'Yes, of course you are. That is why I say *STAY FIRM*. Death is in the pattern: you must not let it push you either way. If you do it could be you who will die.'

Robert had a very slight lisp which gave an edge to what he was saying when he was excited. I was thankful for his clarity of mind: it enabled me not to pull any of the levers that would spell disaster.

When it was getting dark Robert and I, with Ishtar, walked to the café in the village by descending a long flight of wooden steps. It was very crowded.

The electric light dimmed every now and then as it did in Robert's house, Canellun. He said he had given the light to the village some time ago but was not happy with the way they operated it: they seemed to have found a way of doing him down over it, but he could not tell how. This was important, showing him to be an integral part of the community: everyone cared about him, even though their gratitude came and went like the electric light he had given them.

At the café I saw Keith Baines again and Cheeko the Bum who was painting there and selling his pictures in Paris, as well as several others whose faces were dimmed in the heavy cloud of cigarette smoke amid the noise that was deafening. I made a quiet cell of silence inside the roar of music and voices in an attempt to listen to Robert talking about what he called his 'Bête noir, Ben Nicholson' through a huge meal with Spanish wine, which after a day with

Prospero whipping up the sea and later sending Ariel to my help, I cannot now remember. One image remains: Graves' tall figure in a wide brimmed hat in the moonlight as we stood outside afterwards, reminding me that he was going to lecture in America.

'I am an exile too, you know!' he said as we walked slowly back to Canellun with our Roman Emperor.

I slept in William's room: he was away. I don't know where Ishtar slept that night. As I went to sleep, with the din of the café still in my ears, I could not help thinking that there were many strands of destiny that came to Robert's hands to be untangled and woven back into life: in some way a huge novel that he created and lived but never wrote down except perhaps in *I, Claudius*.

At first light I was out on the same road watching the sheep grazing on the terraces under the olive trees, bleating over the dull roar of the ageless sea.

> This is Oceanus, the origin of Gods and Men,
> Ever ebbing and flowing, now forth, now back. . .

which words Homer wrote long before Christ had found his Gesthemane in such a place, where everyone was asleep but I.

Here there was tranquillity. Robert had chosen to live here after his war which was a far worse war than my war, even though you can only be killed once, and death can be your friend. This place resolved the poles of his being: his quest for the Goddess, his life as a poet with a place to write and bring up his family. He wrote prose and lectured for a living, yet shut out the anger and corruption of modern man, as much as possible.

On the silent white road at dawn a figure walked towards me wearing a long dress, with a snake ring on each hand and a snake necklace. It was Ishtar the Snake Goddess, strange and magical in the pale light.

> Upright she stands
> In a sculptured skirt:
> In her ancestral hands
> She holds the serpent and the serpent.
> Her face is the moon above
> And her hair the night:
> A spiral is about her girt —

PROSPERO'S ISLAND

> Mystical woman of other lands,
> Goddess of War and Love,
> Priestess of visionary sight:
> Indifferent to the death of lovers
> Killed by her golden glove.

I had not expected to see her: she came from nowhere.
'I know about it now. Robert told me last night!' My voice was husky.
'About what?' She was perplexed.
'Fergus!'
Her face, framed in her deep blue hair, went stone white. Without an answer she went up the dusty road to the orange grove near the house. I went to the cliff edge. As though looking into my own soul I watched the sea boiling below, feeling the double vertigo which grief and anger bring when combined together, pulling me down like an octopus, knowing I could have picked her up above my head like an insane dancer and thrown her on to the rocks below and myself have followed. I only know that it was by the touch of an invisible hand that I did neither. My whole existence seemed submerged in water. Later I wrote this:

> Hell's last circle Deyá is —
> Come not to rebehold the stars —
> Here the twisted centuries hiss,
> The sea boils in Devils' jars.
>
> Poets haunt the olive groves,
> And twine their hearts with silver snakes
> Destroying where the Goddess moves,
> Fierce where the seascape quakes.
>
> Innocence of children lives not here,
> Nor love in elegance and pride
> Can her lovely emblems wear
> Or the white horse of Beauty ride.
>
> Only the gentle goats and bell-
> Ringing bible-grazing sheep
> Can help my bruised spirit sleep
> Until this dark magic breaks its spell.

Back at the house Robert got breakfast. He started by picking oranges from the trees outside, where he did a good deal of gardening by day. Then he squeezed them through a metal instrument, emphasising the point he was making as the thick juice ran into our cups and the pips slithered over his sensitive fingers. He was very tense.

It was all poetry with him: even when later he took us up a long case of stone steps to a closed courtyard of a Spanish residencia in vicious heat, to see a coloured donkey in which Ishtar was interested for her researches. The creature was fine and brayed as loud as an ancient skin bellows when it saw us moving like flies in amber through the thick sunlight. We talked all the time. The donkey brayed again. I quoted G.K. Chesterton:

> With monstrous head and sickening cry
> And ears like errant wings
> I'm the devil's walking parody
> Of all four-footed things.

I quoted after 25 years and think it was right. But Robert was silent, so I never knew.

From there we went to another house on the edge of a silent village, where a woman stood alone and a linnet in a wicker cage sang in a block of cool shadow: both prisoners for life. Robert had bought the house years before, which he said I could use at any time. It was cool with stone floors and walls, with sparse wooden furniture. In a stone niche there was a glass amphora which seemed to hold the silences of this timeless place. It was the colour of golden honey. Although it was probably light modern glass of no value, it seemed to me to have a simple stateliness of form and I liked it. I thought it was beautiful and remarked about it to Robert.

'Then have it, Sven! You must take it with you. It's yours.'

It was no use resisting Robert when he was like this, even though he might have wished he could have got rid of me as easily, and took it as though he had given me my life back in a new and fragile form – also with a feeling of thankfulness. I handed it to my silent daughter telling her to take it with her as though it was my life, safely back to England.

This she did with devotion.

It was returning down the long flight of steps to Deya that Robert talked of Vaughan Williams. 'What did you think of him?' he asked.

'He was the most humble man I have ever met!' said Ishtar. 'Humble?' replied Robert testily. 'What do you mean by H*UMBLE?* Aren't I humble?'

'Not really Robert. Not in the way he is!'

'But he – Uncle Vaughan Williams was here only last week and we sat in the same café as you were in last night singing songs and drinking wine together. I didn't see anything H*UMBLE* about him!'

Ishtar had touched a raw spot on the wrist of his vanity, and the more it was scratched the worse he got: especially as her humour had quite sharp nails. He wrote to her later: 'If you refrain from using your magic destructively and keep your sense of buxom crazy humour you'll survive. . .'

We moved into laughter.

When we got back, there was a salad with aromatic oils to eat amid the coming of poets, and the drinking of wine, but always with the understanding not to ask for Robert. This made me realise that I had broken the rule on the first day, because, although his presence was always there, he often disappeared to work or be alone or with someone else – perhaps one of the young girls, with whom he seemed to alternately fall in love. I had much to learn.

> He was the magical Enchanter who
> Could love or hurt those too near his flame;
> To occupy his time in Xanadu
> The spellbound women were drawn by his name.

He had that curious gift Shelley is said to have had: of suddenly appearing at your side – which was no more than an awareness of his visibility – then disappearing. Shelley was often naked when he did that: not so Robert: at least not when I was there.

I was shown the garden again and at the back of the house there was a small built-in theatre where Robert produced plays and had poetry readings, none of which I was able to attend. His life on the island was all poetry as far as he could make it so – for its own sake. In spite of his vast scholarship, which sometimes had an almost perverse twist in its interpretation, and might even have been pure invention, he insisted that his prose writings were all money spinners: even Claudius. Lecturing also. He liked lecturing in America because he said they treated him like a demi-god and he could do anything with his audiences.

This intellectual power, which might have made him a less great poet, gave him an overall control when he was lecturing, the lack of which defeated Dylan Thomas who was probably petrified until he was pissed – and was finally spat out as a dead man across the Atlantic: a poet whom Robert could not stand; yet conversely, nor could he have written *Under Milk Wood*, which comes from the raging blood of the people. Robert was a poetic snob who could not stand Charlie Chaplin or Lawrence Durrell, but when I quoted the sonnets he at once looked up and said: 'O yes, Will Shakespeare's all right!' His great friend in America was Robert Frost, whom he praised as a great poet.

My own feeling was that Robert did not like any other poets at all. It was his defence. But he himself was a fine poet: perhaps not a great one – I don't know.

There was a good deal of talking with the *DUENDE* active enough to get everyone excited, except perhaps when I was being aggressive to my host and he was defending his castle from attack with enormous patience. Time did not matter; nor the amount of wine we drank. When you are drinking someone else's wine the supply always seems to be bottomless.

One of the young ladies with long hair came up from the Casa del Pisa that evening to cook a meal, moving silently on bare feet. She was very nervous but we praised her and she was pleased. Beryl very wisely got us to help with the chores – even cracking nuts. Robert was exempt. He was spinning his thread.

When the meal got going with Himself at the head of the table, he started to relate a sequence of events going back to the eighteenth century thus:

'Dr Johnson patted the head of a baby who turned out be be William Blake; he patted the head of a baby who grew up to be Shelley; Shelley patted the head of another baby who was Robert Browning; Browning patted the head of a baby on Putney Hill who was Swinburne and HE patted the head of a baby who was Robert Graves!'

The sequence ran like falling dominoes down the centuries and I at once remembered reading a similar account in a literary magazine of my youth, by a well-known critic whose name stood on my uvula but I would not come out.

'David Gar. . . no not him. Sir Edmund Something!'

'Sir Edmund Gosse!' Beryl supplied the answer from the other end of the table.

'That's it, Sir Edmund Gosse. He was a great friend of Swinburne's I believe.'

'There you are Robert,' she added, correcting him. He went quiet.

It was then I realised there was a kind of contest going on all the time, in which I had inadvertently scored. I never really understood about one-upmanship, if that is what it was – perhaps because I had never gone to public school. I was just let free from inner tension and probably rather excited and pugnacious. Awful how you are when you don't know!

The evening grew through talk of Augustus John chasing Robert's mother round the parlour table, to readings by Robert of Blake's more tendentious prose writings (not very well) and a theory of his about Fanny Brawne and Keats. The impotence of Lawrence of Arabia, of whom Graves was the official biographer – until we finally got stuck on poetry again – and Yeats, whom Robert hated. 'He behaved badly to my father, Sven!' The women having got tired, and perhaps bored, had gone to bed. Robert and I remained till midnight withered into morning.

I was standing up for Yeats not knowing he was in Majorca in earlier days when Robert was with Laura Riding, and something went wrong there. It always stood out as an odd kind of relationship about which Augustus John had written such a puckish pasquinade for Roy Campbell and sent me a copy in a letter:

> Robert Graves met his grave
> By riding Laura Riding:
> Then he got better.

I don't think there was any question of there having been an affair. Yeats' sex life never seemed to get off the ground until he started having his chambermaids as an old man, and writing his last important poems – unless he liked wrapping it in long heavy hair to the call of the curlew. Between the church and the curlew it got delayed.

It was something Yeats said to Laura Riding or Laura Riding to Yeats sparked off a quarrel. Robert said that as a result of this they both had to tell him they would have nothing more to do with him and broke off the friendship.

It seemed paltry to me, who was getting well pissed by now and wanted to get into a real bullroaring argument. But Robert took it all very seriously.

'Anyway, he was a great poet!' I said, obtusely.

'Yeats was a minor poet who bloated himself up, Sven. Greatness is something else!'

'Madness!' I put in. 'Going mad. I don't think you are mad enough, Robert. Where is your tiger?' Robert was very patient with me and defended himself with some dignity.

'My poetry always makes good prose sense.' he said quietly. 'I like to make the heat go everywhere like the Aga, instead of losing it all up the chimney.'

'That's it. That's what I mean. Too local to be always great. Now listen to this.' I opened Yeats at the 'Second Coming' and read in a loud sonorous voice:

> .... somewhere in the sands of the desert
> A shape with a lion's body and head of a man
> With gaze blank and pitiless as the sun,
> Is moving its slow thighs while all about
> Reel shadows of indignant desert birds.
> Darkness drops again; but now I know
> Twenty centuries of stony sleep
> Are vexed to nightmare by a rocking cradle,
> And what rough beast, his hour come round at last
> Slouches toward Bethlehem to be born?

When I had finished the last couplet, letting out the monstrous poetic image with almost a roar, Robert remained silent. Then he won the day completely by saying in a quiet voice: 'You read so beautifully, Sven, that anything in that way would seem like great poetry!'

He then turned on his heel, went through the kitchen, opened the front door and retched, as though he was being sick with anger perhaps. I went quietly to bed.

The next afternoon Beryl drove us to Palma, Robert and I hunched up beside her in the Land Rover down the long mountain road, the others in the back. We went shopping. Robert whipped into the Post Office with Ishtar. It did not occur to me till now, thirty years later, what messages might have been sent – and to whom – before mine.

I waited outside the grocer's while Beryl bought some things and later Robert came in to pay the weekly bill. But they took a long time and I went off to look at the town with its monument set on four tortoises, the bony horses of the carriage drivers, the artists sitting under the wall trying to sell their paintings, and the fierce cathedral where I quietly described a circle round Ishtar while she was looking at the altar and said a prayer looking at the saints in molten fire of the coloured windows. Then we returned and waited for Robert under some plane trees.

'There are no more aeroplanes today' he said as he came up. 'I've booked you in at the hotel over there for the night. I've got to get ready for the trip to America.'

'You didn't get your hair cut Robert!'

'No. I'll do as you said and get it done at Brussels.'

'O Christ!' I ejaculated suddenly. 'I wonder what is going to become of the whole thing!' He started to move away throwing his hat up among the plane trees and catching it as it fell. 'It all depends on the White Goddess! It all depends on the White Goddess, Sven!' he said over and over again.

That is how I last saw him.

When I got back to England the Irishman was gone, but the damage was enough to have broken my marriage and Ishtar left soon after. She went to him and they were married as soon as my divorce proceedings were over. A daughter was born. They lived in Ireland and I heard later that Fergus fell in the Liffey when he was drunk and got washed out to sea, with the rider that it was thought to be an IRA execution, but I was never able to confirm this. Robert was right: death was in the pattern. Had I not taken his advice and stayed firm, it would have been me.

During the period that followed I had a long friendly correspondence with Robert which was sensitive and wise and talked also of poetry – even helping him with one, maybe more, all of which helped me to restore my balance at the fountainhead.

I value this unique friendship. Not again will Prospero open the front door of my cottage to receive me; or on his island act Virgil to guide me through the circles of Hell in search of the Goddess.

For his poetic genius and for his tolerance I thank him. His arrogance I see as a reflection of myself. To the agonies of the heart he gave me no answer, even when I asked:

> You who are an archaeologist of love
> What emblems find you in this pit of wounds?
> What bones lay bare the dried up heart
> That once were girders for the strain of love

And stress that heals the cut of absence?
Heart hollow with love's pain.
Spirits part, calling one another down the years:
Perhaps this glass amphora holds their tears,
Perhaps their stories will one day unwind
To where love's enterprises start!

I thank him for the glass amphora which my daughter got safely home and now stands on my desk. I place in it four stems of corn at harvest time every year – One for Woman. One for the Poetic Moment. One for Love, and one for the Poet making his poem alone.

When I heard of Robert's death in 1985 I had been dying almost to the day, which made it easier to return because the news awakened in my spirit his poetic force and wound me back into life. I kept his newspaper photo on the locker by my hospital bed. For Prospero on his Isle the work was done and his spirit set free.

When a man or woman dies it is always a time for sadness and grief, but when a poet passes it is a matter for the angels. From Homer to the present time this has been so, and will continue through the star-laden centuries to come, as long as the calliper of hard reason does not extinguish the spirit which, like stars touching, can give that spark which lights the unknown, and the human who is able to transmute it into beauty and wisdom, usually at the cost of his own life. It is up to him which level of existence he chooses, but he must never pretend that a mechanical device can create the gold which is the emblem of eternal vision.

ROBERTO GRAVEZ

The old Gods sail their ship of gold
Through the harbours of the sun,
Handmaidens with you gold enfold
Beyond landfall's folding done.

Take the last from the sacred glade –
Poetry of the written word –
Where Homer's form still like a shining blade
Stands sharp as a Saracen sword.
Here the White Goddess keeps

PROSPERO'S ISLAND

Her endless vigil on the wind
Spinning while the poet sleeps
A poetic instance from his mind.

You turned your disillusioned soul away
From our world enclosed in glass,
Where men are dumb before the gold of day
And vultures snatch our children as they pass —

To be a Prince of Poets in a cloak
And wide sombrero hat of black.
Red scarf for passion at the throat
Beyond the legislator's fierce attack.

It was not a burning image forever new
That flashed from your mind's golden rods,
But a poet's even arras made by you
Woven as a weaver for the Gods.

You were the wise Enchanter who
Could love or hurt those too near your flame
To amuse yourself in Xanadu
And bring the spellbound women to your name.

Like Prospero on his Isle, the work was done,
Your spirit free: the Goddess, her magic to perform,
Held your profile to the Spanish sun
And on her double coin struck your form.
Solid on groundswell as you slowly go
Stand for all time firm, Roberto Gravez:
One last toast while on the crest you flow
I drink your gold still molten on the waves.

PREDELLA

In poetic instance me you
come before:
I, in art and love,
no less than you were more.

Cornish tin miner. Drawn ca 1946 on an underground visit to Geevor Mine, Cornwall, with Peter Lanyon and John Wells

PART THREE

KINGS AND QUEENS

There stand stately Kings and Queens
Rulers of the sunset throne
Bathed in light I've never seen,
Monarchs of the wave and stone.

Sven Berlin

The Dark Monarch.

"The Evil one was upon me"
                        Borrow.

The Islands.

CUCKOO TOWN By day, by Night

The Tower. The Brothers. The Painter. The sea, the Earwig, Evil Eye, world of art. The white Goddess. Christof & the Jacket of madness. Gethsemene.

Author's sketch dated ca. 1960

The Dark Monarch

For an artist, when his name grows in the outside world and becomes something to consider, even to be demolished, that world seems to diminish in size and power: the certainty of achievement more possible. To grasp this should be simply to see that there is no empty niche left in the wall with your name on it at the end, or history will say: I wonder what happened to him? – but for no other reason. My own niche had been won but not occupied long enough to prevent it being eroded by shadowy sanctions after I left St. Eia. I was rejected from corporate, national and international recognition, which I had already won.

I have found that for me life goes in sections which are clear cut: when one period is over the arcades of the soul must be swept clean, although there are shifting platforms of experience going on at other levels. This I do by writing a book. It helps me to keep in touch with the workings of history, which is like going down into the main engine rooms somewhere deep in the centre of my ship which are the centre also of life: thus many things are foreseen and many no longer expected. By writing a book about what has happened one is better able to understand the present.

After the war, disgusting and yet moving as it was, I wrote my war book: *I am Lazarus.*

> I am Lazarus come from the dead
> Come back to tell you all: I shall tell you all!

It happened that I waited thirteen years before I found a publisher in Anthony Dent who was to print it. Apart from my biography *Alfred Wallis: Primitive* which was written in the early part of the war, and five years in the hangers, Lazarus was my first book about my life, and it came through well without any over-editing spoiling my natural way of writing, which was to mature into something worth following as an extra art form, when most writing was so bad – based on a clipped-hedge journalism which probably grew out of Hemingway and got stuck in the snow. Anyway I could never see how anyone should have the gall to alter anything one has written any more than they should change one brush stroke in a painting one has done, or a chisel cut in a sculpture. This kind of thing should be limited to nuts and bolts – any kind of spelling or grammatical mistake. But for me it is unforgivable cutting up long paragraphs into small ones and spoiling the natural flow of language – often meaning and poetic statement. Anthony Dent was particularly good about this and when he told me I was the most conceited author he had ever met, though I at least had something to be conceited about, I was encouraged. But he did not have my books vetted for libel, about which I did not know and he did not expect to happen.

There is a frontier where excellence of editing and the poetic statement meet and form a paradox. Only by sensitivity to the writer of what might be a new statement of unique vision can the editor give full chance to poetry and meaning by letting it alone as his best judgement in fulfilling his job.

Lazarus cauterised my mind and assuaged some of the shock which passing through a war imposes: though the shock lasts for life. At least with me it has. I killed a good many creatures when I came back, to my shame: it seemed less cruel than killing a man. Now I would not sacrifice the miracle of engineering that is a mayfly and have gradually climbed out of the blood pit where these things go on. It is for each to realise his life in the way that brings the most out of him to give light to evolution. Yet much in my nature was resolved by going to war. I now understand the destructive force as part of creation and how the flower of greatest beauty grows best on the foulest dung heap. Out of this I would say my answer is that each of us on his way to Xanadu should kill a lion: out of that the sweetness will come and he will be his own man. But the greenstalk who harms an old man cracks the chalice of wisdom which must be kept full in every age: he should be killed.

In writing *The Dark Monarch* I almost killed myself. It was as if, with the innocence of a child, I had thrown a match into an ammunition dump and set it off: like the Crystal Palace firework display of my childhood. It has gone on exploding ever since. It was something I touched without knowing, and have not yet found out what it was unless it was in illuminating the truth that there is the presence of evil in each of us and that we have the onus of victory or defeat, in the end, on our own shoulders.

This happened with my book on Alfred Wallis: after 50 years it is still high explosive – though not so bad as *The Monarch*.

After the period of experience which damaged and ended my marriage to Ishtar – with great sadness but practically no resentment, because it made me realise I was almost impossible to live with – I found myself being, first and foremost, father and mother to four children, three of whom were mine and one a stepson, who with his mother Ishtar had lived in Majorca on a Brixham trawler with her first husband who was a friend of Robert's. Thus it is, when a person leaves, all the threads are trailing everywhere and weaving their own patterns of possibility that impinge on the main arras and become part of it for a time. My problem was to set the domestic framework right. Jasper had been rolled in a sheepskin where he had fallen asleep watching 'telly, on the front room carpet, not knowing what had happened. Ishtar did not say goodbye. He being only eight, I did not know how I should tell him. In fact I didn't. I allowed him to realise over a period of time that she was not there, to avoid any sudden shock that might get lodged in the lower mind as he grew, with its attendant emotions and cause him trouble later. The other children helped me to re-organise, but disintegration had started to set in. When something basic, like a depth charge, happens and no one knows, other things start at once to go wrong.

The first and most vital thing was that the authorities closed down the Children's Zoo, which had been an immediate success and would have held things together because I was already making an income on the plus side, the lack of which was the main difficulty all along because I could not sell my work. No planning permission. I should have fought it in the courts. I had a case to expel some squatters and a divorce already on my hands. With this I could not have gone more than waist deep, because the failure of my marriage had taken my last chance of stability away. Money was getting low. I had kept books, of course, but on the stables side it was a disaster. So the staff had to go and the creatures were sold.

I turned more to writing and asked Dents if I could have a book to follow *Lazarus:* I offered two. Anthony wrote back: 'But do I take it that I can either do *Dark Monarch* or *Spectre* in November 1962? How do we stand about the illustrations for these?'

He chose *The Dark Monarch*.

Behind the experience of meeting and foolishly falling in love with Mai Zetterling, and forming a friendship with Robert Graves, I had my heart trapped under a stone in Cornwall, and it caused me some anguish because I missed my friends and our wild life by the sea. I did not regret getting out of the politics which were of the most vicious kind – like going for a bathe and swimming into a shoal of barracudas. But people like Bryan Wynter were still about, Sydney Graham and Nessie: they could not be replaced by the hard drinking commercial core of the Forest pubs, except for the horse dealers and the gypsies. I suppose this – and a certain wish to find out why it all went wrong in Cornwall when I was at the centre of the creative hurricane that had already made history – made me want to write about it.

Not that alone. I knew Cornwall itself from inside from working on the fields, and living in my Island Tower, was close also to the fishermen. I suddenly realised I was the one person who knew the whole thing. It was one of those moments when the Gods send the message through all the levels of the heart and mind at one instant. I had to go and write. I had seen it all in a single flash that came from the very soul of Zennor Moor and the granite beds of Chysauster, striking the walls of my bruised brain. So in the background of those last difficult months before and after we went to stay with Robert, I wrote into the night when I could not sleep, like Claudius, to get at and preserve the truth: *The Dark Monarch.*

But I was writing a book about my whole experience of Cornwall and the people – not about any one person, except, unavoidably, myself – as so many have thought. It was not a book about Arthur Caddick or Peter Lanyon or whoever got angry with me and served a writ for libel, but about a creative event that hit Cornwall after the war, transmuted into an imaginative novel. It was not a documentary nor was meant to be. Imagination is the sorcerer of art and why literature flags is because this one well of invention is being taken away, gradually replaced by recorded documentary based on fact, dry cleaned of any spiritual content by the advent of the word processor and the law. I touched in Cornwall the source of its magic: as with all such things I found that if it was not used creatively it would destroy those who interfered with its secret working from the fountainhead, at the point where Good and Evil were interlocked.

I cared desperately about being an artist and had suffered considerable setbacks to achieve a footing. In doing this I had evolved writing as an art, instead of simply writing about what happened. With a rich mine of experience already worked over, it was right that I should create this one novel which, for all the disturbance it has caused and the excitement it still causes after thirty years, and the degradation it has suffered, I am both humbled and proud to say has been named a masterpiece. The critics might have killed Keats, but like a Galapagos tortoise I am too hard in the shell to crack open easily. My old age is tough and green enough never to have forgotten my attempted assassination in Fore Street, St. Ives by Peter Lanyon, who drove his car at me, nor one moment of the 30 years' exile about which I am now writing, or the behaviour of the Establishment, which has torn a gaunt hole in the stocking of democracy.

It was also true of myself before I left, that I was trapped by a madman with a knife in my Tower; my wife tried to commit suicide; I rescued my children from a gas-filled room, my cottage was burnt down. An extraordinary string of events to have to record, which are intrinsically woven into this pattern.

At this time in the Forest, after Ishtar had left, I was drinking considerably: it was becoming more a part of my life than I cared to realise.

Fortunately I had an in-built discipline from the hard years — perhaps also from the austerities Sven Hedin was able to impose on himself, going on one occasion something like 70 days without water — to myself correct excess and cut out dangerous habits on the instant, which I did in time to avoid that sort of disaster. But while it lasted I enjoyed it in the boisterous company of publicans and sinners and their attractive women, one of whom became my secretary and helped me through by typing the final copy of *The Dark Monarch*, before it went to the publishers.

I preferred to drink with the country folk because they had the vigour and strength of their calling — be it dealer, farmer or huntsman. It was in this way I met Alice Lenthall who was the wife of the new huntsman at the Foxhound Kennels, recently come to the Forest.

I was in the Mailman's Arms, at the lower end of Lyndhurst and had gone there first to see Jo Jenkins the publican's wife about the script of *The Dark Monarch*, which she had nearly finished, and there was a young girl sitting at the bar who I had not seen before. There was something about her that was arresting: the way her mouth was, the way her hair fell, the blue of her eyes or simply her youth: all these things and yet none of them. It was a feeling she gave out, an overtone that switched me on, like the head of the young Queen Tai I had seen in the British Museum.

'What will you drink, darling?' I said in a low sonorous voice, leaning over her. She looked at me through the engraved mirror opposite her without turning her head, giving me the most comical icy stare with the lid of one eye lowered.

'Brandy!' she answered disdainfully. Jo Jenkins served us with drinks out of the optics, also looking at us through the same mirror, smiling, and saying as she swung back: 'This is Julie, Sven!'

I took the drinks, gave one to Julie and as we said 'Cheers!, I caught sight in the mirror of Alice standing on my left looking just like Queen Elizabeth the First, and behind her, her sister Marj, looking like her Lady-in-waiting. So I pointed down at Julie interrogatively and looked to her in the mirror. She nodded her head. Then I swung round.

'That's right,' said Alice. 'I'm her mother. That's my Julie. Didn't you know?' And I fell in.

Julie's version of this is slightly different but I will go along with my own invisible memory since he is silent Cicerone throughout this story. The great thing and the most extraordinary truth about this meeting came clear almost at once when I asked where they came from.

'Seaton near Beer in Devon!'

This was exactly the same answer I was given when I asked the same question about Alfred Wallis's wife twenty years before: only in reverse.

'Beer near Seaton in Devon!' – 'Do you know anyone called Agland?' I added.

'Yes, of course!' shouted Alice through the low roar of voices, the smoke and electric light chopping off the heads of other people. 'There are two main families – the Annings and the Aglands. I was an Anning, before I married 'im,' she went on, pointing to the strong short figure of her husband, 'Arry, getting drinks.

'The same as Mary Anning who found the big fossil fish?' I bellowed.

'That's right. She lived in Lyme and was a relation.'

As with all countryfolk, it did not matter about a century having passed since then. Just as Benny Wells, the gypsy, talked about the blood of Rufus staining the King's Garn a forest stream, as if he died yesterday. Time is treated as an invisible continuum.

'Why do you ask,' said Alice. Do you know any Aglands?'

'No. But I've written a book about a man called Alfred Wallis who married a Susan Agland born at Beer.'

'That would be either daughter or mother to Julia Agland, whose old man drove his pony and trap over the cliff. Yes we knowd 'en or I didn't, I wasn't born'd then but. . .'

'Where do you fit in?' I said, turning to Julie.

'Well that's my Mum. Her Dad was my Granfer Anning from Seaton and he married an Agland from Beer, bringing the two families together; and I was named after Julia Agland, so my name is JULIA, not Julie.' That put me in my place.

'Was Granfer Anning a fisherman as well?'

'He was a builder. He built half Seaton, including the school, but his partner suddenly ran away with all the money and he spent the rest of his life fishing, which he had been brought up to.'

This was the most perfect and original introduction to an attractive young woman, who I was trying to get off with in a pub, I have ever known; and the pattern in which it was set going back about 150 years was also a complete pedigree of the true peasant and fisherfolk who have held England together for centuries; let alone being linked to Alfred Wallis, of whom I had made a searching biography some years before. At the end of an evening with my new friends I felt they were already part of my life.

Julie came to the pub the next night, saying she had just dropped in after seeing her mate, Sue, on the bus, to see if her Mum was about and we sat talking for a long time about the Valley of Kings, where I said I hoped one day to go. At the end of this I said I would drive her home to Kennels if she promised not to try and get me. She kept her promise. She told me later that she had said to her mother that she had been out with this strange man who had been deserted by his wife and was drinking heavily; he had holes in his cardigan and was looking rough. 'Why don't you ask him if you can go up and help out in the mornings. He needs someone!'

So it was that this great friendly countrywoman, Alice, came to work for us in the cottage each morning. The result was magnetic: the boys loved her. Paul, who had gone to work in the forests of Sweden after his mother died a year or two before, was now back. Willie had stayed when his mother left and Jasper was indeed too young to be without a mother. Jan was with us but courting a young man from another large Forest family, the Witneys. The balance was exact. So Alice – as she was known to all or the 'White Tornado' because of her energy when she hoovered the cottage with a fag hanging out of her mouth – became for that time the earth mother to my family and we all felt safe again: even myself.

The other staff had already gone, since there was no longer any stud; save one Appaloosa which belonged to Willie and was sold to help him get through his 'O' and 'A' Levels in Southampton. No Children's Zoo – save the macaws who were my friends and flew free in the Forest, often pitching down on my shoulder when I went for a walk or was in town shopping, as my tame jackdaw used to do earlier when I was living rough. They would also dive bomb the retired colonels when they went to the inn for an early gin: until one was shot in mistake for a jay and the other was stolen by visitors.

The Barbary doe escaped into the Forest and successfully integrated with the fallow deer. A toucan was lost, and a coypu. All the other creatures were found homes: I have always hoped good ones. You can never tell.

This extra-evolutionary extension of our lives gave me a feeling of belonging to a greater aggregate than I had ever felt before, which made it even more tragic that we had to close.

Sir Gavin de Beer, Director of the Natural History Museum in London – who celebrated getting his knighthood by drinking rum with me out of a jam jar in the field at Edie Gailor's while he imitated my bantam cockerel exactly – would have been the one person who could have helped keep the Zoo open, had he not died that week and the silent ghosts of the planners closed my doors to the younger apes of our origins.

Meantime *The Dark Monarch* was published.

When a book is published after the months, often years, of holding the mind to the theme like a knife to a stone, till its edge is sharp and pitiless, there is a pause as before a great battle, and then a silent explosion. In this case the impact was terrific, almost a psychological shock through the art world – and in the pub where I had the shelves filled with copies between the whisky and gin bottles and the tough countrymen even were buying it. In Cornwall they were buying as many as thirty copies at a time. But almost immediately, within eight days, it was withdrawn owing to four writs for libel being served against it. 575 copies were sold. Under court order, the publishers instructed booksellers and libraries to return the rest to them. Many did not. But the shock was considerable and the effect on me devastating. Voltaire had his books burnt: mine were pulped – the exact opposite of creation.

My friends and the establishment had taken it as a direct attack on them and many were deeply hurt. I, who had written a portrait from within could not comprehend or believe this until those long legal envelopes started to fall through my letter box with the silence of bombs through bomb doors. Francis Bacon always said he went into another room to paint a portrait because he did not want his friends to know what he did to them. I did not Baconize them. I re-created truthfully: perhaps that is the same thing. . . if they were the same transmutations? God help Art for God's sake!

I was asked by the publisher to lift one word from the description of a man I had named Haddock; one chapter about a woman called Bendix; one line about a lady named Gannet. That is all. If I did this, they told me the book would be re-issued immediately and would be a best seller. I refused to do it on the grounds that I did not intentionally mean to hurt my friends and in this sense I was contrite. That it was a work of art and would be spoiled by altering it and making it into something that was not a genuine novel. And I wrote it because I was the one person who knew from inside the nature of the Cornish people growing out of their own land into the superimposed cone of abstract art that was now enclosing it. My refusal caused great hardship to myself, but has made *The Dark Monarch* a permanent part of English Literature.

As I write this now I am able to say that in 1991 I was offered the chance of republishing *The Dark Monarch* in its original form, which would have been an immediate sell out. I refused because I did not want to be responsible for the forces it would release. It remains mine – and England's.

Robert Graves wrote at this time: '. . .There is such heat and power in the book. I was horrified to hear from the publishers that *The Dark Monarch* had been withdrawn: it is a remarkable picture of colony life. I am reading it with great interest but slowly. . . I am so grieved about your book and the wolf or jackal pack. Why I never had the same thing happen to me I don't know. Born lucky, I guess!'

Lawrence Durrell was equally sympathetic – and Mai Zetterling, who knew from her later films and plays what such opposition could mean. No wonder she won: she was tougher than I was. I hadn't thought of that.

'What is the matter with everyone?' I said to my lawyer, Michael Rubenstein. 'Why are they all like that?'

'You have told the truth, Mr Berlin, and everybody is going to make a lot of money out of you – including myself!'

DARK MONARCH

The Dark Monarch was the final nail in the Crucifixion after which no Pietá was intended, but Anthony Dent, like Aramathea, came to my help. He turned up at my cottage with a lady friend whom I had not met, when on that morning the solicitor had written to say that the prosecution were going to make me bankrupt. I was in a nervous state when they came. I had to speak out and tell him this, first apologising to his friend. He was very good about it. He said that he could not reply there and then, but he would do so that day, and they went. I waited anxiously. At midnight he phoned to say it would be all right. He had made an arrangement but would not say any more than that I need not worry. And he kept his word. I don't know even now what he did, but am deeply glad that he did it.

He even got his firm to honour the contract for *Jonah's Dream:* a Meditation on Fishing, which came out two years later, in 1964 and became a classic both here and in America, though I did not make a penny out of it. According to a journalist on a national newspaper, who told me so on the telephone, *The Dark Monarch* book had cost £7,800 up to that point. Dents were insured and a lot of it was covered that way. I knew I could not pay my final bill for costs to my solicitor. I wrote and told him, asking if I could send him a sculpture of a dove instead, ending the letter:

'Bleeding in all pockets – *SVEN.*'

He agreed. The beautiful alabaster dove filled with translucent light, and twice as big as the head of a man, was sent by carrier to London. After it had left I sent a telegram:

DOVE LEFT THE ARK
THIS MORNING: LOVE NOAH.

Madonna

Following the fall of *The Dark Monarch* there was a period of dejection, which comes anyway when a book is published, partly from exhaustion, having given everything to its making, and partly because it takes some weeks for it to be absorbed and understood from outside. But in this case there was one terrific electric shock as though I had hit a pylon wire in my flight path and crashed in flames, leaving no hope of good reviews or expectation of success and a little money. I felt the edifice of life had crumbled about me too many times to be comfortable: that I was doing something wrong or had something wrong within me that caused it to happen. I have learned since that if you keep the doors of the whole mind, zenith and nadir, open wide enough to let the life force through to drive the processes of creation, a slipstream of evil is generated and will drive in the other direction to destroy you. It is by these opposing forces that the law of life works, as well as of death; and why so many creative people have such a hard time or an appalling end. I was right when I wrote instinctively on the fly leaf of my book just before it was published, six words from George Borrow:

THE EVIL ONE WAS UPON ME!

I refused to alter a word. In a micro-poem that came later, I wrote:
>Like Pontius Pilate
>'I have written what I have written.'
>That is my fate:
>Even though I got bitten
>I remained obdurate.

Although a man choosing his own direction in life, for whatever reason, has to get used to being alone, I was not lonely as when I was One in a Tower. I had the family round me, and although they did not know a great deal about what was going on, save that I had given the manuscript to Paul and Janet to read before I sent it to be published, their presence was an extension of life that made it worth continuing – they were there, grazing near – although I was a lone bison away from the pack most of the time, finding it difficult to work.

Paul was quite a giant of a young man by now, with a good physique on which to hang his handsome bearded look, working in the Forest as a woodman like his Grandfather Kalle before him. My stepson, Willie, who was curiously comical in a maddening sort of way, would walk about in a silk top hat and Wellington boots, looking just like Harpo Marx, as if it was the normal thing to sit like this at table or help Paul to dig a ditch, or go off in the morning to college. Jasper was still at elementary school, in a magical setting by a forest stream at Minstead, to which I drove and fetched him every day for those seven years before conceptual thought intrudes on the dream of childhood. They were all in gear with each other and played Alice up like mad, but she went along with it and, in her loud country voice, threatened to smack their legs when they tormented her. But she was fulcrum and I did not have to worry, as with the other staff who had all sorts of recondite experiences which seemed to go on – especially when I was away.

Julie was working in Timothy White's in Southampton, so I could only see her some evenings and at weekends. Occasional friends from Cornwall came and went. I was grateful for letters from Robert Graves and Lawrence Durrell sympathising over *The Dark Monarch* and especially for advice from Robert:

> 'There is such heat and power in the book that too much of
> it goes roaring up the chimney, instead of heating the room.
> If only you could apply the Aga principle of heat-
> conservation to it, instead of being so spendthrift. . .'

This was a comfort from someone who knew about my marital troubles and wrote continuously for about a year. The two problems were bound together: the failure of my book and the failure of my marriage, which formed a double negative to overcome. To remove the blockage from work was of paramount importance. During this period, Ishtar was back in St. Ives.

I sat in my huge workshop one day thinking how, in the tiny room in my Tower in Cornwall, 10 foot square, I used to cut out my images almost without knowing. Here in my converted barn, 30ft × 20ft × 30ft high, I could not lift a hammer. The energies were closed: La rue fermée! I looked up at the tall two-ton block of alabaster I had ordered for the lonely Priest when I was broke, standing now on a sunken pedestal still waiting to be carved. I heard a voice shout out loud:

'THE MADONNA!' And the voice was my own, telling me what to do. Carve the Madonna. The Priestess of Motherhood! Image of Woman! The Mysterious Female: base from which heaven and earth sprang. The Queen of Heaven.

As the words came to me I felt the spirit move and the energies start to pour through my mind as though the dykes had broken. The image was clear because I had done the drawings a long time before and it had been able to mature: it was ready to be taken from the stone. I now climbed the steps set up by her and began to mark out in thick red paint the direction her form would take inside the stone. By going down the steps into the pit I could draw continuous lines from crown to foot, then up and round her again, working in a spiral as always since my dancing days and the ammonites of Lyme Regis, the tunnel graves of County Meath, shaft graves of Mycenae going back to the beginning of time. And then, to mark her beginning, I took a pitching tool, and climbing just above her, struck off large chunks of stone, down to where the shoulder and indeed the child were. I could feel their form and would not go beyond it. At such a moment, if you strike right along with the crystal formation, careful not to bruise it, the stone falls away along the exact frontier required, although with alabaster, as with a woman, it is not always predictable. When I left the workshop that day the main image that had been in my mind was fixed also in the stone where it had been waiting since timeless beginnings stirred. The spell had been broken: the flat surface penetrated and a new dimension entered; as always at this moment it was like peeling an orange. Subjective and objective meet and are the same, which, behind invisibility, is true in the first place, as when you meet the woman who is within you, and for whom you are searching. This is a metaphysical and a spiritual truth.

From now on it was a matter of continuous work from day to day which unified my mind and body in a way that it had not been for a considerable time. But I knew now the wholeness would remain and the parts of my life would continue to come together. That the terrific blow that had shattered it like a dome of glass had now lost its energy and in cutting this new sculpture a new period in my life would begin. A Virgin birth in stone.

I knew of the four stages of woman: Eve the biological woman of creation. Helen the Anima symbol of love and beauty. Mary the woman of heavenly and spiritual worship, and Sophia of unsurpassable wisdom. My Madonna would be an aggregate of all these women containing the highest values of Heaven and Earth. She was the Queen of Heaven so I gave her a crown. The child would be the spiritual emblem of the highest achievement of mankind at every level of life taking us into the future. Herein is contained my First Principle, my Aesthetic and my Ethic of life and creation.

To live this was another matter: to make an image that contained it was possible.

I was always about early, even if I had come home late and fallen in among the musk roses and stayed there half the night. Vikings are tough men and hard drinkers: it has always been like that.

I liked to get to the workshop between five and six in the morning and with my head clear as a Forest pool, pick up my hammer and get into the stone: it is the toughest prayer I know and is answered at all levels. At eight o'clock I walked up to the cottage where Alice had breakfast laid on a table under the apple tree by the back door where my macaws lived. When they saw me coming they greeted me from the top branch with 'Allo!' and started to climb down the other branches, all now stripped into streets and flyovers, under-passes and bridges, on grey prehistoric feet; feathers of scarlet, turquoise, and viridian.

Often Ollie was there alone and one morning as she climbed from the tree onto the top of the aviary a kitten crossed her path. Without a sound she bit off the kitten's tail so quickly the kitten didn't even notice. But the she-cat did. There was a sudden rush and she leaped on to the aviary hissing at the macaw with her ears back.

'Christ, Alice! cat and bird!' I exclaimed. Alice, a plate of eggs and bacon in her hand, paused.

'Never mind that, your breakfast will get cold!'

'Wait just a minute and see what happens.'

In a little while the macaw again said 'Allo!' – this time to the cat, blushed on her veined white cheeks, crested her comb and made her way past the angry cat to the back of my chair, took the fried bread I offered in one of her reptilian feet and stood on the other eating it like a Rabbi who had found a sixpence.

'Well I never!' said Alice. 'I've never seen anything like that before. Now come along young man get this down yer before it gets cold. And don't get that stone dust all over my clean cloth.'

"Drummer" oil ca. 1985, drawn at the annual Wimborne Summer Festival

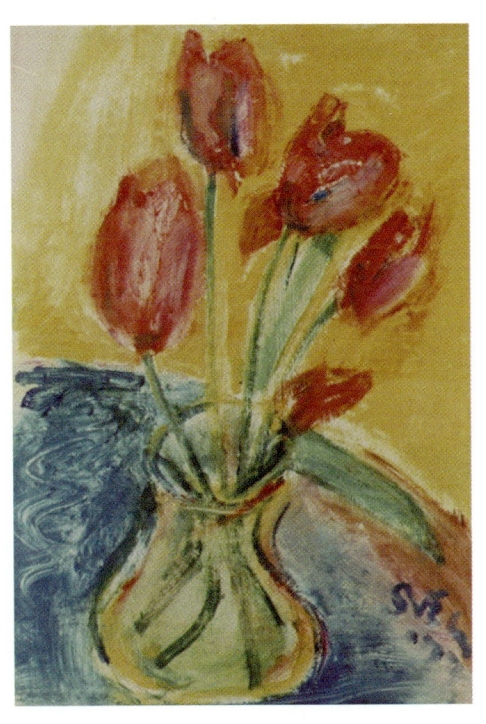

"Tulips" oil ca. 1977

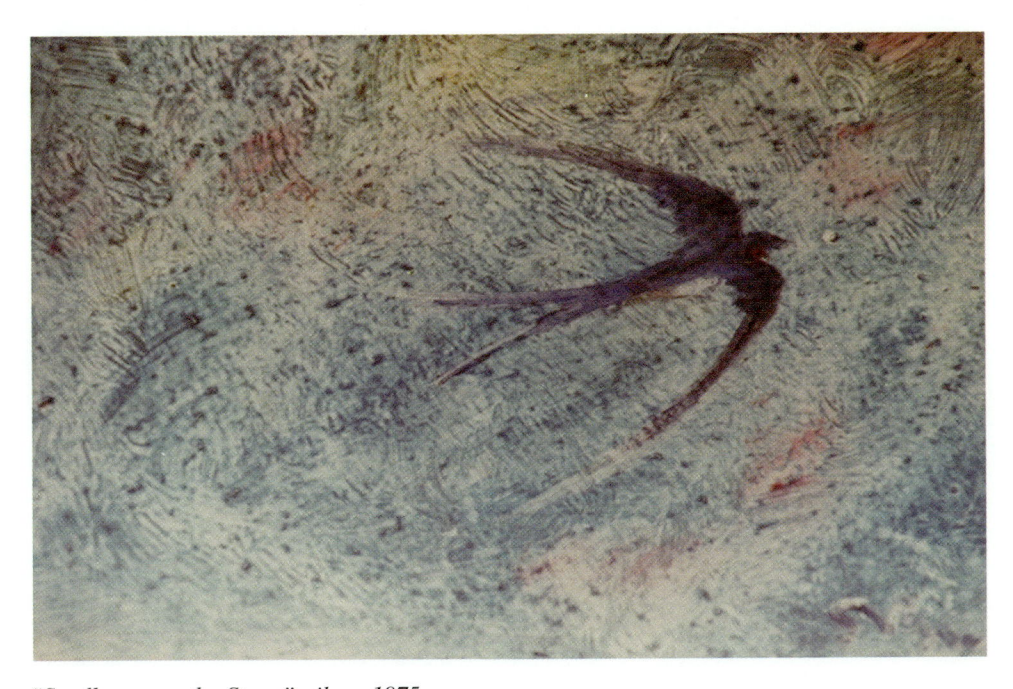

"Swallow over the Stour" oil ca. 1975

"Gypsies Dancing" watercolour, New Forest, ca. 1954

"John Paddy Brown" (poet) watercolour, ca. 1985

"Winter Scene by the Stour" oil ca. 1970

MADONNA

'Yes, alright Alice, but sit down for a moment. I want to tell you a story about Ollie.' Alice sat down and lit a fag while I pushed my breakfast down.

'Well go on!'

'When I started the Zoo I had a pair of scarlets, like Ollie, a blue and a toucan. . .'

'What's the toucan got to do with it?'

'I'll tell you if you'll shut up and listen. The red macaws hated the blue one — see? They set traps to kill her. Stalked after her on those terrible feet, conscious of murder.'

'Why?' said Alice.'

'Jealous of her colour, blue and yellow like the Swedish flag or of a love fix she had with one of the scarlets — kept flashing her fanny at him. I kept watch all one day and they nearly got her, but I changed her roost. They stay out all night now but at first they shared the same house. I changed it that night and put the blue in the toucan's house and the toucan in with the scarlets — but in a large parrot cage. Got it?'

'Yes!' said Alice listening carefully. 'I've got it so far.'

'But the state of murder was still in the scarlets and they transferred it to the toucan. I hadn't thought of that.'

'I expect it was territorial!' said Alice, who knew about creatures.

'Yes, I expect it was now, but the thing is it was there and very strong. They climbed down from their perches to the parrot cage where the toucan was, making terrifying shrieks as they went, and either out of terror or self-defence, the toucan put its long beak out through the bars of the cage and the macaws took it in a vice-like grip and pulled at it till the toucan was hung. I came in just too late, when I was checking last thing before I went out.'

Alice was not upset because she lived in kennels and was not easily shocked.

'I don't doubt it, mind you. You don't have to be a toucan to get that done to you: not in the Forest. We aren't much different!' she said and gave out a great laugh, which startled Ollie, the scarlet bird with me, and she flew off my shoulder.

'There she goes!' I said as I watched her fly into the blue sky.

'O, look,' shouted Alice, pointing. 'What are those other birds going for her?'

'They are jackdaws and rooks. With her flat head and curved beak they think she is a hawk. They are mobbing her!'

MADONNA

'Hope she'll be all right!' 'Did I tell you about Vi Biddlecome who lives up South Lodge?' said Alice. 'The other day she was out in the field and His Lordship come along and suddenly said to her: "I say Violet, there's buzzards about!" And she said to 'en: 'Bizzards? Bizzards, M'Lord? Them's ain't no bizzards. Them's Mister Berlin's pirrits!"'

That gave me a great laugh as I went off to feed Caliban the swine, thinking what a rare person Alice was and how lucky I was to find her and what an exciting daughter she had.

'Look!' called Alice as I turned round. 'There's Charlie!' her voice excited. On the green of the low hill was a big dog fox. He stopped in his tracks and looked down at us, showing the long curve of his back going into his brush.

'Christ!' I shouted. 'It's the black fox. He's a big bastard, isn't he!'

'Yes,' Alice shouted. 'He's quite an old man. They say 'eve bin round for a long time.'

'Like me!' I answered and went off.

'You're not done by a long chalk, you 'ole bugger!' she shouted after me. My desolation had gone.

Alice and Harry had been at the West Kent Kennels before they came to the Forest and their deep Devon and Somerset tongues were turned by the sounds of Kent (where I was born) and all that it had gathered from London over the centuries. It was precisely this London brogue in Julie's voice and her own wonderful humour that drew me to her in the first place. Somehow it all linked up with my childhood, long before the trappings of art had touched my young head and my innocence had been worn by the rough tongues of survival where love cannot last. Now I had eaten 'the bitter bread of banishment' I longed for a mouth to kiss:

> O, a kiss
> Long as my exile, sweet as my revenge!

What a beautiful enigma to be solved!

I went back each day to my new sculpture, feeling it grow under my hands as I hauled it into existence with a net of chisel cuts as if bringing it from the bottom of the sea, sunk there with a lost civilisation. I did not know that she had a special destiny attached to her that was to nearly cost me my life some years later. Perhaps the stones in their antiquity carry more than that with which we impregnate them.

Alabaster is a strange stone to work. Like a woman, it will bruise if

MADONNA

you strike it too hard: if you go at her pace she will go with you, eventually giving up her secrets and radiating her gentle beauty around you, especially if you are carving a woman. Don't be harsh or leave her in the open for too long or she will grieve, her luminous spirit will disappear, her substance erode. Keep her in a shrine, a quiet room or a dry stable: she will give sanctuary to your watchfulness, smile at you in sun or moonlight, and never reject the love in your heart because you have made her in the image of your own soul. She is enduring and fragile. The years will not take her nor vile mind corrupt her, or correct her harshly against invisibility. She is the Empress of Stone, Tsarina of Everlasting: who opposes her will die.

When a man goes into a stone he takes with him his own history into the ancient darkness of tomorrow; he is between the hinges of each day's turning, as doors open and close. It is a journey he takes alone. It is not only his technical knowledge he uses, but the experience of how to undo that knowledge to get at the answer to each new problem. Only he can do that in the way he discovers to bend his spirit like Ulysses' bow and fire through the bronze axe of truth.

That is how it was with the Madonna which took two years to complete. From the first chisel-cut, she carried my destiny into old age.

Marriage

My daughter, Janet Elizabeth, as I had named her when she was born in Cornwall in the midst of war, was getting married, and I put up a marquee in the paddock to celebrate, wiring it with loudspeakers from the chalet, so that the trees roared with music, and invited a cross section of local society to join in: countrymen, farmers, dealers, gypsies, bank managers, solicitors, doctors, builders, millionaires, poets, painters and sculptors, generals, TV producers, huntsmen, foresters and Annie and Lily Bright from the cottage on the corner. All gathered together to wish the young people a harmonious and not too tangled a life. There were no speeches, with slightly filthy innuendoes and marital advice, for the young know it all by watching the middle-aged, and the old have either forgotten it or let all their experience distil into wisdom. The music and drink were enough and many were speechless anyway. There was a great feeling of a life-force, having risen up through the ground, as a way of confirming that an important holy ritual had taken place with delight; like a Roman banquet but with a certain English decorum under the huge golden umbrella of the sun the gods had spread in a clearing of the Forest where Pan still lived.

Among the guests moved the animals left over from the Zoo: a four-horned St. Kilda goat, a Barbary ram, a llama, and a jack donkey. There was one peacock left who showed his glory to a common little bantam hen who pretended not to notice; and Caliban the swine snorted round the legs of a judge.

How does my Honour? Let me lick thy shoe!

The llama had already eaten the general's rose and spat at the millionaire; she moved on looking disdainfully at everyone as though she was as accustomed to garden parties as a royal flamingo. There was a certain snobbery coming from all the animal kingdom. The ram horned an American lady journalist and the macaw bit a gay man's ear.

The animal presence gave an extended view of the human psyche. Even a young cockerel flew on the back of a lady and tried to tread her as she bent over to take a sandwich. This, and an attractive barmaid from the pub, was enough to liquefy all hope of sobriety, even though I was host.

'Well, yes,' the colonel was saying, in answer to my question about Roger Casement, whose bones Harold Wilson had just had dug up and sent back to Eire, 'I don't really know anything about the fella. It all seems very cloak and dagger to me!'

We were picking up a conversation we had at a party in his cottage the night before, where Montgomery Hyde was trying to tell his story about Yeats. I had butted in saying how difficult it was to write a poem about Casement after Yeats' thundering couplet:

> The Ghost of Roger Casement
> It's beating on the door!

I shouted this: 'I have only one couplet of my own and that has the same beat:

> They broke the thigh of Ireland
> The day they murdered him!

But Montgomery Hyde – a small vigorous man – obviously couldn't hear me, and went on with his own story about the poet.

'I must tell you this now, while the ladies aren't listening. I had asked Yeats what he thought about the Catholics and he said (Montgomery was shouting also by now but did not notice): "The trouble with the Catholics, Montgomery, is THEY WON'T LET YOU PUT IT IN AND THEY WON'T LET YOU TAKE IT OUT!"'

The story broke all sound barriers and shattered the room like a pane of glass – far more than the broken thigh of my poetry. The ladies pretended not to hear, but were all roaring with laughter enjoying the joke.

And now, at the wedding party the next day, I was hoping the same little colonel, if not Montgomery Hyde, would tell me more about Roger Casement. All he would say was:

'No, old chap, I'm afraid I can't help you there. I'm strictly a bow and arrow man myself!'

I somehow missed Montgomery after that. A pity!

At this point somebody bumped into the colonel and upset his drink down his throat and choked him. It was a young artist who fell drunk among the bales of straw I had strewn around for people to sit on. Terence Carroll, an ITV producer, sat on one of these in top boots playing flamenco music on the guitar and like a domino was hit too, but not hurt.

My happy daughter and good-looking young husband, who absolutely adored her, started to jive on the grass outside to the loud-speakers. I noticed how similar the modern open dancing was to the old country dances although it was more inventive, and the whole gathering took on a Breughel atmosphere in the sunlight, joined into or watched by guests on both sides, making me suddenly aware that I had a whole company of new relations some of whom I did not know.

Janet's new father-in-law, whom I knew well, and who loved his whisky and beer as much as I, suddenly threw back his head with his Mephisthophelean beard jutting into the sky and toasted me as the best drunken father outlaw in the Forest. We were both from London and had a common humour and understanding in these matters, until he died ten years later. I continued the friendship with his sculptress wife into old age, after the young couple had long parted, but first honoured me with two grand-children, Jason and Anna.

Now it was time for them to be going away I was feeling a bit bewildered as I watched them dance from inside the marquee, smelling the grass and straw mixed with the sour stench of beer, thinking how in the South of France at Les Saintes Maries, some Russian gypsies had tried to buy her from me for a thousand pieces of gold, a Cadillac and a bicycle; and the difficulty I had resisting them while a lovely young gypsy woman served us with tea from a samovar, laced with strawberries. She was now given away to the man of her choice with love. It was right she should dance for it out there, since it was with her mother I had danced round England in the Thirties. I had said goodbye earlier to avoid the emotions. Suddenly the barmaid, who was liquefying my corner gaze while she cleaned the glasses, shouted across to me: 'Look who's here!'

Coming in from the sunlight as if from history, was Alice looking more than ever like Queen Elizabeth the First, and Julie like the Egyptian Queen Tai. It was a good job they came: being alone I was already casting a stitch with the barmaid. I have always preferred women, because they don't have to say anything to switch the dynamo on. They too work the magic shuttle for you more than anyone. It is prison without a woman: and it is prison with.

'Am I glad you came!' I said. 'I didn't think you would make it.'

MARRIAGE

'Well we are here,' said Alice, ordering a gin and tonic. 'Brandy, Ju?'

'But I thought Julie had to work!'

'I did too but my boss, Mrs Hanham, relented!' Julie said in her country voice, honed to a London edge.

'What about Dad? He said he would come in scarlet and play "Gone away!" on his hunting horn. Too late now.'

'He'll be along,' said Alice. 'That's if Sir Newton lets him go in time and he's not too tired after hounds have been fed and bedded down. It's first cubbing. They've been out since four o'clock this morning. Mad lot of buggers!'

It was difficult for me to realise how much in control of their lives the Master was. And it took me a long time to understand what a tough job it was being a hunt servant.

Julie in a grey suit was younger than I thought. Eighteen, in fact. I was fifty-one. It did not seem odd to want to talk with her. Her honesty and simplicity were good to see: rare. Her physical attraction, marvellous: unspoiled. Her vitality and happiness: magical. Humour broad enough for me to call her 'Football 'ed' and be safe. Hair on to her shoulders: near blonde. Full mouth. The aggregate was a young English woman made by the sea and the hills, instead of the concrete towers of the city in which I was brought up.

I recognised these things in the cool of the marquee with my daughter dancing out the last of her youth in a sunfix dream. A tooth in the great unseen wheel that marks out our lives clicked into place.

Before long the people started to move back into the tent to get more drinks and get cool, so we moved just outside where there was shade under the ash trees. And here several men, younger than I, started to move round Julie and chat her up. They were all television people. John Boorman, Michael Croucher, Terence Carroll.

'Isn't she marvellous!' said one.

'Just like a beautiful peach!' said another.

'Just ripe!'

'Ready to pluck!'

'I know. We must get you a job down at ITV and have you around. What about that?'

Julie with that overall expression in which even her hair smiles when she is happy, gave some quick answers, obviously used to dealing with the country boys and friends of her brother.

'That's all right. I'll have two. They're rather small!' (Meaning the men).

'That's it,' said another. 'We'll fix her up with a job in Southampton. Then she can't get away.'

'Yes,' said I, 'but what a pity you can't pluck her. She's mine!'

Taking Julie by the hand I snatched her away from the crowd with a smile and not a murmur from anyone. She did not resist but came with me and we felt joined as we walked across a field, leaving my guests and Julie's suitors to go on drinking. I felt like Ulysses.

As we walked I ran my fingers through the rye and wheat grass, blue scabious and milky thistle. The doves flew in a victory flight overhead – always the doves. I was silent. Insects leaped on and off my hand. 'What are you thinking?' she asked.

'Grass. That's all simply GRASS!'

'Of course, but why do you say it like that?'

'Because most people want to turn it into concrete and money!'

'I don't,' she said. 'I take it for granted. There has always been grass!'

'But you are a country girl. I come from the town. No matter how long I live in the country and know more about the countryside than most countryfolk, I can never alter that; even though the fields in North Kent still came nearly to our doorways when I was a kid, and there were plenty of orchards left where we used to go scrumping; but there was already something more urban than rural by then. The spirit of the country was stealing away in the night to join its own kind. After a time it goes altogether and one is locked in brick and paving stones and wire and noise. Then it's gone and you wonder why. And you can't ever replace it no matter how the planners perform. At best they save a little, but that is not the trees that spoke to the moon every night.'

Julie listened to me, then spoke.

'You are right. The country people love grass because it is part of their lives. It almost grows out of us.' As she spoke her fair hair fell forward. Her excitement showed in the broadening of her voice and the quiver of her hand as it touched mine, ferrying through the grass. 'Things that grow, I mean. You are right – it is like the spirit of things: trees and that. My mother always says she wants to be buried, not cremated, because a rose tree might grow where she has been, like going back into the actual things themselves. You aren't country, but you know what I mean.'

'But my father came from the country in Sweden rather like you from Devon – only there was a great lake. Yes, I know what you mean. I feel the same.'

'How did you know I was from Devon?'

'Your mother Alice told me, remember? She works for me now!' Julie laughed as the breeze lifted her hair. 'Of course, Mush. How silly of me!'

'Mush is a gypsy word. Do you know any gypsies?' I asked.

'Yes. In Kent. My Dad was huntsman there before we came here. I told you. Well in summer, we girls used to go fruit picking. There were lots of gypsies would come down from London every year. My mum still uses gypsy words: like MUI for face, and POSH that's a gypsy word. MOOMLI is a candle.'

'You almost rokkra the jin!' I said, teasing her.

'What's that?'

'Speak the language. I don't speak the language properly. I only have a few phrases and words I have picked up when I was living rough with them because I was broke. Lovely people.'

'Like what? What would you call me?'

'Kushti rakli! Lovely girl!'

'Who's that going down the field now?' she asked, pointing beyond the farm buildings.

'They're gypsies. Cliff Lee and his wife Sheila with Ken, their son, and two girls. They've come all the way from Liverpool for Janet's wedding. They usually stay at Augustus John's field but he's getting on, so they have started to stay here sometimes. We had a terrific party in Augustus's field last year, with Mai Zetterling and her husband and a few others. But I think the old man was busy working – anyway he couldn't come but sent us a message.'

'And the tall boy with a top hat on?'

'Oh, HIM. That's my stepson Willie. He and Jasper are great pals. He stayed here when his mother left, but is going to Jamaica to look for his real dad soon.'

'Are you divorced?' she asked suddenly and quite seriously.

'Yes. I am waiting for it to become absolute!'

'How long does that take?'

'Three months and then I can marry again.'

'Are you going to?'

'I might.'

Julie was looking at the big metal building we were approaching. It was painted blue and had tall chimney stacks like a Mississippi steam boat. 'What is that place?' she asked. 'I've often wondered!'

'It's my workshop where I do all my sculpture. The wooden building next to it is my paint shop where I paint, and the chalet in the paddock where the party is going on is another studio for painting. I write my books indoors, in my study.'

'By painting shop you mean an artist's studio?'

'That's right.' 'You are an artist?'

'I am. And that is the nicest thing you have said to me today — Thank you!'

I took her into the blue building which was a converted Dutch barn. Like most sculptors' workshops it had blocks of stone with a central gantry for lifting the heavy ones.

'I love stone. Sculpture for me is a matter of stone. It is truthful, has simplicity. You can't pretend with stone or falsify its forms.'

Julie looked up at the Madonna, emerging out of the alabaster in the afternoon sunlight. She seemed over-awed.

'Isn't it beautiful! You are a clever old Mush. Do you know that?'

'No. Not really. Stone is something special. To cut it is quite a rare thing really I mean, so it lives. I just happen to be able to do it.'

There was a fist of Cornish granite flashing with quartz and spar. Also a large block of green marble that had just arrived from Connemara, glowing as if it was under the sea, covered with a kelp of weed showing an Irish King, half formed, waking from a long sleep.

I realised she had never seen anything like this and could feel her mind open like a flower.

On the benches were sets of chisels, hammers, files, grinders, polishers and other tools.

'You keep the tools nice — its like a tack room in stables!' she remarked.

'But of course. If you know that, you know also that you can't work else. Tools must be right.'

'That's what my Dad says about harness and that. Even his skinning knives are sharp and clean.'

At the far end were the furnaces: one for melting the wax from the mould and one for melting the metal to be poured. And a forge for tempering my chisels and heating metal for wrought iron. Rows of crucibles, carrying shanks.

There was a set of hammers by the anvil and different tongs. But although Julie understood my workshop discipline, it was before the images she stood, each in turn, and marvelled.

'It's like being in a cathedral,' she said. 'Or one of them tombs in Egypt where they lay their kings!'

'That's how I started, when they found Tutankamen in the Twenties. I was only twelve then. But I got very excited and wanted to do that.

'Be an explorer?'

'Yea, and when I couldn't, I wanted to find things in my mind and carve them. I'm still doing that I suppose.'

Julie walked a little way down the long workshop in her grey suit with scarlet chiffon at the throat, her hair forward as if thinking, and suddenly said 'Do you think they carry men's sorrow?'

I was amazed at the question; it was not conscious or intellectual; simple, spontaneous and natural. I was excited.

'Of course. The sorrows of men and women and the joys, the tragedy of war, the love and evil. That is the true theme of sculpture and poetry. Not the superficialities.' I pointed to a great stone back of a woman leaning over her son. 'I see grief there and I ask myself: is it because it is a great stone rising before me that I feel that, or is it because it is there, come out of my hand as I worked – from my mind?'

Julie looked at me thoughtfully but without puzzlement. 'It's man's destiny!' she said. 'It's like you found a language for creation and God. The Great Man who is always there.'

'I feel that too. When I'm working at my best is when someone else takes over like a presence at my shoulder, and the stone falls away as if it were snow. That is the most strange thing of all. And it never goes wrong. I call him The Violet Man who has just come out of the dark mind. The Naskapi Indians said the same thing exactly. They referred to the Great Man inside who helped them push the sun across the sky each day.

It was the gift of this girl that she was as simple, original and primitive as those people at the same fountainhead of which the world has lost sight in an agnostic technology; yet in art is returning to the primitive to save its face. It was like finding a jewel in the grass and for the first time confirmed the simple faith I was too timid to talk about. She knew instinctively what civilised man had forgotten.

'Stone is a marvellous thing!' I said as we went to the door and I waited for her to pick up a drop of bronze from the floor, fallen from the furnace at the last firing.

'Can I keep this?' she asked. 'It's been marvellous talking to you, Mush. I want this to remember it by. And thanks,' she added, shaking my hand with considerable strength. 'It's not often you meet a bloke you can talk about things. I've been longing for this for years.'

There was such honesty and innocence in her face I could hardly believe it: that I should be trusted with something that could be so easily made corrupt or smashed. More than ever she reminded me of the young Queen Tai; exactly her double, save for the fair hair and blue eye of the north.

I kissed her gently on the mouth. 'Goodness me,' I said. 'All those people. I had forgotten about them!' When we got back to the tents nearly everyone had gone except for Alice and Harry who were waiting anxiously for Julie. I gave them a huge bunch of flowers out of one of the vases and drove them home.

Exactly a year later, after what Julie insisted was a proper courting, we were married. I had not got the nerve to ask Harry so Julie did. 'Sven wants to know if I can marry him, Dad?'

'That's all right, my Svenner. But look after her,' he said.

I promised I would. As I was older than he was we had a good laugh over it. And my eldest son was three years older than Julie – the exact ratio of Alfred Wallis' age to that of his stepson when he married Susan Agland twenty-one years his senior and related directly to Julie. If that isn't destiny cleaning up the edges of a tapestry with a firm cross stitch – then I'm the devil's agent, thirty three years older.

Twelve months to the day, the marquee went up again, the drinks flowed down the throats of the Forest worthies and unworthies. We had hoped to be married by a friend – an ancient priest who like Tiresias was blind, but the Church had unfrocked him because he had married his wife's sister, and they rejected me because I was married twice before. This was a real disappointment for Julie who had always been a serious church-goer and with her beautiful contralto voice sang in the choir. But I, being an old campaigner who had always worked best outside the orthodoxy, felt it was a loss to the Church when it so blindly shut its doors to sin and with it the way to our not being sinners. It would have moved me profoundly had they left them open, especially as I live always on the edges of conversion.

Harry kept his promise also. After the celebrations were underway, Julie and I said our farewells amid a huge human wish for our happiness – lords and ladies, gypsies and clerks, publicans and sinners all joining in and as we drove off in the Humber Hawk I called the

MARRIAGE

White Goddess, Harry, dressed in hunting scarlet, blew 'Gone Away' on his hunting horn, which echoed round the Forest and made all the creatures pause to listen.

We caught our plane and flew south, but wished afterwards we had stayed with the celebration which went on till the next day.

The Sacrifice

It was Annie and Lily Bright who lived in the cottage at the top of our lane who kept the real spirit of the Forest going, for they were a hidden Forest stream that knew and remembered the secret life of the place itself as it had gone on for centuries. It is only in this century that things have leapt forward with such astonishing change. Before that it had been a continuum that had not been questioned, at least among the country folk, and not long since they had lived in mud huts and shelters. Only the gentry whom they served had any kind of security or opulence. Outside that there were dealers – like Brixy Veal who handled everything legal and illegal; Jack Homer with his smallholding, who ran a milk round with his pony and float; charcoal burners and other types of ancient Briton who had unknown occupations and were interwoven with the gypsies. When the big families went down there were left a few of the strange lives still afloat and that was the time Julie and I lived among them; Julie's people being hunt servants in the Forest.

It was Annie Bright who used to do her rounds of the restaurants and shops in Lyndhurst, collecting swill in her barrow on bike wheels to feed her pig, and the huge capon they kept every year, as images of sacrifice at Christmas; and I was given half a pig's face as my share, along with gifts of stale bacon and cake from the barrow every week 'for Feyther' as they called me after their own father with whom they had stayed at home till he died. In return Julie made them up a basket of tea, sugar, eggs and a bottle of wine.

They were both spinsters. This was because, since the day they saw their men off under the Faggot Tree, which was the great oak at the end of Silver Street, they never set eyes on them again; both were killed – Jack and Arthur – marriages never to be. Both stayed faithful to their memory. All their lives they kept their images in their heads and their dreams were of their dead lovers.

The years brought fragile beauty and happiness through poverty and the simplicity of their needs; shrewdness from surviving on the hard edge; they were without fear. The thatched cottage in which they lived was stuffed with wood faggots, old tins of food, piles of newspapers and geraniums flowering behind dirty lace curtains. The floor was carpeted with hessian potato sacks; the grate was full of hot ash from a fire that had never gone out for perhaps a hundred years or more, where they cooked and talked by candle or oil lamp all their lives. No phone, no wireless, no TV, no washing machine, no electricity, no car, not even a bicycle – only bicycle wheels on a barrow.

Theirs was the lowliness of Mary and Martha, but they sent the vicar running if he called.

'We don't want the likes of 'ee round 'ere, interfering,' Annie would say, looking up at me with her blue eyes. 'Do we Feyther? We can do without 'en!'

She was a tiny woman with a long skirt and a shawl and an old crimson hat from which the dye stained her forehead. They were like two little pottery figures in and out of the day.

Everywhere there were butterflies attracted by the pink sedam flower outside. The garden was stacked with shoulder sticks brought in from walks in the Forest. Old crocks, rusty horse bits, parts of harness, chains, prongs and a centre dung-heap from the chicken and pig and the huge cockerel which Julie and I said was the ghost of Arthur who had died in the first World War: Annie's long-lost sweetheart and now kept in a wire cage. He and his sucessors were eaten every year. Simple people with simple answers to big problems. Only by being simple could you understand them.

Lily had a limp with her right foot at quarter past the hour from not having a break set some years before, and cracked glasses from a car accident when someone had taken them for a ride, as I often did so they could visit relations. Annie had a cuckoo brooch I had given her on her 80th birthday. Whenever I looked at the brooch, when she called at my cottage, she remembered the great apple tree she called the Merry Tree when it flowered each year in the top corner of my field that was opposite her, like a huge man reclining in the snow. One year it fell in a storm and the axeman came and took it away. Ever since she sang a wild little song, for it was then I gave her the brooch.

> Merry Tree! Merry!
> Lover come back to me!
> Cuckoo! Cuckoo! Cuckoo!

getting the exact note of the bird which is rare.

'That's bin on my coat since Feyther pinned it there and it will

THE SACRIFICE

stay there till I doie!' she said to Julie one day. She loved Julie because she was a country girl. Julie picked her daisies from the field or a rose from the garden. They were friends.

'There 'ee are, Annie' she said laughing one day. 'Daisies to put in yer 'at like when you was a maid!' 'When Oi was a maid. I loikes that, you saucy thing! Just loike Wild Jack used to gimme!'

Wild Jack had a milk round till some years before. Annie's mind was clear as a crystal stream in the Forest, reflecting images and feelings. I wondered if Wild Jack might have been her lover, as Arthur Cockerel was. 'Jack,' said Annie one day, 'Ee come to me just before he doied, in the dead of winter. It was a winter loik the one when Mister Buckle froze to death in 'is shepherd's 'ut an we found 'en. And just after,' she went, on pointing to me, 'Feyther there come down the road from the woods to save the life of 'iz little son Jasper. Tarrable it was. Tarrable snow. You see I remembers. Wal Jack come along on 'iz milk float and looks at me standing there in the snow. 'Annie,' he say.' I ain't got long!' Just loik that. And I remember one o' they doves come down and couldn't get away again because of the oice. What do you think 'ee did? 'Ee got down from the milk float, took up the bird. Twistezes 'is neck and gob'n to me dead. Without another word 'ee clime on 'is milk float and drove away 'ome. The very next day 'ee was gorn dead izelf!'

Annie was still smiling when she had finished her story, as if the passing of her lover was the snow from her hat.

'Ever since, I called the black fox wild Jack. 'Ee went some time late almost on the one day I says to Lily: "Can you 'ear 'ounds 'ollerin?" We listened together. They come nearer. Then Lil said they was out cubbin' and must 'ave crossed the vixen's path. I was watching the 'ole in the 'edge.

'That ain't no vixen', I says. 'Ee'll come through there in a minute. The ole devil was after my chicken this morning. It's the black 'un I calls after my Jack. And just at that moment 'ee come through so close I could see the grey hairs on's face. Good teeth still as 'ee lifted his lip and stopped, seeing us. Lil, her bad foot was in the way with 'er the 'edge, and me the other side, then the cottage. Instead of leaping through the gate 'ee turned into the porch just as 'ounds came through. I 'eard a cry and they tore 'en to bit before our eyes.

'Then huntsman blew 'iz 'orn and they was orf. Lily was shouting at 'n for breakin her fence and messing up the garden. Then the butterflies come back and it all went quiet. And that old colenel come along. You know'd 'en. The frisky one, with a limp. "Killed on top I see!" esez "Jolly good show!" "Silly ol' fool", I sez to myself. What does 'ee know about it. But fancy that ol' black fox going loik that! It was afore you had took over!'

She looked to Julie, having told her tale and left us at our gate, then walked up the lane with the basket of things Julie had made up for her. The lights were on in the houses and the village was quiet. I stood looking at a pair of pyjamas the Idiot Boy had thrown up there in the telephone wires earlier in the day. The Forest closed, keeping its secrets, its brutality, its sacrifice, its silence as the nightjar whirred on a dead fragment of the merry tree and the night heron flew toward the lake calling: FUK FUK. I went down to see to my furnaces that contained an image to come back from the dead. Before I entered I stood looking at the stars and thought I heard a faint call on the night air: the voice of one crucified on nails of ivory and blood.

Fiery Furnace

Jasper had advanced to secondary school before going on to Technical College and had his own life to live in his own way. I did not see him so often now, although he had helped me a good deal in my workshop, particularly with bronzes where I could not do the whole process myself without another man to help pour if the image was over a certain size. So it was a great delight to find the workshop door ajar and him inside when I went in to see if the mould I was melting out had drained completely clear of wax and cooled enough to lift to the casting pit and pour. A clean strong young man with close cut hair and a lively expression, because he was always smiling, stood before me. Strong because I insisted my sons always worked hard in the fields or some other tough job while they were young and so avoid having the greenstick arms of most young men of their day, and they enjoyed it. And a strong young man was exactly what I needed at this moment. 'Just the man I need!' I said. 'But what are you doing here?'

'Well I was round this way and called in. Julie said she thought you were going to pour tonight if you could find someone to help – so I came down. I was going on a piss-up and wouldn't be in till late otherwise. I didn't feel like that anyway. It gets boring after a time.'

'But you've set all the gear out,' I exclaimed looking round. 'That's a real help. I was up most of the night melting the wax out of the mould and seeing it safe till morning, then I closed the furnace down for it to cool when it seemed clear. But you can never tell. If you get a lump lodged up inside somewhere and the hot metal goes in, it can blow up or split the mould. But you know all that by now. I got a bit of a kip in but couldn't really sleep in the day, so I walked round the lake and had a cast for that old pike, but he didn't stir. Just as well to get him because he is eating all the small fish. The otter was down there about dawn. When I appeared – and I was going ever so quietly – I thought myself invisible, but he picked me up at once. Gave two sharp whistles, just like old Kalle used to when he called a taxi in the city – that warned his mate and he disappeared. I could just see his trail in the water – like a spirit moving. I don't mind them though. They work two lakes – the one down by kennels as well, and the salmon steps in between, and that's it. But the pike is lake-bound and he takes the ducklings – following up behind the mother – one by one.'

Jasper listened patiently knowing that fishing was a mania with me – at least till I had written *Jonah's Dream* which I was on at that time. Because it was away from art and artists it turned out to have a curious mystical poetry which defeats reason and I could never retrieve. It wrote itself.

Jasper had laid out the gear which I started to check. Crucible set ready in the narrow throat of the Morgan furnace, the top of which was at ground level, the main part sunken in the floor was to take 80lbs of metal. I looked at him.

'I guessed it,' he said, 'by the size of the mould. Bit over I reckon.'

'That's OK. It will give me plenty, but put out two waste moulds to take the overflow and warm them first: everything warm and dry.'

We went through the sequence. Lifting tongs, carrying shank in place across the front, goggles, asbestos gauntlets, wood stack, coke stack, and every detail of each thing in place.

'What are you casting, Dad?'

'A stag beetle!'

'With that? You won't need 80lbs of metal for a stag beetle. It's tiny.'

'No, Jas, it's at least ten times life-size. Like a prehistoric creature – which it is really. It should be terrifying if it comes out well. You will see it as a flea sees a ladybird – a huge structure like a moon-module lurching, with those great antlers poised to crush you or grip its female in copulation. It has an exo-skeleton like the mechanical structures of our time which dominate us with about the same psychological power within them. The strength of a stag beetle at great size could pick up 50 tons. A really big one I mean. This one will be a study for the big one, about a foot high. But I need lifting gear and all sorts of extras to do it bigger. I hope I can because such an image relates to our environment and to our evolution at one glance. And is an image of the Forest of course, with all its fierceness and brutality, as well as its prehistory.

'I thought you were going to cast Lazarus.' Jasper was disappointed.

'I was, Jas. I've done a small maquette and it's come out well with a huge hand shielding his eyes against the sudden daylight and the light of the Christ combined. The moment of the actual experience must have been terrific. But the practical problems are not the same in the big casting: they are much greater.'

'You said the BBC were going to do it with John Boorman.'

'They were or we thought they were – until I worked out the extra cost. Then they ditched it. John was as fed up about it as I was.' 'Pity!' said Jasper. 'I liked the documentary he did of you. *A Portrait in Time*. This one could have been even better. Especially when he ran all those self-portraits one into the other covering about thirty years.'

'Yes' I said. 'That made me feel quite strange: as though my soul was going through a revolving door at enormous speed and was both outside and inside existence at one and the same time. Think of a complete man doing it: it would probably kill him: murder by documentary!'

Jasper smiled as he cut the last of the wood and we went over to the wax furnace and cleared a space round the mould carrying the giant stag beetle. 'Christ the Stag Beetle!' I said as we got a good footing and were able to hold the mould with our asbestos gauntlets on our hands. I felt tense and serious. I knew from experience that this moment was critical. Inside the fragile mould was only the space where the wax image had been – now a spirit image – with the inner core fixed to the outer tunic by copper nails: a jolt would shift it although it was a very small core because I wanted to cast almost solid to get the weight feeling of the beetle. We leaned over the edge from each side and down into the furnace, taking the mould in our four hands. It was heavy, but we could put no pressure on it because it might break: it had not baked too hard. As it emerged we rested it on the edge of the furnace. I saw that a fire-brick upon which the mould had been standing had melted and stuck to the bottom. If it was fused into the mould everything would smash when I tried to separate it: if it was partly stuck it would come off. Without hesitation I took a small mallet and struck it smartly – it came away.

'That was lucky!' said Jasper.

'Not luck, Jas – instinct. It was as instant as a Samurai cut. If I had hesitated, it would not have happened! Now turn the whole thing over so that the holes are at the top. That's it. Now gently, carry it to the pouring station. . . on to your knees and lower it into the pit as smooth as silk. Done!'

As we dropped to our knees and set it in the hole in the sand made for it there was not a jerk of any kind, both in perfect unison, both streaming with sweat, both anxious. Then we took off our great fingerless gloves and started to pack red Mansfield sand round the fragile mould carefully, tamping and pressing it firmly to strengthen the sides but not strain them, ready to take the pressure of the hot metal when it is poured in. It was always amazing that such a fragile container could take such an intrusion shooting within it like lifeblood. This was very much the forceful creative act completed by perfect gentleness of recession. Finally we built in a steel collar to the level of the top surface of the mould, leaving only the pouring hole and air vents open: these were temporarily covered with strips of thin metal to stop the sand falling down them.

'Thank heavens that is safe and over!' I said, still on my knees feeling tired and dirty, very much alight but still cautious. 'Safe, Jasper. If there is no wax in there nothing much can go wrong – if we pour well. Nothing in there but a spirit form waiting for the transfusion into life.'

Jasper had already packed the paper and wood round the crucible in the Morgan furnace, so we lit it right away with the top and the fire-door open, allowing it to start up under a natural draught. Then we put the tray of metals on the old wax furnace to get warm but forgot the waste moulds. I scattered Mansfield sand over the concrete floor to save any hot metal hitting its surface direct, which was dangerous, especially round the carrying shank placed in front of the furnace. Then we threw sticks of wood and handfuls of coke in to feed the fire, until it reached the rim of the plumbago crucible, closed the fire door, turned on the forced draught from the in-built electric fan, which whined like an air-raid siren, till an orange and clear blue flame holding pink and green roared out of the circular vent in the top cover. We put on our green goggles and asbestos gauntlets and worked like two moon men feeding the fire until the crucible was white hot. Then, with hand tongs, we started to feed the crucible with metal: 88% copper, 10% tin, 2% zinc. The copper first skulked, became sugary, collapsed and was suddenly liquid. The tin shrieked and vanished like a silver serpent. The zinc belched an acrid ochre smoke and then a marvellous emerald flame gave us sick heads.

'The cry of tin!' I shouted, bending a three-star rod to my ear to hear its structure break. I can hear it weep.'

'Yes, Dad, I know. You've told me before – lots of times!'

In an hour all the metals were melted. I threw in some charcoal to clear them of gases and a DS tube which helps de-oxidise the metal. Then plunged a cold rod into the red heart and withdrew it immediately. It came out clean – and we were ready to pour.

'That's it mate. We are ready to pour!' I shouted and opened the top of the furnace which had a sliding movement, to one side. The fire round the white crucible was about 1100° Centigrade, burned orange in our faces with tongues of violet and blue licking us as we lowered the great two-handled tongs into the furnace and gripped the crucible round the centre.

'Hup!' We lifted it out of the furnace and set it in the carrying shank on the concrete in front. I stopped and bound it by a safety chain that hooked onto the lip and scraped the scum from the surface of the molten metal by tilting it forward. It was so close it seemed for a moment the skin would run shrieking from my face. Then, again at an exact signal from me, we lifted together and stepped forward to the pouring station where the mould rested like a woman with her pouring hole open.

Always before the moment of pouring I felt tense and had to call on all the energies at my command, for only at my end of the shank was there the controlling handle. Together, as we leaned forward, the stream of hot metal flowed into the hole. Air and gasses hissed from the vents. I could almost hear the stag beetle inside clapping his antlers, screaming to be born. A drop of hot metal hit the cold concrete between the sand and jumped on to my boot. I smelt it burn through the leather but felt no pain. I did not flinch because to stop pouring and start again would bring about a cold-shut in the metal, which is a seam where bronze of two different temperatures have met but not merged. It was like pouring out the whole of my life at one single moment of time. Jasper was steady: for a moment I felt myself tremble. Then the great moment came when the mould overflowed, the air gas vents also were filled with bronze from inside. We poured a little longer to allow for contraction or for any air pockets to clear, and then moved over to the waste moulds, which we had both forgotten to warm.

The immediate impact of the metal on the cold iron caused it to shoot upwards in the air and come down towards Jasper. I saw him look up and watch it come down towards his back. With intuitive speed he twisted sideways, still holding the shank, slid the metal off the back of his loose shirt in one solid pad at the exact moment it touched before it could burn into him. This was a miracle that could not happen by calculation or another means except total awareness of mind and spirit. Yet he held the crucible upright, did not loosen his grip and let the molten metal go everywhere. My control would have gone if he had dropped his end.

I stayed silent. We both did, while we poured the remaining metal into the sand heap at the side of the mould for safety, and set the crucible upside-down in the carrying shank against the wall and left it to cool. The operation was over. Both of us were safe. The bronze for the transfusion that would bring the image to life had passed through.

It is helpful and quite important to say here that all my bronzes during the ten years I ran my small foundry, teaching myself as I went, were cast by the direct cire perdu (lost wax) process, where only one casting is possible because the mould is destroyed as the form is released. This means that if anything goes seriously wrong, the work is lost. This only happened once: but often there were blow-holes and distortions which improved the work and the casting could be used. The final image was unique. This was the method used by Cellini to create his *Perseus* which can never be repeated from the same mould. The excitement of the whole experience of casting is recorded in his life, not read by sculptors today because they don't cast or know anything of the sacred transfusion of spirit into metal, but leave all the responsibility to the founder to make an 'edition of eight': good for business but bad for the soul. Each artist should cast his small solids in secret and know what happens because he lives it: and leave the big ones to the master founder: who in the end, is indispensable.

Next day Jasper went away, waving to me sadly in the snow with doves flying over him, both wondering when we should meet again, but knowing something had been transfused that would always be an emblem of permanence of love, and complete trust between us.

After I had freed the bronze from the investment next day and had cut away the runners, I had before me an image unique − not for its perfection − but that, because of scorching, finning, a few blow-holes and all manner of irregularities that became part of its size and form, was like a creature thrown down by a fiery hand at the beginning of time, never before seen on land or sea. A new image to meet in the dark green dioptase of the Forest. A work of art even though it was an industrial reject, in praise of imperfection.

FIERY FURNACE

I did not machine it, but left it with all its faults like the burnt leaves on the Forest floor. I did some highly finished perfect ones which, as the gypsies would say, were 'too kushti'.

Inverted World

One of the rare forms of magic that I was able to enjoy with a modicum of skill and considerable insight that came from nowhere was fishing. Somehow I always knew about fish and what they were doing in their underwater world – that inverted world which was so different from ours: how they behaved, where they were, how they tasted food from a distance round the corner of a bank, almost what they thought, if thought they had – or shall I say some aqua-psyche that was joined to me in an invisible way, that was sending messages from centuries ago which were just reaching me like the sight of stars thousands of light years away.

Nothing in this world is single!

said Shelley, which is perhaps a simpler way of saying what I think I mean.

It was this that impressed Terry Frost when he came to visit me one day with Roger Hilton, whom I had not met before. When you show other artists your sculpture and paintings there is usually an embarrassing silence, which is either because they think it is awful, parochial, mundane or, more likely when they are silent, you have done at least one good piece they are learning from or preparing to steal. I was going through one of these unbearable silences, wishing I could become invisible, when it was broken by a minute friend who had come in on chance to fix a date to next go on a fishing expedition on the Dorset Stour. His name was Ronnie King and he was a small compact human with confident aplomb set against my more awkward height of six feet, he being less than five, which amused Terry. My skills were largely taught me by Ronnie, who was an expert fly fisherman and could tie his own flies. I once remarked that he tied himself and that is why he was such a good fisherman, which shaft of humour synchronised with his, and was part of our reason for being good friends. He also taught me to catch a pike, which is no mean achievement if it is done well. He had no interest in my work and had hopped in to our world of art in my huge workshop like a jackdaw for this one purpose, and hopped out again when I had given him a day.

After he had gone I explained to my visitors that he was an estate agent with whom I went fishing, which led me to tell them of the extraordinary thing I had about it, mostly when I went on my own and how it had become a kind of meditation as a solitary art; although it was destructive rather than creative, there was this telepathy with the Gods – or perhaps with a Fish God. Terry at least listened with generous attention when I told how I was working at the bench on some wax image for bronze, which is a completely absorbing and quite difficult process, when I suddenly felt I knew where a giant pike was lying in the Dorset Stour thirty miles away. I stopped work, got my rods and gear into the car and drove to Wimborne where I bought some live bait at Newman's boat-house and went on the White Mill across the medieval bridge near Sturminster Marshall. From there I walked across the fields to a place where there was a run of dead Cooper reed that resembled a broken jaw sticking out of the water quite near to the bank, keeping well back and silent while I set up my rod with a dace transfixed on a treble hook. This is the one certain but most diabolical form of fishing known to man: I finally had to give it up for the sake of my own soul as well as for the crucified fish. I cast the fish gently between the rows of sharp hollow reed with the large coloured bung like an abstract form in a painting, floating on top. I waited some hours until my whole being was quite still and in harmony with my surroundings and towards late afternoon, when the winter landscape was losing light, the bung went under. I waited nervously until it started to travel out to mid-stream and stop. This I knew was the crucial moment. The pike, which always takes its prey across the back, was using the main stream to turn it head down to swallow. Then the final move as he swam off. I simply leaned back, holding the rod almost upright and the movement drove the treble hook into his jaw. The bait was flung off and swam away bleeding, but the great fish raced downstream. I let him go and as I drew him back he ran like a long dog on the surface, unable to stand the pressure. I wound him back a little and then let him go again to kill him by his own strength. Gradually he weakened and finally came obediently to bank, his mouth open like an African mask. I slipped the gaff in the integument at the point of his lower jaw and, holding the line tight with the other hand, moved quickly up the bank into the field where I laid the rod pointing at him on the grass and removed the gaff. I then slipped a spring gag into his great mouth with its seemingly thousands of teeth and removed the hooks with a pair of arterial forceps, my entire hand entering to get at the ones in the back of the jaw where the oesophagus would have closed over the bait, had it not got flung free. He lay supine looking at me with a familiar and ancient eye that only I could understand as I took him with gentleness under the belly and returned him to his own element, watching him swim slowly out of visible range to his own dungeons of healing. He was at least twenty pounds in weight and lay exactly in the place where my precognition had directed.

Terry did not get such a full account, but that is how it happened, and he listened eagerly. Roger was not interested in the story and said nothing. I don't think my work distracted him because he obviously didn't like it. Terry was also very excited by the run of windows down one side of my workshop with the handles all at different angles. I've often wondered if he got a painting out of them, I expect so.

After this I took my friends down the track at the side of my fields where I no longer grew corn now the horses were gone and which were mostly empty, simply because if I rented them to the local farmers they took over and I could not get them out again. Occasional ladies of the horse used them for grazing and that is all, other than Julie who ran her long-dog there. The fox too, passed through, carrying off the farm cat in winter and the deer fed there silently at night. But I wanted to show Terry and Roger the Forest lake where I often fished for perch and carp – possibly because it was like the Crystal Palace lake where I used to fish with my brother as a boy and tasted the first enchantment of fishing with a hook, in a childhood which, like the walls of Jericho, were later to fall to the strident blasts of reality. A still and beautiful place surrounded by trees. A place where the reflected fish swam silently through the mind in an inverted world. I was nervous of saying much to the two other artists, both of considerable perception. I had a certain rapport with Terry because I had known him in early days when I was in my Tower and we had shared the same hardships and enthusiasms after the horrors of war, when the creative hurricane had started to whirl round and within us. And I knew also that he had wanted to be a sculptor and once worked with Barbara Hepworth, which I refused to do.

I did finally remark how the trees grew downward into the water with their roots at the top – an experience which always amazed me as an active fact characteristic of my inverted world and Terry reacted at once, as he had about the window handles in my workshop. It wasn't that I wanted to teach them anything because I am not a teacher and never could be, but wanted to share any experience of nature I might have discovered in my Forest as they in their Cornwall, which was so different and dominated their vision, whereas I had by now cast it off. Terry mentioned this when we got back. I think I asked if anything they had seen excited them at all.

'Yes,' he said. 'Particularly the trees growing upside-down into the water Didn't you Roger?'

'Yes,' said Roger. 'But I don't like to be told!'

This quite aggressive remark was addressed across Terry directly at me, which I understood at once because any original artist does like most to make his own discoveries, so I left it at that! Had I known Roger was a whisky drinker I would have minded less than I did, because at that time I was also one myself and knew how short-tempered and aggressive it makes you if you are in the habit of holding the golden goddess by the throat to kiss her too often and too hard: she holds you fast, you cannot get away, and finally kills you, which is what happened to Roger – and she spoilt his later work before he died.

Perhaps that is why I went fishing so often alone, and preferred to do so even without my level headed, humorous auctioneer friend, so like a fly he himself had tied; for although he taught me to kill the Tiger of the River there was always a celebration after with a bottle of whisky. On one holiday when I went with him to Eire to catch a salmon in Lough Conn at Crossmolina and look upon Yeats's grave under bare Ben Bulben in Sligo, we drank enough Powers' whisky to fill the Liffey.

Being alone in the matter was to be also without the Goddess, who is indeed a fisher of men, but also able to hold you by the sheer intoxication of her not being near and the world gradually brought peace, healed my fragmented mind by the austere discipline of waiting – even though it was to be joined to a great fish in the green dungeons under water by the same agony, watching the pilot float of liberated colour, blue and yellow as such, move midstream, knowing but an eyelash in the eye, a nerve in the system, a single thought in the ether could break the gossamer thread that held me to the fish and his prehistoric brain listening through the row of windows in his side, as the line tightened and pointed a finger of pain at his head. It was I alone who was opponent against this armoured dragon, this Japanese warrior of the water.

When I had packed my things and drove home to where I belonged, it was not with a hangover or murder in my heart having known how a creature lives and dies. But I returned with a green river in my head and the blood of a sunset that never heals, waiting to be processed into another struggle with another magician at a different time. If you asked me why, I would say: 'I don't know. And I don't like being told!'

It was all so different in Cornwall, where we worked in a group as individuals but were drawn into a common pool and therefore a common language of paint which varied in each but was as a uniform that also identified each. There was no escape. With the network of intrigue, love and hate, and calculated control by the invisible faction, a person was not so free until he divested himself of it – sought his own invention and discovery. So Roger Hilton's remark was more significant than it might seem. And perhaps my inverted world where the trees grew upside-down (certainly they did at night when I fell among the musk roses) and the blood of a dragon stained the sky, was not so odd after all, and quite a rediscovery of the experience I had with my brother in the Crystal Palace lake where the giant prehistoric cast-iron animals watched over the tops of the trees. It was to culminate in *Jonah's Dream*: a book that was derided in the pubs of Hampshire by the River Men when it came out, and later measured beside Thoreau, Melville and Hemingway. I still want to carve my King Pike from green Connemara Marble to complete my mission: to be the only pike in the history of art, except the one in a cave at Perche Merle in the Dordogne intaglioed in mud.

This was my inverted world which I did not like to talk about, even to my short friend, with whom, like Paganini with his tiny manager, I went about the rivers and lakes fishing. He knew more about it than I, but I think he was dismayed at the poetry it awakened in me. And yet it was Terry Frost who was so awed by what I told him and still talks about the day I left my workshop at the call of the Gods and drove thirty miles to catch a giant pike I knew was there and to be on the feed, which means, waiting to be caught.

The important thing is that each of us is looking for a lost key to unlock a treasure hidden somewhere under the sea, on top of a mountain or inside a woman, and by doing so add a little stardust to our sleeve or lazuli of wonder if Beauty touches us with her skirt as she swings round to glance at what we are doing. That is the magic of our art. With Terry it is the sheer love of life, the brilliance and gaiety, the joy uppermost that takes on a changing and destructive world, ephemeral and vital, whereas I, perhaps an over-serious searcher of the depths, miss in his work the plunge into profundity. What we create is no less than what we become in doing it – no more than our failure to hold in winning: the aggregate of all being the deposit of radium our particular dementia allows us to leave behind in the saucer of history, after it had been excoriated into truth.

The demonic anger and despair that sometimes scorched my days was usually in the decreasing possibility of founding my name in exile without the help of good companions in a foreign dock, for since the publication of the *Dark Monarch* no official help was possible, it seemed. A curious position because everybody knew about me, but did not any longer know my work, which is the worst part because, although one does not work for fame, the end purpose of art is to communicate your discoveries and what has been created out of them. Without this madness ensues. As the *I Ching* says: 'The wise man gladly leaves fame to others!'

I wondered, after my friends had eaten with me and gone away, if they had been sent by the Arts Council to see if I was doing anything worthwhile. Several visits of this kind ensued but nothing ever came of them.

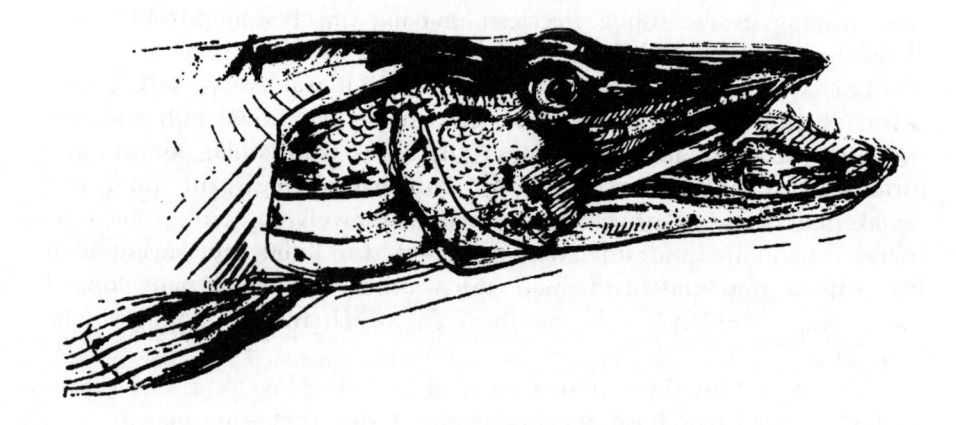

Queen of Heaven

I am more than ever convinced as I write this book that at certain moments certain people are contracted by destiny to be at a special time available for help or direction or guidance of some kind. In early years it was Frank Turk, Jack Wilson and Arthur Hambly, recorded in *The Coat of Many Colours*, followed by Adrian Stokes, Naum Gabo, Ben Nicholson, Bernard Leach, all before my exile. Then much later when I was already an old man and fairly near suicide from despair, that shrewd connoisseur and collector of art, Monty Bloom, appeared and bought a painting, which set a whole sequence of events going, out of which came Irving Grose, who was to buy up most of my sculpture and give me three consecutive shows in London, so bringing to an end my time in exile and restoring to me my place in contemporary art. And Bloom continued to collect over a long period, which ended also the endlessly slippery slope of incessant poverty.* I exhibited in the Tate Gallery exhibition in London in 1985* – that clinched it.

But that was twenty years ahead of the point about which I am now writing, when I was newly married to Julie and trying to build a future for us both. The one person I needed at this point to survive and keep faith in my work, came into my life as follows: Elizabeth Trehane, with her husband Richard became M'sieu et Madame les Patrons of my artistic destiny – Virgo in exile who seemed to be rowing so hard and going nowhere because the current was running in the other direction, making progress impossible.

Richard was Chairman of the Milk Marketing Board. A tall courteous, silent man with little to say unless it was worth saying and a friendly smile, searching gaze before which one should not blink an eye. But Elizabeth had much to say that was worthwhile, for the life force poured out of this equally tall lady with her elegant but lively countenance and satanic humour who was well cut out to be our friend. But at first I resisted the friendship and Julie kept saying that the lady we had met in the pub one evening kept on phoning to ask

* Marty Bloom died suddenly: January 1996, while I was correcting this text. Both Lowry and myself survived on his patronage. He became also a dear friend.
* St Ives 1939–64 Tate Gallery, London 13 Feb – 14 Apr. 1985.

if she could come and see us. I was very morose and did not want any intrusion because working alone was so difficult, and I was terrified she might be one of these art buffs who wanted only to talk about art.

'O, balls to her, Julie. Tell her I'm not in. I'm still in the workshop. Anything you like.'

'But I can't, Mush. It's so rude. I can't keep saying no. She's a nice lady. You must tell her yourself!' As we nearly had a row I gave in.

When she came of course we got on like two rivers meeting, simply because Liz was in love with artists and all that they did. Also she had at one time been an actress, which gave her that uninhibited fluency of speech which is the hallmark of all 'pros and which I so missed after I left that world and lived among amateurs, especially in St. Ives where so few were down-to-earth professionals at their job: that is an illness from which art suffers. In some ways Liz became Queen of Chelsea without the wilful decadence. She was an off-shoot of Irish gentry which linked her to Lavery and other artists of her time. Her father had been a major in the Raj and her connections among what are called 'THEM' by the underprivileged, were complete.

She seemed to have an instinctive understanding of a good sculpture or painting and loved everything I did.

'But darling, you must have a show in London!'

Having not had one since my initial show at Lefevre in 1946, followed by one at St. George's Gallery and some mixed shows at Tooths, I was pleased and flattered by this. And the remarkable thing was that she arranged it, and Richard opened it, all within a few months. And I started to sell. Nor was any dealer's commission payable – or only when it was connected with charity.

This gave a good charge of energy to my work, but in no way interfered with the way I did it – even when I was doing a commission, which was as little as possible. I did do one for the Cattle Breeders Association, of a young bull in bronze to be presented each year by Richard and Liz to the best breeder. It was part of their humour and tolerance that, because I cast it solid, it weighed about 15 lbs, and was almost too heavy to lift so there was great difficulty in her actually giving it to the winner each year – almost a comical situation. I think it was finally phased out to the Australian branch of the association where they were probably much stronger. But nothing was ever said.

"Bride" watercolour ca. 1986, drawn at Wimborne Minster

"Self-Portrait" oil ca. 1975

"Maintenance Boat at Cowes" oil ca. 1972

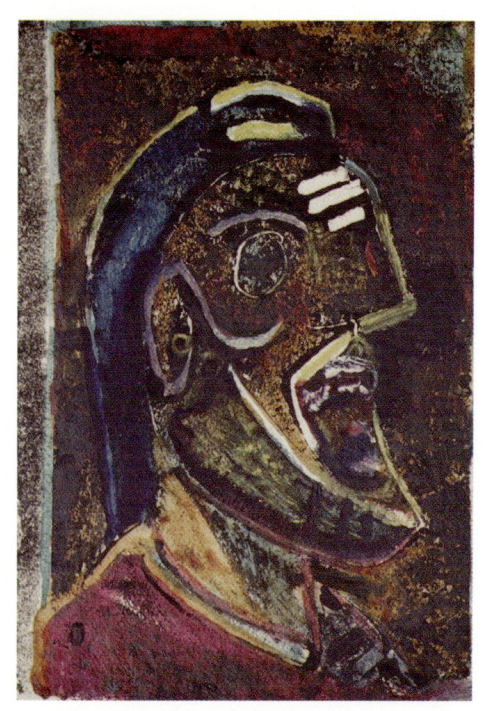

"Carol Singer" Coloured monotype ("Svenotype") coll. Brit. Museum, ca. 1948

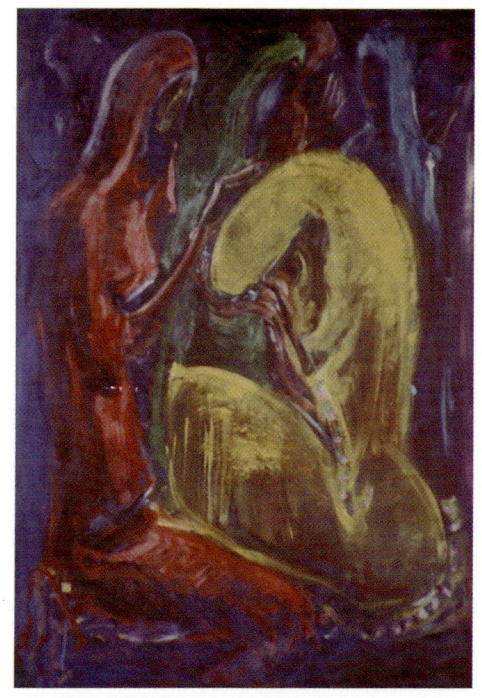

"Women Weeping" (Stations of the Cross) oil, ca. 1973

"Houses by the Sea" (St Ives) watercolour, ca. 1947

Richard was finally knighted for the work he had done for the farmers who thought so highly of him. There was no change. The event was only marked by 'an extra drinkies' and a remark which I shall always remember her making when I had been a long time at the toilet.

'What have you been doing – putting down the red carpet for me, darling?' she said when I came back.

'No Liz. I'm not like that!' She smiled.

Being the daughter of a huntsman, Julie had been brought up with gentry always around, like the Cazalets and the Gazelies who entertained both royals and celebrities like Noel Coward, Richard Burton and Elizabeth Taylor, Douglas Fairbanks Junior and the Queen Mother who always brought her slippers so that she could wear them at dinner: so she saw the whole facade from both sides, yet remained with her strong peasant roots of which she is always so proud. Being unsophisticated gave her a cutting edge to her humour which none of us could match, and insight to her knowledge.

In spite of the fact that Liz sold quite a few small sculptures to the businessmen of the big advertising firms where I had my one-man shows, I was still outside the circle of the Arts Council and British Council, who, since the war, had held in their hands the destiny of most British artists and I was excluded for my naive behaviour in Cornwall, which meant also exclusion from national and regional collections. I called it my Berlin Wall which now, thirty years after, seems to be falling under the weight of its own injustice.

I decided to build my own principality outside the City Gates, as the gypsies had done outside Paris in the fourteenth century in order that I would be a vital organic point of creation belonging to no school or group and surviving to work and grow in my own way, being as Marcus Aurelius the Good Emperor once wrote, 'neither tyrant nor slave to any man'. For this I am now grateful.

I held shows everywhere: in pubs, art shops, art galleries, churches, workshops, studios, stables, publishing and business houses and, through Liz and Richard, as far away as Texas. I did not sell much but was able to climb out of the provincial pound to be again an individual artist of some force. This at least gave renewed meaning to my art without which it is impossible to continue. And with the example of Van Gogh, down whose path I had travelled a good distance in the past, I knew that, and what was ahead if I was not able to correct it.

Although I had avoided bankruptcy over *The Dark Monarch* – just – my small fortress had suffered a lethal blow and I had to sell parts of it off; cut down in all directions, always hoping for the big commission or sale that would right the boat. It did not come.

I did one, a Rain God in aluminium bronze for an irrigation firm in Ringwood, Wright Rains, but they paid only with a year's free salmon fishing on the Hampshire Avon. I caught nothing. Then one day I was offered a chance of placing my Madonna, which was now complete.

The thing that few people know is that these images are images of the soul and once the transition to the outside world begins it can be quite painful although it is so needful.

We met the Rev Leslie Yorke, who was in charge of the Priory of Christchurch, acting Sky Pilot at an Air Force Show at Sopley where Julie and I were judging a display of paintings. It was quite a piss-up. The Rev Yorke who was in need of a drink and quite sober, asked me if I would like to leave my mark on the Priory. The request shot like a tracer bullet through a haze of alcohol and set me on fire.

'Christchurch! Not half. When can I come?'

'Tomorrow!'

The sun shone the next day. We were there!

This was exciting to me because life had changed levels so much that it had become like a web of fly-overs that could send me in many directions. The concentrated and compacted effort of earlier years trying to be an artist; travelling by horse and waggon on the road; dancing as a professional on the music halls; fighting it out in the Tower; each was a powerful discipline from day to day but now I was an artist the chances were that I would make for shallow water and lose my intensity of purpose. This chance offer of doing something for the Priory was like being given direction to go deep-sea fishing, because this was a place of great holiness – also of Presence. T.S. Eliot's lines returned at once:

> Who is that who walks always beside you?
> When I count there are only you and I together
> But when I look ahead up the white road
> There is always another one walking beside
> Gliding wrapt in brown mantle, hooded
> I do not know whether man or woman
> – But who is that on the other side of you?

It was just THAT as I hurried through the sunlight towards the Priory: 'Who is that on the other side of you?' Nowhere at any other time had I felt it so real. And that is what I had been searching for. Perhaps I grasped it too eagerly and lost it. I don't know.

Leslie Yorke told me of a legend that the Priory was sited on the other side of the river originally, but when the stones arrived and were piled up ready for the builders they were moved overnight by a hooded figure to the present site. Everyone was so overawed that the Priory was built there, between two great rivers – Avon and Stour, running to the sea.

Since a boy I always had this mystical sense of being someone else – an extra-spiritual extension of myself perhaps. It was the nearest experience I had that fitted in with what the orthodoxy were on about; although I always felt they had extinguished the spirit for the word by intellect; at least that is how it affected me. As a consequence I worked far better outside, where the spirit was not a refuge but a companion and guided me through the shadow as well as the light. In the church there was no shadow, so I felt unworthy of being there – because I had one.

But Christchurch did not do this to me, perhaps because I came with an offering from my own spirit: an act of humanity like one of the three wise Kings – my Madonna, Queen of Heaven.

I think Leslie Yorke had something smaller in mind, when he came to see me in the Forest with his kindly wife and heavenly daughter. I took them into my workshop and there was the Madonna in amber alabaster standing in her own translucent light, giving out an aura of pure beauty I had never seen before because I had never been far enough away. Now at this moment she seemed to have passed into her own world as though someone else had created her – he who was on the other side of me, I don't know whether man or woman.

The miracle also affected Leslie Yorke and his wife, and Christina his daughter who was limping a little from a wounded knee, which I, indeed, felt holy enough at that moment to have healed. The experience was between us and therefore I felt I had taken on extra spiritual state as they in turn had also done from my sculpture. It was an immediate and unanimous wish that the sculpture should go to the Priory.

The next day I drove to Christchurch where the front door of the Vicarage was opened by Christina and I spent a short but delightful

QUEEN OF HEAVEN

time in the sunlit kitchen talking with her: every word, every moment, every image and every feeling was in complete harmony and understanding, so that her father's appearance could only be a regretted conclusion. Then we went to the Priory where Mrs Yorke was arranging flowers for the Harvest Festival. Then to the Lady Chapel where, in the cool silence by the altar, a stone pillar dreamed upward by a tall window where the light streamed through.

'There!' I said. 'That's where she must go. Set her on a block of stone about four feet high and she will gather the light into her, smile and levitate over those who adore her!' I had never felt so sure of anything. The others agreed.

Afterwards the women took me along to the Garden of Remembrance where we discussed a possibility of a tall figure carved out of rose marble looking down into a long water with fish moving through the reflection. As we walked there it was an excitement in the sunlight and I shouted: 'Who is that on the other side of you?'

One of the things that took me, apart from the friendly majesty of this great building, was that they had a memorial to the poet Shelley, with whom I was saturated all my early life: so much so that I still want all my writings to be published under the canopy title: *The Dome of the Glass*, from Shelley's poem written on the death of Keats:

> The One remains the many change and pass:
> Life like a dome of many-coloured glass
> Stains the white radiance of Eternity.

H.S. Ede promised me he would have Gaudier Brzeska's name written in gold letters at Kettles Yard, in Cambridge, and failed. I would wish this title printed for me by someone who would not fail.

There were other works of art displayed at the Priory which I did not like, because they seemed self-conscious and not very good, mostly by students at Winchester Art College; except for one crucifix in bronze which inhibited admiration by having broken legs.

A mural in a spandrel of one of the flying arches recently painted by a Polish refugee had caused some disquiet because one figure had a crown and Leslie Yorke had let it through without diocesan permission: he had been summoned before a consistory court to explain this, which had upset him and seemed a wholly medieval way of doing things. It is such behaviour which serves to isolate the Church, rather than the faith it represents.

Julie had gone to her mother that day, but came with me on the next occasion when Leslie Yorke took us down to the quay where quite an intense life went on and many boats were moored. He spoke to a fisherman with a short beard who might have been one of the apostles waiting for the Master. We all went aboard his boat and were rowed downstream, where the two rivers met in a considerable cross current before narrowing into the mouth at Mudeford where houses lined the banks of sand. The priest remained calm, so did I, disturbed though I was. Julie who came of fisher-folk remained happy and laughing till her yellow plastic hat blew off. I, looking round for a moment thought she was overboard, when she made some killingly funny remark behind me, like:

'O dear I thought I'd lost my bonce. I'm glad I'm not still inside my 'at!' as we watched it twist and turn and vanish under the water.

I had an idea that Leslie had taken us on this trip, not only as a treat, but to test us out as people in an unstable situation, just as Robert Graves had done with me over the circles of Hell in Majorca.

The apostle remained unmoved, rowing with slow deliberate strokes upstream. To be a fisherman is like being an actor in an inner world other people are not able to penetrate. I thanked him when we got back but don't know if I should have paid. Leslie didn't. I think it was on the Holy Ghost.

During the following week the Parochial Committee came to the Forest and fell for the Madonna. They were a quiet, human, loving group of natural simplicity. They made their report. The finance was arranged without the embarrassment and suspicion I have met since in dealing with the Church, as though one was a common tradesman trying to dice for Christ's clothing under the cross: much to be deplored. Everything was then sent to the Diocesan Committee. I was asked to keep the proceedings 'sub rosa' during that time, but a young photographer who knew about it earlier when he was taking shots of the Madonna, leaked the information to the BBC in advance, with news that my Madonna was going into the Priory being broadcast the next morning, which made me curl up. My son Paul heard it and sent me a telegram to say how proud and pleased he was. But I was devastated. What the gentlemen of the cloth in Winchester thought, I don't know.

There were weeks of indecision and I had the feeling, awakened by a resident guilt, that they thought I was trying to smuggle the Devil in under the Madonna's skirt. After a second Diocesan Meeting it was decided to send a delegation to my workshop to view the sculpture, because the photographs were felt not to give an accurate portrayal. This was wise because sculpture is always in another dimension and cannot be seen on a flat surface; and the clergy were not sure of their art.

A day was fixed.

Those chosen were no more than two. The first was a delightful canon from Romsey Abbey, Chairman of the Diocesan Committee whom Hugh Walpole might have created especially for the occasion: wearing knee breeches, a long clerical coat and hat with wide brim which was supported by cords each side. A pale face with faded blue eyes smiling over his circular smooth white collar. He was courteous, talkative and a little nervous, and said he did not know about modern art, but was illuminated when I told him my Madonna was inspired by one I had seen at Chartres Cathedral: with hindsight, this comment might have been misguided, since he was not catholic.

The second nominee was one of those wilful non-persons − fragile, anaemic and pale in a grey suit, and seemingly voiceless. He refused coffee with a lift of the hand. The canon introduced him as Principal of Winchester Art College, which made me feel like a first year student under his accipitral eye.

On my side I had Julie, my wife and Lady Trehane − or Elizabeth as she now liked to be known. Patroness of the arts who behaved with dignity and charm, acting PRO as our little cortège walked down to the workshop in the autumn sunlight to view my Madonna, who was in splendour but in silence.

There was no comment AT ALL.

They left almost at once: the canon to his Abbey to continue his devotions and the little Master of Arts to his College to teach his pupils to be artists.

A few days later I got a letter to say that my Madonna was not considered suitable to be in the Priory. This completely negative answer after so much exultation and joy was a shock to the spirit and destructive to the mind. The Establishment had won again, shattering my belief that I had been drawn by destiny to have my work housed in this most beautiful and most profoundly spiritual home.

By the correspondence that passed among the clergy, some of

which I have seen, it seems that the roots of the objection go back to the Cult of the Virgin in the later Middle Ages and it was precisely that cult and the excesses associated with it which was one of the things rejected by the Church of England at the Reformation. The Roman Catholic Church on the other hand developed it. So in the heart of the Church as well as in the heart of the Establishment there seems to have been a fundamental objection to my work. And why? It was said to be out of sympathy with this medieval building and too large for it.

In my own immediate contemporary terms it meant that the deep note on the timpani had been struck twice: once with the withdrawal of *The Dark Monarch* and now, as if an immediate repercussion, the rejection of the Madonna, on the advice of a member of the Establishment which thought my book was directed at them on the one hand; on the other because the image I had created was related to a medieval cult of excessive behaviour – and she wore a crown.

My own turret rocked on its foundation as my Anima Spiritus was derogated to oblivion. After nearly thirty years I am still unable to understand this. But there is more to tell in the next stage of the Madonna's strange history and how she seems to have a power of her own which nearly cost me my life. Perhaps in the end that is what she will demand.

Pietá

'This is the Flesh House!' said Little 'Arry as he showed me round the kennels at Furzey Green. We had been through the buildings where hounds had their lodges, all whitewashed and made with clean straw. There was a grass yard outside where they were exercised and trained, kept in by a high fence. Being an outsider it was strange for me to see so many creatures together. They gave out a curious, almost ghostly feeling of being gentle, because they were entirely worked out: no spare fat, clean limbs, huge sad eyes: they were killers – and themselves knew death; lived under the inflexible law of Harry's tongue, his will, his mind and the end of his whip, with which he could flick from yards away an exact hound answering to name to bring into line. Every hound was completely individual in markings, temperament and behaviour. Harry had this same pattern fixed in his quick mind: he never made a mistake. They were his children, his soul, his secret love. He cared for them with his life. He did once take me among hounds, late at night and I realised what an amazing force was in his charge: one switch of his mind could release it. I was not afraid but remained absolutely calm and still, laying my soul in his hand. Like a child asleep it did not move: he accepted my trust as I had his and the whole psyche that governed the creatures remained still also – otherwise the fate of Acteon.

But to me this world was a new experience, even though I had been on the battlefield and seen the things men do to each other: unbelievable until one was in a state of permanent shock. To watch a man you knew and to whom you had just been talking dying with his liver hanging out on a pool of blood, was an event you somehow absorbed – or watching a flame-thrower at work. This here was quite different. It was a still, echoing place with dead animals on the floor waiting to be skinned and cut up for meat to feed hounds. There was nothing cruel about it. Harry didn't kill them – unless it was by special order and decision by the master to do so. The carcasses brought in by farmers or foresters were of cattle killed on the road or were old sick creatures put down by the vet for one reason or another.

Blown cows on the fields of France were no different: they looked ridiculous in a charging position when a shell had hit them – the

PIETÁ

head a few feet away perhaps with some wire, a few metal plates from a tank and a human hand making a construction that would create a Kandinsky, a Miro or a mobile that obliterates the haunting beauty of a Bryan Wynter or John Wells painting.

The animals here were also ridiculous when they had been skinned and the meat cut away, but the head and hoof still left on the bone with the eyes watching. Because death IS ridiculous and so many toys make it so on the nursery floor where all our killings are started:

> Who broke all the dolls
> Strewn on the nursery floor:
> The dead one with the bloody mask
> And the boy with the broken jaw?
>
> Ask who got it geared up
> To smash the beautiful girl:
> To crack her face against the door
> And her teeth of Mother of Pearl.
>
> O, who split the second leg
> Of the man on the trampoline
> And broke the heart of Auntie Meg
> And her bleed'n baby, Sin?
> Just like a field of battle
> With a barrage coming down:
> They've broken the Devil's rattle
> Belonging to the clown.
>
> Who broke the ceremonial sword
> Of the Admiral of the Fleet,
> Took from his hat the magic bird
> And trampt it under feet?
>
> Set on her throne is the angry Queen
> Over the Nursery floor,
> And by her side where Love had been
> They've set the God of War.

That is why, after hauling out the bodies from a bombed German

PIETÁ

city during the war, Francis Bacon became The Cardinal of Hell, Priest of Abattoirs robed in gralloch to perform his satanic surgery and re-invent the screaming forms of life: a toothed vaginal hand, cosmetic puss of paint pushed into the face of a man, in his Vatican of Blood. A dying sphinx who interlocked Beauty with Abomination.

We had to be unclothed by his knife.

Ever since I saw Rembrandt's noble ox, like the golden carcass of a God, I wanted to paint it: after his *Anatomy Lesson*, I wanted to get my own carcass as Michelangelo did from the Santa Spiritus Chapel, to paint: the case of the spirit, the kennel of the mind. Glimpses of the old slaughter houses of London as a child must have started it – and the story of the Crucifixion, the greatest tale of horror in history, enacted on Golgotha, the place of skulls. Perhaps I should have been a surgeon as my mother wanted?

Now I was standing before a horse crucified, hung up on a hook by its head, its legs helpless and limp. The knife had already slit the belly from throat to scrotum in a single cut, releasing the blue stench of gralloch which poured onto the floor and from shoulder to shoulder completing the Sign of the Cross: hung there in the Image of Creatures as One Other had hung in the Image of Christ the Man – his galloping fields of love gathered into him. At this point I thought I heard a voice: Cri de Merlin, perhaps, his spirit unredeemed, still wandering in the Forest. I regret I did no drawing that day.

Harry, a strong, stout, short little man in a plastic apron and cap was High Priest with knife in hand ready to cut away the stringy flesh, remove the pink lungs and aubergine liver from the great pillars of golden fat round the domed frame of the ribcase holding in its ivory girders the roof of the heart, tearing away the blue fascia from the spandrels of shoulder blade, to reveal the beautiful dark cathedral within.

All this was made into a giant pudding cooked in the copper vats steaming nearby to feed the hounds. The hoofs to go for glue and to make cosmetics for beautiful women; the bones to be ground up to feed the fields of far grazing and to grow tomorrow's roses.

> I sometimes think that never blows so red
> The rose as where some buried Caesar bled;

I knew nothing of the centuries-old secrets of kennels: rituals of breeding, healing, training and otherwise, or of course the mysterious

PIETÁ

(that is a right word here) relationship between huntsman and fox. All this was for the people themselves who lived an almost monastic life within their vocation. I was simply concerned with the thing that was there – as I was with war – and tried to understand it. They would not have told me anyway. Their code is esoteric and will remain so.

Julie had been brought up in this world and could perform the skills and rites as expertly as her father: had passed the initiation. And where I was squeamish or disturbed, she laughed at me and thought nothing of it. She spent most of her free childhood in kennels and reared any Nizzletripe* pup the Master had ordered to be put down as unsuitable for service. The standards of perfection were high in a world so severe in its selection that love dare not tread and grief was terminal. There was place only for beauty whose name was death from a bruised heart. So it was with considerably suppressed emotion and secret care she worked for the values of life and indeed, love. After this visit to the Flesh House, I wrote:

> I met these creatures
> In their long sleep,
> Unjacketed
> With full features,
> Eyeless head,
> And feet
> As though they had forgotten
> To remove their shoes
> Before entering the temple
> Of the dead and the woe-begotten.
>
> O, such gentleness,
> Such meekness,
> Bleakness!
> Such submission of innocence
> Untouch'd, unlick'd, unspoil'd
> Looking through the dull red odour of death:
> And the intestinal smile
> Of the sacred cow
> And the sweet sheep asleep –

---

* Nizzletripe: Somerset or Devon term for a runt, the smallest of the litter.

PIETÁ

> Their spirit done with life,
> Severed from the flesh by the skinner's knife:
> Sacrificial images who once passed through
> Tunnels of bright breath.

About this time I carved a huge *Pietá*, from a 2½ ton block of alabaster which I had sent down from Hixon Mines in Staffordshire.

It was springtime and all the skulls would be flowering with campion, meadowsweet and hyssop ready for the remembrance. I am sure the realities of the sacrifice are realised by only a few, for nature covers her stage with a beautiful curtain so soon after the event and all is beautiful:

> Golgotha in the Spring grows the rose
> Through the skulls of men who died before,
> When on this place once a High Priest chose
> To kill a Man it took a miracle to restore.
> Out of the agony of each man's dying
> Grows the root of Creation's power:
> From the stench of life there outlying
> Breathes the beauty of the finest flower.
> And he whom a woman spurns in love
> From his anguish will create a dream
> And plant another tree in Beautygrove,
> A silver fish in the sacred stream.
> Under a tree marked for Time's erection,
> In death's dark leaves, we rot into resurrection.

After the rejection of my Madonna, I think I had upon me all the grief of the centuries, which the meeting with Julie, so much younger than I, coming as she had, out of the sea and the people of the sea — out of the earth and the people of the earth — made it possible to pass through this crisis in which the image of my Anima had been expelled, holding for me the deeper core of life's meaning, that perhaps most people don't think about.

The battlefield had been the first stripping away of the jacket of blood, and during it I was consecrated by fire. But I didn't know how to deal with this till I found myself in the eye of the hurricane in Cornwall on my return, my visit to the Isles to meet Johnny Wells and live, in his words, for eight days 'in all directions at once': then the years of intense creation that followed.

PIETÁ

The exile in which this culminated was my journey into Egypt which I believe all men called by destiny have to take in one form or another. That I had that strange Jewish ancestor whom I did not know about till old age has made it none-the-less apparent. I could have even been working out what he failed to achieve. The failure of our forefathers is far more likely to make a man of destiny, than if you are a child of a gifted parent under whose shadow you must live: which is one of life's dirty tricks because, with such an impediment, there is less time to discover the genius in your own soul which each of us has.

When Ishtar left I felt doomed. Had it not been for the friendship and understanding of Robert Graves I am sure the mermaids would have enticed me into a deeper sea of whisky than I was already in – and its siren sister suicide, who is always ready to call you to the deep.

Julie and her people were no saviours, but they would pull you out of a rough sea, as any hard-drinking, tough fisherfolk would do, but with humour instead of tears. In Harry's Temple I saw the truth of this: what the under belly of the shark was really like. They 'took me in and made me safe', as Susan Agland had done to Alfred Wallis.

As I write this, I have been married to Julie for 31 years and quite recently my book on Wallis was re-printed after 40 years. I corrected the proofs looking across Seaton Bay to Beer where Susan was born, which is another of those pauses to make one more end-string in the tapestry safe.

If I had stayed on in Cornwall I would have gone with the others and become famous, or gone under. But I was moving now in quite a different sphere from the art world, which seemed more and more unreal against the rough hessian of my new family, and I did not talk about the momentous changes that had been going on inside me. I had to learn to be my own judge and jury. It was probably this that awakened the image of the *Pietá*, which was one of the most dramatic things I have ever attempted to carve, and the most profound image. It obsessed my whole life for a considerable time during the sixties, carved I think, after the Madonna was finished and before the time when the Church rejected her. I have no complete record. The Madonna carried me through on the transition between marriages and the *Pietá* consolidated my new life but was the final extinction of my youth, which had been delayed in the whirlpool of Cornwall – as with so many.

PIETÁ

It happened also at a time when terrible things were happening. Riots in America had resulted in students being shot down on the campus and their young women leaning over them as they died. Also the disaster at Aberfan in which school children were buried under a moving slag heap. The underlying disturbances in the world, now the war was a decade or more behind, began to be apparent and the news of such things became more frequent, the television coverage more uncompromising, until in this later day we have a serial horror story which seems to have no ending and points to the truth that Francis Bacon should have been canonised before he died and the directors of great art galleries should take a course at the abattoirs.

At the time I was working on this huge sculpture of the Pietá these things were mostly like a seismic tremor on the Richter Scale, and the marvellous creative expression of the early sixties among the ordinary people, which was an extension of what happened in Cornwall in the forties, began to die down; the Isle of Wight Pop Festival was a search for a lost Messiah, before the pendulum started to swing back in its enantiodromic change to the period of destruction that must inevitably follow until somebody makes death obsolete and we become invisible.

I chose my son Paul for the model for the young Christ. He was back now from the Swedish forests, had abandoned music by smashing up his piano before he went away, after passing his exams on the organ at Winchester Cathedral under Alwyn Surplice. Instead he worked for me around the farm and helped keep things going – like Jasper, pouring metal and digging ditches, with Willie also, in his top hat. It was good to have them around. And fortunate in this case. Paul with his black beard, thick black hair and slightly Jewish countenance inherited from Brody-Berlin 200 years before: he was an exact image. His body was well developed from working in the northern forests, giving an aspect of both physical and spiritual beauty it would have been hard for me to find elsewhere. And he submitted to the endless hours of drawing with complete un-self-consciousness, which, to anyone who knows the rigours of drawing the same figure over and over until he has extracted every ounce it can give, is a blessing – even to the hands which were wide and large from using an axe.

For the Mother I did not use a model. I let her remain faceless and her form nameless – growing out of the stone it seemed on its own volition – and might in this way have been humble and true

PIETÁ

enough to be the image of a celestial Queen because for all the glory she has been given, and the protection from excess, it was from the dark uncouthness of a stable that she emerged.

I had not thought any of this out. I simply had this huge image inside my mind, like a rock submerged by the sea, and knew that the job that confronted me was to release it from the stone. That is the sculptor's task.

It is in the mind: when you cut deep it is in the stone. You unpeel it – who knows how? As Harry unjacketed his creatures – only in reverse, back into life – as a surgeon takes a child from the womb in a caesarian section. Thus death and birth are the whole truth.

There was a considerable amount of stone to be cut away to reveal the image. I tried to bring it off in sections as large as I could, so that they could be used for smaller sculpture, but the crystal formation made this difficult. This slowed me down. I had no cutting wheel to oppose this, for which I am thankful, even though it often meant extra work, except when it suddenly went by its own nature. At one point a large slab set itself free when I was still on the ladder and slipped past me quite of a sudden. I was quick enough to drop tools and catch it in both hands and fall with it – some hundred-weight landing squarely on two well-shod feet. Thanks to my dancer's body and mind, I was not hurt and used the same impetus without a pause to swing it on to the bench made of solid railway sleepers.

'A fish!' I shouted. 'Christ the Fish!' Later I completed it into a separate and very beautiful sculpture. The obstinacy I speak of is a feature of alabaster. With marble and oolitic stones, even igneous granite if you get it right, it will fall away like chunks of ice.

The pain of the work was considerable: the expenditure of life-force great: both things which quieten a man as though in an isolated process of prayer. This is not to do with the technical conquest of stone, though possibly an instinctive infusion with its nature, for it is a material that has been there since the first fires left it to cool, far nearer to the initial creation than we are now. But it is to do with the movement of more profound emotions which otherwise might transmute into volcanic behaviour, murder and suicide, that we are also concerned about such principles of Beauty, and Truth, about which we know so little yet their effect is contained also in the same metaphysic of our own origins as the origins of

PIETÁ

stone, possibly from an identical root. And out of respect for these matters should also grow our ethic – which means goodness.

Meanwhile one is an ordinary workman with hammer and chisel cutting out a dream by a very slow process of destruction, until that inner form is reached and changes it gradually into a process of creation. Like all important happenings it is enantiodromic and the law of life and death also depends on it.

My image made a diagonal curve in the block of stone with the reclining figure at the base and the hooded Mother leaning over it, all contained in an isosceles triangle lying horizontally. As I excavated to exhume the Christ, the Mother's image started to rise above me like the curve of a great wave that had not been there before, and with this happening all the strength left me as it grew until I had to stop. I did not know what was taking place, for it was like a geological movement of the earth and was indeed a transfusion of forces from myself as a man entering the stone. The grief of centuries, the agony of sacrifice, the meaning of life in the heart's core and in the stone: the meaning and understanding of death, I realised after.

I went away from it and slept for several days.

When I returned, there before me was the Mother's back, a ghostly form leaning over her son as a huge wave containing grief: but being translucent, she, and the roughly carved form of her son also, gave out an aura of light. It was not I, but the miracle of stone that made it happen. I knew I was looking upon beauty radiating in the form of light as a Presence might do; and I felt strangely frightened after the wonder had passed. Could it be that, like Acteon, I had looked upon forbidden beauty for the first time and would be changed into a stag, whom the hounds I had released from my mind would tear to pieces?

None but I know how that thought came to be true. Face thy agony, Man of Stone – in silence.

I had learned from my new father-in-law, Little 'Arry, how to deal with the business of death as a creative fact of living and in this way my fears left me. Whenever he told me things I listened intently, but I could not always understand his broad Somerset accent. When he sat a horse in scarlet, he rode by in majesty without taking notice, hounds kelped around him. I was outside the Temple Gate. He knew nothing of how he helped me cut the Pietá: which held a truth: the king must die – be it horse or man.

PIETÁ

When Harry retired from hunting, he had to give up his hounds and horses with which he was so deeply involved. He made the change-over amazingly by looking after his wife, Alice, in an old people's bungalow and by following hounds once a week. But this was not enough and he became suddenly struck down with a mystery illness which surgeons and medical experts fought for months but found nothing wrong – even at the point of death. When he emerged he was silent with no wish to live; like a spent fox he had gone to ground. 'I should never have given up my hounds!' he said – or had he glimpsed a beauty and love beyond telling and from which there is no redemption – who can tell? He died soon after, with a secret none of us will ever know!

Julie was devastated as he vanished in his coat of fire.

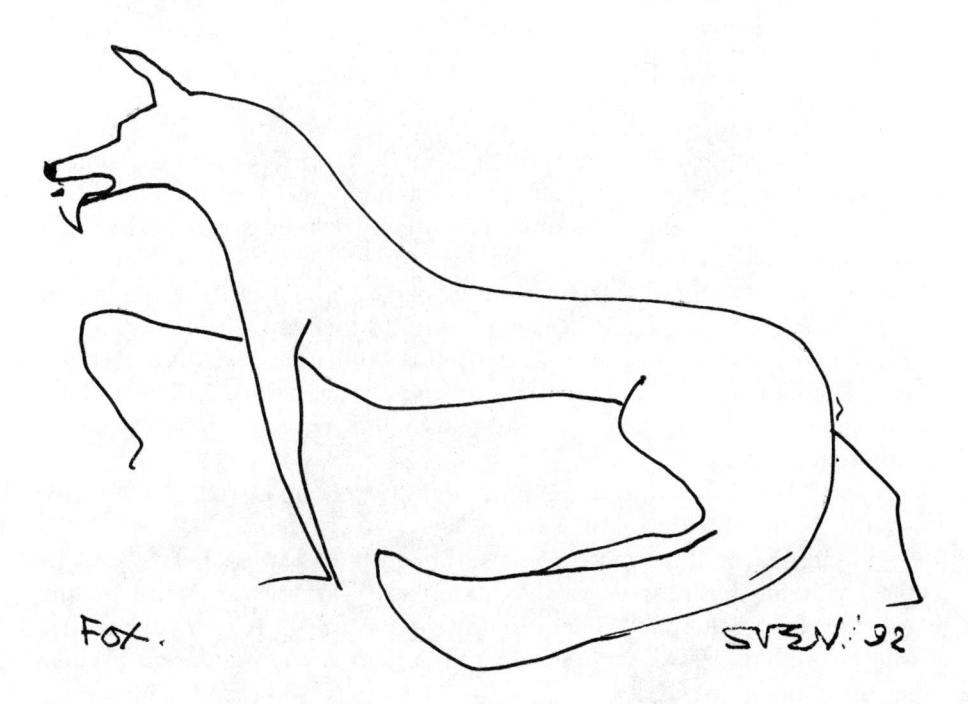

Self-portrait. Early days in the New Forest

PART FOUR

THE FLOATING WORLD

All that we see or seem
Is but a dream within a dream

Edgar Alan Poe.

Drill monkey. Drawn at London Zoo, ca 1948

The Forest Show

Like Rembrandt with his Saskia, I was riotously happy with my Julia. One of the most enjoyable happenings was to paint a great full-length double portrait drinking wine with her and her favourite whippet, Flash, at her feet. It took all my skills of drawing as well as using paint; but I found as always that to get right up in front of nature and make my transmutation was a sovereign test of my powers, both in the act of painting and the performance of living through it – reminding me that the structures would look after themselves, but that the symphony of the soul came out of the heart of man and woman through the esoteric enigma of paint. That was the difficult part and demanded everything, but not consciously.

It was after one of these morning sessions of painting Julie that I said: 'How would you like to go to the Forest Show, Mush?'

'Cor Yea! I'd forgotten all about that. Harry's showing hounds too. I'd like that. It's a bit boring sitting 'ere like a stuffed dummy. I'll go and get changed. See you at the gate. Oh, and while you're waiting check if Harriet Wells has taken the old clothes and stuff I left in the outhouse for her. I told her it was there some days ago and I don't want those rats to get into it.'

I went to the gate and leaned on it for a time, watching the two great oak trees in the field opposite spreading their branches like nervous systems where, for two centuries, ten thousand birds had found sanctuary and watched the stars in their courses, among whispering acorns of regeneration.

Then I was aware of someone at my side. It was a gypsy, in her soiled black skirt and white shirt, red diclo at her throat; she had a cast in her eye set in a brown face under greasy black hair, looking into mine with the tip of her breast touching my shoulder like an electric iron.

This was uncanny because I did not know her but had been writing about her during the night in my book called *Merlin*, and a man from the East carrying a hawk. Both inventions of the mind now projected before me. I carried on as though it was not unusual, but felt disturbed because I was in a strangely extended state.

'Ow you then?' she said, as I looked round.

'All right. You?'

'Yea. Looking for the hawk.' Her touch was powerful: a woman can catch you – like that. Suddenly I thought of Merlin when he was alone in the wood with Vivian.

> 'Where one of Satan's shepherdesses caught
> And meant to stamp him with her master's
> mark.'

I hesitated, knowing Julie would be out any moment and the gypsy would run like a hare. I felt in danger.

'Where did you lose the bird?' She turned on her full power, facing me.

'Somewhere near here. We flew him at a rabbit; he missed, but wouldn't return. Otaka wants it back. He's Hawk Man!' This I knew. I had heard she lived with a Japanese traveller who carried a hawk.

I tried to deflect her by asking when Harriet was going to collect the things Julie had left out. She said that Harriet was doing that now, and made a movement with her head. I looked in the outhouse and saw the older woman with a hooked nose and steel blue eyes coming away, bent double with the weight of a huge bundle she had made up from the things Julie left there, slung over her shoulder. I moved forward to help her.

'No that's all right, my chiel. I can manage,' and she pushed past me through the gate, off down the road, knowing as with a horse, that if you stopped with a heavy load you could not get restarted so easily. Manners were pointless.

'Otaka want her back!' she said when Harriet had gone.

'What, the falcon?'

'Yes!' She gripped the gate till her hands went white, like claws.

'Does that bother you?' I asked.

'Not really!' But she was lying. There was something going on I could not understand and because I had been painting for several hours I was open and vulnerable. I could feel her heartbeat as if she was joined to me. It was something only a primitive woman could do. But I was helpless and began to feel paralysed. Had it been sex, where a man and woman are drawn together like arrow to target, it could be dealt with. It was not so. It was something else: as though she had been flown at me. Then she reversed the energy and I nearly passed out. Quite suddenly she was gone and I got free. She must have heard the house door go.

FOREST SHOW

This projection reminded me of Alexandra David Neil in the Himalayas. She met a man who stopped and talked: after a while she saw a devil on his shoulder, but said nothing. Later a local peasant told her the man was an artist who had just come from painting a wall in the Temple. The image on his shoulder was one of the devils he had been painting.

Julie appeared at the end of the drive walking towards me and seeing I was pale, said: 'You all right, Mush?'

'Yes. I'm OK. I thought I had passed out for a moment. It was probably that hydrochloric acid I was using early this morning to stain the stag beetle bronze I cast with Jasper. Dr Willis told me to wear a mask but I forgot.'

'You haven't been drinking?'

'You know I don't drink when I'm working. Anyway I've been painting you all morning, since!'

'You sure? Shall I send for Willis now?' she persisted. I got irritated.

'Let's get down to the Forest Show before the traffic builds up!'

'What was that Gypsy woman doing here?' said Julie, sensing something was wrong.

'She was with Harriet collecting the gear you left for them to take down the compound. And she was looking for a hawk they had lost.'

'O yeah?'

After a pause watching the ducks being herded by a Chinese goose who had become head duck since her gander had been killed by a car, I said to Julie: 'Do you believe in black magic?'

'Of course. Why do you ask, Mush? There's plenty of it around here. You know that!'

The goose, with her neck outstretched near to the ground, was honking while the ivory Aylesburys with their banana-skin beaks and garnet eyes passed under the gate and crossed the road to the field where the two great oak trees stood.

'Ducks!' I exclaimed. 'Grant Watson always says they are joined to the landscape in some way. It must be to do with water: they think they are joined to the land as well. When I come back I want to be a duck. A wild duck with arctic snow on my back and ice under my feet. To hell with this human being lark.'

We got into the shooting brake and drove to the show being held in the middle of the Forest, forgetting about the gypsy for the time being. But a voice was saying:

FOREST SHOW

Why did you leave me for dead,
Hawk Girl?
Split head,
Heart torn,
Liver bled.

Only the song
I sang on my branch
Was wrong,
Made you blanch,
Not what I said,
Hawk Girl – Shrike!

Why did you leave me for dead
Why did you strike?

The first time I ever went to the Forest Show was with Benny Wells, brother to Harriet, when I was living rough in the trees. To get in we did a gypsy roll under the barbed wire. You stand erect, hands at your side, quite rigid: fall forward and as you touch the ground, roll under the bottom wire and by the same impetus stand up on the other side without a scratch. Today we drove to the entrance, parked the car and paid to go in.

It was a fine day: every Foresters' heart was full of joy, his belly full of beer. It would be a tragedy if it rained. After we got away from the lines of horse-boxes and cattle lorries the spectacle began. Countrymen in box jackets, breeches and cord caps: women in summer dresses and large hats: labourers in their best: gentlemen, gypsies, cattlemen, huntsmen flowed in one river to see the show. Massed bands were playing and I could see the brass flashing and hear their silver and gold sea-lion sounds. Flower stalls, vegetable shows, implements of bright colours like great coloured insects from a forgotten age, stood in lines. Children ran in and out, and through the crowds I saw the lone figure of Otaka, the Japanese traveller, with his black beard and slotted black eyes in a skin of potato gold carrying his falcon hooded on his arm with a glove and the jesse coiled in his fingers.

There were praying mantis hedge-cutters; ditch-digging dinosaurs; giant beetle tractors, laughing-man muck-spreaders; there were dragonfly helicopter sprayers and a combine-harvester like a yellow House of Death or Village of Fear.

FOREST SHOW

Even a bank with a fine fist of notes, green as a forest leaf and coins as silver as a forest trout with loans for sub-luminary farming sons of God.

There was show-jumping, dressage, a cattle parade, Hackney cart driving. Great horses descended from Agincourt. Great bulls from Hereford and Charollais. Great horsemen from Sweden, St Cyr, Vienna and the Don Plains of Russia. So vital and so multi-splendoured an array as defies description and needs at least as careful an eye as Richard Jefferies recording Amaryllis at the Fair. A complete trompe l'oeil and indeed, trompe de la plume, beyond my powers.

As we grow there are blank areas left in the memory that become clear later. Julie says she does not remember me taking her to the Forest Show and, although it was probably the last time I went to one and often refused her in later years, I did do that, and myself remember how excited she was by everything: especially when her father, Little 'Arry, dressed in scarlet with white breeches and top boots, a column of rosettes on each arm and black velvet huntsman's cap, paraded hounds with Sir Newton, to the delight of the crowd in the enclosure.

Alice was there, Queen of the tough countrymen and women who fitted like a cog into the gentry. They respected her for fearlessness in the face of conspiracy and for speaking the truth: the most deadly serum of all for snakebite: and her humour.

Julie was with her mother, Alice and I lost sight of them for a time. When I was looking to find them again I went into the beer tent, thinking they might be there. But everyone else was – and I only just managed to get through to buy a pint across the counters swimming with spilt beer. Charl Penny, Jimmy Biddlecomb, Rig, Ammer, Charcoal John and my own drunken father-outlaw, Roland Witney, tall and bearded, singing a ballad, just as after in the pub Little 'Arry would sing his 'Jolly Laughing Policeman's Song' and get them all going.

I was sipping my beer on the edge of this tangle of human bodies when I realised the gypsy was pressing against me once more. I could smell her body and took a drag of a fag like powdered glass. Next thing I had blacked out: only for a moment they said, but felt clear in the head afterwards, as after an orgasm. She had gone. Everyone looked afraid. Only I was clear: a new man, as though I had died. A young Welsh dealer named Gwydir bought me a brandy and I stood outside the tented air and human sweat into the gold of the sun.

'You must carve that angel for me!' he said.

'Yes. I will soon, Gwydir. Don't worry. I've been so busy. I want to get a peaceful space to work in.' He smiled with pleasure and went away in the crowd.

My passing out could have been due to recurrence of a bronchial condition which had dogged me since I lived in the Forest and my doctor had discovered how certain chemicals were affecting the haemoglobin corpuscles of my blood and I had myself noticed that when there was a physical disorder it was often paralleled by a fault in the psyche. When I returned from the war I used often to black out for no known reason. Then one day when the deep green of the harbour at St. Ives suddenly beckoned me at neap tide and I dived in with all my clothes on and swam to the other side, I was suddenly cured. I continued to do this because I no longer blacked out and I saw exactly what I must do to become a good painter after the experience of the battlefield. I remember Peter Lanyon saying I was showing off and denouncing me on the wharf for doing it within sight of my family. This might seem irrelevant to record, were it not for a concomitant event not long after these new blackouts, which I have ascribed to self-protection against the gypsy woman, in which there was involved a curious death wish such as I think the rabbit has before the stoat or the falcon take it. Or was it simply bronchial troubles from too much smoking and drinking, coupled with inhaling chemical fumes? But none of these hypotheses satisfied me completely. There was always a missing factor, until one day soon after a stranger said to me in a crowded pub, as though he was going to hand me a writ:

'You're Sven Berlin, aren't you?' I said that I was. 'Did you know that your friend Peter Lanyon has died after crashing in his glider?' He showed me a paper, then went away as though his mission was to give me this news, which was a punch in the brain. I stood under the evening sky wondering how this could be, and if it was anything to do with my blacking-out – a precognition, perhaps? I saw quite clearly the scene, eighteen years before, almost to the day, when I was talking in the sunlit Fore Street in St. Ives to a friend. The crowds suddenly started to part and a small green drop-head coupé car drove straight at me. The driver behind the wheel, his mouth set and his blue eyes fixed ahead, was quite cold and without passion. It was

Peter Lanyon. I did a perfect *pas de chat* onto the side walk and he missed. It was like Van Gogh trying to kill Gauguin, but in each case it failed and the line of force followed the aggressor. On the long shore of the mind many a wave of unspent force crashes years after if the event that set it going has not been completed: the gypsy woman trying to take me with her hawk mind was like a metronome being in time with other unresolved events colliding in psyche. In this case again I was cured of my *petit-mal* and it has never returned. Nor has the gypsy.

I have remained silent but haunted by this event for many years, and it has caused considerable anguish. I have mentioned before how I believe the velocity of a force that has passed by its victim floating on water, and has homed elsewhere, might be de-energised, but it seems now that it must otherwise continue like a shuttle in space for all time and is therefore a possible threat in the future. And because it has been troubling me in this way from its ethic as well as its danger, I have recorded it without bias in this unusual way, *believing* I have done the right thing to defuse it into the mass psyche and might add a fragment of wisdom rather than unsolicited pain or death.

As the massed bands marched out of the arena, what I should have expected was to have seen – as a form of ancient sacrifice – the falconers to ride on, each man with a falcon, and dismount; a man following on foot with a cadge of hawks wearing hoods. And for this to be a remarkable and almost medieval sight. Not simply a display of using the lure and flying the bird at it or returning him by it, with, like the Portuguese bullfight, no kill. But instead, the gypsy woman to have released a hare into the arena and Otaka fly his hawk at that, as it ran for safety. With perfect timing and a few wingbeats, the bird – its opened talons wide apart – would lift and glide to take the hare in a death struggle, ending in covering her prey with her wings save for a visible emission of sperm and a twitching of the legs. A terrifying and fiercely beautiful sight which would horrify some and excite others; but silence everybody with the truth, until a Giant's Voice gritted its teeth on the public address system and said: 'Will the competitor who flew the last hawk report to the Organisers Tent immediately!' But not to explain that the truth of sacrifice, like the Crucifixion, speaks the language of both death and creation without which we would be forever unredeemed and become extinct. It just did not happen, and the gypsy was nowhere to be seen: nor her partner from the Orient.

I pretended to be flirting with a tall girl in a skirt suit and boots: it was Julie with her mother Alice. They were roaring with laughter at my apparent mistake:

'That's a turn up for the book!' shouted Alice. 'Trying to get off with his own wife. You wait till I tell 'Arry!'

Then Julie came in with: 'And what were you doing in the beer tent talking to that old gypsy woman – chatting her up? You want to watch out. She ain't no bloody good and that's fer sure. She's no good, feller. And she'll get a bunch a fives if she comes near me.'

'I expect she'd make a good bundle!' I retorted, teasing Julie. 'I like a bit of spare.'

'You do, my Cocker, and just see what you get!'

'What will that be?' I asked a little nervously.

'A knuckle sandwich right in that bloody girt cake 'ole a yours, 'an no messin!'

'Now then, you two,' said Alice, seeing Julie was angry, 'let's watch the Hackney carriages'.

By this time the sartorial gentlemen were already parading round the ring, each with a whip poised in a four-wheeled light carriage behind a high-stepping Hackney horse, with his head drawn well in to show the crest of his neck. Each driver was as well groomed as his horse, with an apron across his knees. Mostly men of sixty years' experience. The animals, originally ladies' horses, stepped out like ballet dancers with high elegance and nobility. Thick necks, convex heads, full manes and tails held high and absolutely silent in their beautiful action, save for the jingle of the harness. These old gentlemen performed the figures and patterns invisibly in their minds for them, so that there was perfect union between them and the psyche of the animal. They brought to mind a time of skill, a time of courtesy, a time of grace that passed from the world at the moment the single bullet was fired at Archduke Ferdinand of Sarajevo and sent seven million men to their death. As we savoured this touch of English elegance they drove off the field to the final judging in the paddock and the Giant's Voice said: 'Ladies and Gentlemen – the Russian Cossacks!'

A torrent of life force entered the arena, a stream of men riding low in the saddle with absolute fluency on horses with golden coats, black manes and tails from the Don Plains in the Caucasus. They wore sheep-skin hats, skirted coats of crimson, deep blue or yellow, with brass cartridge holders across the breast and riding boots. Short strong men with yellow Tartar faces, whose life was the horse, spirit and body, since the days when Genghis Khan crossed Asia with his hordes. They performed marvellously, firing their rifles under the horse's belly and hanging on one stirrup: horse and rider one animal. I felt their exhilaration rise in me from ancient places. Men who rode to live into death. The same who pursued the tanks of Hitler's army on the snowbound plains, leapt on to the turret and dropped a Molotov Cocktail inside – then sprang back to the saddle before it exploded.

Alice and Julie were both excited by their manliness and skill and, unlike others, did not give a tepid reception in case war should break out, but clapped with most of the other country women. It was a sheer delight for everyone who could accept it. I had seen them and talked to them in the Ginnet's Circus at the Crystal Palace when I was a boy: now, as then, the Cossacks had their own reward as they rippled away out of sight.

Realising the afternoon was nearing its end, I went to get the car and drove to the entrance where the women waited for me to take them home before the traffic built up. It worked well and we got back to town quite easily, Harry to follow later to the pub after he had seen to the horses and fed hounds, bedding them down for the night at Kennels.

This whole day had been a complete immersion with the people into whom I had married. I felt curiously happy and safe after those long years in the Tower at starvation level. Art and life were no longer separate activities but one a spontaneous interpretation of the other, in which the experience, and the meaning of the experience, were concomitant. I think that is why the blockages of the inner life were cleared automatically, as a goat will find its own antidote to eating laurel, if it is not tethered: I was now free to seek the cure to past evils and had instinctively found them, though not fully understood the process by which it came about – only that the cracks and fissures formed in the psyche by shock were equally important as those for which we might find medical solutions and that the larger Cosmic Psyche might well contain a natural process of healing if we leave it to work by its own law: then the murdered man will no longer seek or condemn his murderer.

The evening of that day was the same, and as it built up I remember standing a round of drinks for no fewer than sixteen of Julie's relations, come from different parts to be with us – all their happy faces crowding round.

'Five pints of beer, four gin-and-tonics. Two brandys, two whiskys, three halves of bitter. That will be five pounds exactly!' said Ken McCarthy the young good-looking landlord. 'You lucky man!' By which remark I knew he had a crush on Julie.

In fact, all the young men had a crush on my Julie, because of her magnetic attraction and personality, also her Rabelaisian humour which fearlessly cut down the more abusive Romeos who were angry that she had chosen someone so much older than herself. When that did not work, I settled one with a quick right to the mouth, for which she called me her 'Ulysses Man': the others fell into line or fell also. But Ken was always friendly and respected us both. He had made all the arrangements and supplied the drinks when I put up the marquee for our wedding.

'Never mind, Ken,' I said to him as I paid for the drinks, 'you are lucky in another way. Look at all these relations! Next time, if this doesn't work, I'm going to marry a bloody orphan!' – this made him throw his head back laughing.

The next day I continued painting the great double-portrait of Julie and myself. It presented a difficult problem in that Julie was there before me sitting in her chair with her glass of wine cradled in her hand; her guilty but beautiful whippet at her feet; she in a suede suit of dull gold and red boots. But I, standing behind her, had to be reflected in a tall mirror which, not large enough to contain us both, only extended me into space like a ghost of my past but presented my image in reverse. This was an equation I had to work out. I decided on the two images being painted in this way because it somehow symbolised the reversal of time – and forced me to look back as well as being joined to the present, which proved right and it came out well in the end, with a curious overtone of mystery. As with Rembrandt and Saskia it was also a celebration of life.

Aurochs

The Creation

> I have gone the whole round of Creation:
> I saw and I spoke!

These lines from Browning's poem *Saul* have recurred with such regularity from the early days, and with such solemn intention, that they have become a ritual chant in my working life. Art was no longer another innovation of isosceles triangles to mark an avant garde progress started by the Princess of Parallelograms. It was a process of the soul which emerged from the daily experience of evolution in the world about me seeking a meaningful way out. Since my active life was so much in the deep Forest, concerned with fish, insects, plants and animals, it is normal that my meditations also were concerned with these things and by a natural process my art should turn towards them, whether I cast a praying mantis in bronze, or cut out a beautiful woman in stone. Out of this, the moment came when I wanted to house this experience of the first creation in one larger work which took the form of a Cycle of Paintings, based on the Book of Genesis, which I called the *Creation Cycle*.

As winter came on and the golden days of October spent themselves in November mists and the fires of another year burnt out, I started this huge task of reaching into the universe to paint the whole of Creation.

At that time I painted in a wooden chalet – the one that I had put up in Edie Gailor's field and later moved to Home Farm – set up at the bottom of the paddock where the two weddings had taken place and away from the cottage. It was always my way to start work early and go to my place of work before first light when the world was lit by starlight which glittered on the sealskin grass as I crunched it under foot.

The only creature who made me conscious of being a man was the ass who stood in green light as if carved from volcanic dust, frozen like diamond boart over his back and loins to make as a habergeon of ice casing his spine, scorched by the black cross, his ancient head held high against the moon like a hewn stone. His jewelled eye, set in fur, had a saurian glow, reflecting my image; and as I approached he arched his neck, bared his long teeth, working

THE CREATION

of Sweden with its lonely eagles and the spinning propellers of childhood.

To dream deep would be to paint well and interpret my subject by reaching the Old Testament colours that had matured in the depths of the mind from the beginning of time. In this way the Spirit swirled like a great fish stirring the bed of the universe, and Adam was made. When this happened I knew the others would follow and my hand be guided if I worked with devotion: my endless search into nature, where I set out to draw the whole cycle of creation to the minutest insect, was now to be used in one eruption for which I was the Volcano.

God created the Insects
God created the Grasses
God created the Birds and the Fishes
God created the Animals
God created Adam

And then, in the pale light of an unfathomable experience

God created Eve.

This was my *Anima Humanus* floating over me: the pain in my left side.

I painted with red calling to gold, blue recumbent with fertile green and umber earth-stained by Abel. I painted with wings of light and the deep ground-swell of darkness under the sea. I painted with pinched yellow extracting life from stung scarlet and the agony of ice blue open to arctic air. I painted through luminous forests of diaptose green and the tall growth of violet spreading to ochre elegance in the secret interiors of aubergine. I painted bone-wise with fountains of flesh. I painted with joy. I painted with anger and oil over the tigerous fury of fire and the tall smooth excellence of love that excelled prayer and profited forked emerald and black. Puss puce entering and exhalting oracles of orange. I painted absolute and out of mind.

As I was walking back in the evening after working on one of these paintings – for I had to stop as light faded and clean my brushes if not too tired – the moon was rising yellow behind the trees and the ass was arranging his archetypal dreams for the night.

THE CREATION

I was victim of that fatigue which has only once been described: the utter agony of body and spirit Michelangelo felt when working on the Sistine Chapel. Although I hardly dare couple his name with mine, I called it my Sistine Chapel.

> Crosswise I strain me like a Syrian bow;
> Whence false and quaint I know
> Must be the fruit of squinting brain and eye;
> For ill can I aim the gun that bends awry.
> Come then, Giovanni, try
> To succour my dead pictures and my fame
> Since foul I fare and painting is my shame.

And the sonnet fits.

I knew that, however my work turned out to be, and whatever agony was dispensed as stipend, this was a release of creative force within me so strong I could hardly stand it, and the like of which I might not know again: nor the manic depression that followed each burst. I went with it, feeling myself to be only the shadow of my own man as such. When I was not working, like Angelo, I drank wine or slept or wept or was silent, so that I would not have to talk about what I was doing, which I dislike at all times, saving the capital of energy for the next session. The journalist is free to shout his facts: the painter deals with experience he has not known before and is inarticulate until he creates his new image.

During this time, because I was interned and not giving myself outwardly to the world, there was little enough return in the way of money and the task lasted all winter into the following year. The world withholds its gifts from those who are gifted because it thinks nothing is being given; or it knows that the gold being smelted cannot be paid for in bronze coin; or it smells its own jealousy in the green fur of the night because only creation can bring light into the world. I had no income. It was with increased anxiety I loaded my home with loans and debts, so that in the end I was the frog eating the leaf upon which he was floating to stay alive. A perilous position in which I had been many times. But not as Man of the Road, for then I had nothing to lose and did not care a fuck. It was difficult for Julie, but as the daughter of an itinerant hunt servant she was used to making do. Our Jaguar Mark 10 masked our troubles. I had to finish the Creation.

THE CREATION

I was never a good churchman and always conducted my devotions best outside the Orthodoxy, and making only tentative relationships with such as Leslie Yorke who was inspired by my Madonna: but that would have been the same in any lane of life because he simply understood what I was talking about and we got on. It was the same with the Reverend Tom McArdle, who in my time at Lyndhurst, was parish priest and walked about the town in his long robe as John the Baptist would have done, and was equally fitted to announce one who came last but was preferred first. He had the spiritual drive that I missed in most men of the cloth.

Since he was in charge of the church with its fine altarpiece of the *Foolish Virgins* by the Pre-Raphaelite Burne-Jones, I was curious to know what he would think of my Creation Cycle of paintings when they were done, and asked him down to have a look. The result was dynamic and he immediately asked to have them in the church. There was no way of hanging them on the stone walls without professional help and – as a temporary arrangement – we balanced them on the pew-ends against the stone, which showed the colour quite well. This caused much excitement among the parishioners and the local paper took it up, but attacked Tom McArdle for allowing into the church a panel of Adam and Eve embracing, because the figures were in the nude. But my friend defended himself, and myself, quite eloquently and refused to move them from where he had hung them very cleverly in the baptistery which had a wrought iron fence round it. When I was asked if I thought it was pornographic or was intended to be, I replied no.

'Adam and Eve were obviously in love and that was the only time I had made it last forever!' To which Tom gave a wry smile and the press went silent. Alan Hutchinson and Roy Hall of the Bournemouth and Poole College of Further Education, having seen the controversy in the papers, followed this up by asking if the Creation Cycle could be exhibited in the Great Lecture Hall at the College during their Arts Festival. To this I consented and it was sent from the church to the college to be hung, much to my delight, because on those vast walls it could be seen as a complete work. Indeed, it was like having my own Sistine Chapel. But when the Festival was over no one wanted it moved, including myself; especially as it was not only where all the important lectures took place, but also where the students sat many of their exams, and it became a privilege to have it there. This led, on Julia's inspiration, to Julia and myself making

THE CREATION

a gift of the Creation Cycle to the staff and students for all time, with a presentation arranged and presided over by the then Principal, Alan Hutchinson and Roy Hall, Head of Arts and Social Studies. For the first time the sectarian and non-sectarian factions of society had come together in taking my work seriously as a lone artist to be in constant close contact with the ordinary people for whom it is intended. I was grateful.

This event did much to strengthen my spirit and make me feel part of a communicating world, with a device in place by which I could connect with the inner life of others without noise or ostentation – almost as an anonymous person, for it seemed otherwise that the guns of destiny, like those in the Maginot Line, pointed only in one direction and it would take a long time to go round them. All official bodies continued to ignore my work. There is one secret weapon used in the world of art. If a painting or a sculpture (or artist) is blacked, the people will leave it: if it is praised, they will take it. A dealer will tell you that the painting he has just bought is the most beautiful thing he has seen: when he sells it to another dealer the next day it is rubbish. That is how it works. But that is only example. To go into the world of dealers is another matter: it is for someone with more courage than I. Among them I have known the best of men. Only they know when it had not been so. But the Establishment is always polite and silent: faceless and seldom forgives: like a sculpture in ice, its promises melt away.

I am recording the way it can go: no more. Because the mesh is small only the best can get through, which is as it should be. But I am not excluding those beautiful people who are always there and never question the truth or fullness of one's work, even when they might not understand it. The companions of loyalty, the invisible spirits who direct the way or make it possible to draw from the wells of poetry:

> Where are the Beautiful People now?
> Tall ones with sapphire eyes
> And those upright of lesser height,
> Fine as a steeple in the skies
> Who gave out that special light
> And joy to see you by surprise:
> The Beautiful People who pass at night.

THE CREATION

Where did the men of laughter go?
And women whose only melody
Was loving deep, played time on time,
Counterpointed pointing south,
Body on beautiful body glowing,
Silver gown on golden going,
Spirits flowing mouth to mouth.

Where are the dynamos of youth?
Souls on mountain summits standing,
Man of vision, girl of truth
Starshod for a journey north,
Secret skirt of understanding,
Universe a cloak remade
To fit her moonlit shoulder blade.

All have dissolved at evening time,
The Beautiful People of long ago,
Proud in elegance sublime:
We can't forget this fragile show
Who trod in turn a turning stage
And read the oracle in rhyme
'Being beautiful is all we know!'
As they pass into another age.

Robert Graves, Augustus John, Vaughan Williams, Mai Zetterling: these are the Beautiful People who pass in every age. The sadness is that they seem to pass like ghosts in a floating world without your knowing and you are alone. The lone Creator – must make his own laws for his own Creation: be Lord of the Dragonflies, Master of Mammoths and Priest of Fishes in their dark sacristies. There is also a shadowy companion who is possibly the questing self, always at my side and for whom I am the antennae.

Unlike the Tower, when physical aloneness was the emblem, this was the aloneness of having been where none other has been, while keeping vigil over a furnace at night, entering a stone by day, or going to one's devotions in paint when starlit ice armoured the arse of my jackass at dawn braying the helpless challenge of a Creation, which it was my lot, each new morning, to take up.

The Reluctant Angel

Marrying Julie, I married the Forest. On the same tapestry was woven the lives of Annie and Lily Bright who lived in the cottage at the end of our lane. My work then was a kind of secret life and a kind of magic also; the Foresters accepted it as something I did, but would take the piss unmercifully if I showed off, with a humour to be matched only by London men and women, with whom they were in contact and did trade. Among the Forest horse dealers in those days there was a ring that stretched back to Wales and forward to London, down to them again, and anything of real value was laundered along this route so silently that it was not easy to detect. I discovered this too late when a year or two before I met Julie a whole stable of rare saddles belonging to Ishtar was stolen overnight. Some came from as far away as Mongolia and Mexico and formed a unique collection. They were never found.

A Forester would drink with you while his son stole your Muscovy ducks, and sell them back to you the next day. 'Sting 'ee loike a Forest floie!' – and laugh! So it was with total acceptance also that I drank with them after work and fell among the roses when I got home, or how could I face Jack Donkey in the morning? That is how it was.

Among those I suspected of stealing the saddles was Gwydir, the young Welshman who stood me a brandy when I had passed out in the beer tent at the Forest Show. He was about in the pubs, and would then vanish for weeks, though I think he had a property somewhere in the Forest. I never went there but did drink with him because that is simply how it was, as I say. We all had our secret lives or terrors or fleeting joys. The meeting place, where all these things were submarine, moving like shadowy creatures below the surface, was in the public houses. The Waterloo Arms, the Mailman's Arms, The New Forest Inn or the Volunteer Arms and Fox and Hounds. Laughter and talking were uppermost, joking and spoofing, buying each other drinks, remained a common exchange. The surge and flow of the evening was linked to this – sometimes breaking into a song, a moment of anger or a good fight but always weaving one life into another giving and taking, strength, love, hatred and devilry with a good deal of laughter. This was the local core that belonged to the place – not interfered with by visitors and the artificial behaviour

THE RELUCTANT ANGEL

they now bring to what had been a historic meeting place for thieves, poachers, gamekeepers, farmers and dealers. Possibly the occasional artist such as George Morland who frequented these pubs or later myself who was of that ilk. Just at the time I was there it was so. All too soon it was over-run by an invasion of retired television people and factory managers, politicians and horsewomen to the exclusion of the Lords of Little Egypt who were born among the trees.

Gwydir was of these, but younger than most of the dyed-in-the-green Foresters, like Charl Penny, Buffy Mansbridge and Brixy Veal who kept the inner life of the Forest going. Buffy and the others drank hard and while they drank, they played a game called spoofing, which is quite well known under other names and simply consisted of hiding three matchsticks behind your back and getting your opponent to guess which was the shortest. The stakes were a Panatella cigar or a pint of bitter. Occasionally small amounts of money. It could go on all evening while others talked and exchanged the news.

When Gwydir entered, things changed because he was one of those humans who had an extra charge of energy which electrified those around him. He was middle height, slim with black hair and blue eyes of a Celt, clean white teeth, and a complexion seen only among countrymen – brown with red cheeks like a pomegranate. He would stand drinks all round and start spoofing; first for Panatellas and then suddenly change it to a fiver, double or quits, a tenner and so on, winning all the time till the others dropped out.

Left alone he would always pick on me to talk to, and ask about the angel he wanted me to carve for his wife who had recently died. He told me extraordinary stories about her, which differed and seemed to be invented. I liked the idea of carving an angel which would be as difficult as the Nike of Samothrace if the wings were spread, and told him I would do it, especially now I was free from the Creation Cycle of Paintings, about which I had not told him. I said I would do it but that it would not be a conventional angel and he would have to go along with that if it was a successful sculpture. He agreed, but was reticent about money. I wanted the whole story to help me cut a whole angel.

If Julie was there, he was more reticent with me, but talked to her most of the time about animals of which – with her background – she knew a great deal. He was probably attracted to her like the others, but both having extra vitality it was interesting and not vulgar. He gave her a set of buttons, each with a fox's head on, and we never avoided seeing and talking to him if he came in. Only occasionally, when I was alone and he started talking about the angel for his dead wife, did I try to avoid him.

He did come to the cottage once or twice – I can't be sure, but not often. We never knew him enough to expect him. So one Christmas when there was a loud knock on the door and I was out the back in mild weather, drinking wine, I swore.

'Oh, who's that? You go Ju. It will be Annie with the pig's face she always gives me at Christmas. Last year I came in pissed and there it was looking up at me with its blue eye from the sink where it was soaking in salt water. Frightened me to death!'

'I expect you were looking in the mirror and didn't know!' said Julie, taking up the basket full of tea, sugar, wine, butter, eggs, she made up for Annie and her sister for Christmas.

'I'll go,' she said, 'but just keep your cake 'ole shut till she's gone, or I'll never get rid of her.'

'Yes get her off as quick as you can. I can't deal with it tonight!'

'Shhh. She'll hear you. Don't be so unkind!' With this Julie went to the door but was back in a moment looking pale. 'It's not Annie at all. It's that young Welshman we met in the pub, Gwydir. The one who asked you to carve an angel. He wants to borrow a gun. He says the fox is worrying his chicken.'

'Lend him one then!'

'I would rather you saw to him!' she said. But just then I saw Annie.

'Look, here comes Annie now, up the back path. Hallo, Annie!' I greeted and turning to Julie said: 'Don't be silly. Lend him the twelve-bore, the Belgian one in my study. It's just by the door. There's some buck shot if he wants.' Julie went off angry.

'Have a drink, Annie!' Annie crinkled up her old face: a smile in a paper bag.

'And there is a nice pig's face for 'ee Feyther. Git the young lady to make 'ee a brawn!' I looked down at the half-face with a blue jellied eye. It seemed to flick its ear.

'See, Annie, he smiled at me and winked his eye!'

'Gor'n, Feyther, 'ee be dead. 'Ee can't do that.'

'Where's your sister, Lily?'

'She got a cold and can't come this year, but sends 'er love. She says to tell you she had a dream an' you were dying. She was trying to help you but couldn't get you back because she wasn't strong 'nuff. I

THE RELUCTANT ANGEL

told 'er you was all right but she wants you to know, because it was a dream and that means somp'n!' I thought of the gypsy at the gate and wondered if they had been watching. All the strange machinery that stored power in the Forest was still active behind the trees. Julie came in looking serious. 'All right?' She nodded, and took her drink.

'We calls 'en Feyther because. . .'

'He is like your Father,' pre-empted Julie. 'You told me. Annie. A happy Christmas!' – and turning to me – 'I didn't like the look of him!'

'Who, Gwydir? What, did he try and get you?'

'No not that,' she said. 'Don't you ever think of anything but sex?'

'No!'

'Well try for once. HE LOOKED MAD that's all!' she said in a loud whisper.

Annie, quick as a magpie to pick things up, asked: "Who do 'ee mean?'

'That young horse dealer from Wales whose wife committed suicide!'

'Im? Never on your life! No sich thing.' retorted Annie. 'Ee never 'ad a wife!'

'Of course he had,' I said. 'He must have had a wife because he asked me to carve an angel for her grave!'

'Nonsense from the pair of 'ee.' said Annie with great emphasis, showing the crimson dye on her hair as she moved her old velour hat. 'Pigs ear! That's what 'ee be. You can't make nutt'n of 'en.'

I was astonished at this but I never argued with Annie about Forest matters, because she walked the town and the village every day collecting the swill on her cart with bicycle wheels, and collected also the debris of human destinies as she went. She knew what went on under the green halls of silence.

'Then whose photograph was it he showed me?' I asked.

'I don't know, but it wazn't 'is wife. That's fer sure. 'Ee 'aven't got no wife!' I sensed Annie knew more and tried to draw her out. 'Do you think he is a gypsy then?'

'Its no use arstin' me, Feyther. I shouldn't be frightened if 'ee 'ad some in 'en. There's plenty of it in the Forest – more'n you know. But 'ee's from Wales and I knows there's a net of dealers stretching from down there in West Country to 'ere, an' on up to Lunnon. Taz they that stealed your saddles – not the gypsies. The gypsies might do it all right but not to 'ee, Feyther, not to 'ee!'

'I only thought he might be a gypsy because he is so dark. There are gypsies in Wales. Whole families.'

'Jazus was gypsy then. 'Ee be dark!' put in Annie, impishly.

'Perhaps he is a Diddy?' added Julie.

'No. He's too clever and too quick.' I said. 'Diddies are like mules and the Spanish say of the mule "He has no pride of ancestry and no hope of posterity!" That's true but he is seen in high places and nobody knows. He is laughing because he has all the cunning of the gypsy and all the cruelty of the Gawjo. Gwydir is clever and when drunk, he falls into a Welsh accent, gambling excitedly as though narrowing his own violence to a single point of victory and always winning. A magnetic person! Is he good looking, Ju?'

'Not bad, with his black hair and blue eyes. Like my Dad that – another Celt, But too violent for me. It isn't that. There's something wrong with the man. He makes me feel uneasy.' Julie caught my glance. 'O yes, THAT as well. I would not like to be alone with him for too long. But otherwise I always felt sorry for him. I don't know why.'

'Arrrr! the cunnin', of the feller to make 'ee feel sorry for 'en!' growled Annie 'Like Wild Jack when 'ee broked up at my feet. I didn't feel sorry for 'en, the wicked 'ole bugger. I didn't care!'

'The first time I saw Gwydir,' I said to Julie, 'he took no notice of me, but talked to you all the time. I was furious.'

'You weren't at all. You were gettin orft with that terrible blonde with 'orn rimmed glasses. I don't know what you could see in 'er, silly cow!'

'But you're not a man!'

'No, and thank Christ for that. I told 'er to sling 'er bloody boomerang and when it comes back, I hoped it 'ud hit her in the fanny. Then she'd be no use to any man. I was just listening to Gwydir: that was all. He was in trouble. He wanted to talk about his children: how he played with them and went shopping for their school uniforms. How much money it cost. He promised to bring them here to see our animals in the Zoo before the Council closed us down. And then it was he gave me the fox buttons for my waistcoat.' Julie was both cross and excited.

'What about the wife 'ee talked on?' put in Annie.

'Well that's just it. She was 'orft with another man most of the time. Then he said she'd come back. And next time I saw him he had great gashes in his face which he said she did with her nails. You remember that.' She glanced at me and went on. 'He said the children were with his people, because she was off again. Tears were rolling down his face – and Matey here,' Julie pointed to me – 'he leaves me when this happens and goes after that bloody blonde and nearly gets into a fight.'

'And why not?' I said, getting nasty. 'They're all after you because I am so much older than you are, but they know I've still got a punch like the kick of a mule and I wasn't going to lose you to that randy sod, so I thought I'd play at your own game.'

'All right, Big Mush. Keep yer hair on!' said Julie trying to quieten me down because Annie was there. 'You'd better look out though.'

'Feyther'll show 'en, won't 'ee!'

'Too sure I will, Annie.' I answered feeling bombastic. 'Have another drink, my dear. Lets get plastered!'

'Niver on your life, Feyther. You know I don't do things like that. But I'll 'ave one with 'ee for Christmas.'

'So will I' said Julie. 'Now shut your gob and let me get on with my story.' She lit a cigarette while I filled her glass with wine. 'It was so bewildering: the sudden changes. He'd be talking away, really upset. Then one of his mates would call him for a matchstick spoof. He'd switch over just as though it was another person, force the stakes up and win. It was his power to win that nobody could understand – as though he read their brains. Buffy Mansbridge – 'ee looks just like a little Chinese magician – doesn't 'ee Mush, with his cunning smile and twinkling eyes: 'ee couldn't deal with a sudden attack from Gwydir. Like 'awk 'ee was! A drunk, a gambler, violent and crooked yet so nice when he showed photos of his kids and his woman. But they were strange photos: lonely, like people you see in the newspaper who have been murdered. Far away. Know what I mean?' Annie listened intently but said nothing.

I asked Julie:

'Do you think he murdered her?'

'Yes I do!' She replied quite vehemently. 'Others too. You remember that young girl Brixy found in a shallow grave when he was looking for his pigs?'

'Ar,' said Annie, 'They said that was Conches' maid!'

'The one up Wood Fiddley, you mean?'

'Yea! that's the one. What do you think, Big Mush?'

'I don't know. Anything can happen in the Forest. That probably wasn't him. But I wish you had stopped me lending him that gun earlier!'

'I tried to, didn't I? Well if you want to know, I didn't lend it to him. But you are so hurtful. You don't listen to anything I say and just brush me aside, so I kept my trap shut. I do have my opinion you know. You pig-headed old. . .'

'Never mind that now, Ju. I'm sorry if I hurt you. We can talk about it. But what did you say to him?'

'I didn't. When I got back he'd gone. He must have heard us arguing!'

'Now then you two,' said Annie. 'Not so much of it. I never 'ad a man and I niver 'ad a chiel but you makes up for it. Now why shouldn't the man 'ave a gun. You know how bad it is when the fox is raidin' the chicken. He 'ad your white peacock. I seed 'en go up the tree and along the long branch where it was roostin, down near the chalet where Feyther paints.'

I was so relieved about what Julie had told me that I let Annie go on. Was Gwydir that bad? He had come to me for a headstone for his wife, but not if he had murdered her, surely! Perhaps he had killed her lover? Then out loud, I said: 'He showed me one of those glossy photos. It was after a long absence: "She is dead! Will you carve an angel for her?" he said in a toneless voice. I said I would.'

'Did 'ee carve it, Feyther?' Annie asked eagerly.

'No I did not. It looks as though I must because I promised. He won't like it anyway and I bet he won't pay me. When I looked at the sweet far away young woman in the photo and said: "Is she dead? It can't be!" he was weeping and told me she had TB, but his eyes were guilty like a fox. I got angry and asked him if he had killed her. He was frightened and would not speak. "What about her lover?" I snapped, sensing I was on to something. I got in a corner of the bar where he could not move and the juke-box was blazing, the crowd talking, the smoke from the Panatellas cutting us off. I shouted at him trying to rat out the truth, but he was silent with terror. Suddenly he snatched his strong arms away from my grip and left.'

'The next time I saw him he had red streaks round his neck, as from a whip or perhaps a serious fight. "Rope, brother. Rope!" he said when I asked.'

"Trying to top yourself I suppose?" He would not answer. Then suddenly he was transformed again, in a second as you say, as though he was another person. He lit a Panatella, pulled out a £10 note, stood everyone in the bar a drink, tossed the landlord, George Jenkins, double or quits for the bill, won and left the pub all like a dream in lightning.'

'Are you going to carve the angel?' said Julie sipping a brandy, as if to know this would give us the final clue to the whole enigma.

'I intend to carve him an angel, and if we can get it inside the church, I will carve it in alabaster so that she shines with her own light. It will have to be done. I think an act of this kind would run deep and produce a good image, because, whatever is wrong with Gwydir, I am convinced he is in love with that young woman in the photo, whether she be alive or dead and that is something you can't pretend. If he killed her, I owe it to her more than to him, because Love has no wall of good or evil and Art has no morality. But whether I can get there and cut it out is another matter. If I can it will be waiting inside the stone. I don't really want to know what happened any more.'

'Niver 'iz wife!' said Annie.

Julie answered 'I expect you are right, Annie. But it seems certain she died. One evening he talked about tablets. On another he said she harnessed the pony and trap he'd bought at market for her and the kids, then drove it at an oncoming car. The inquest was put off for weeks.'

'I heard this too,' I said. 'He told me the same story. I said then to him it was no use carving an angel if his wife had committed suicide: she would not be allowed in consecrated ground. I doubt if permission would be given to put it up elsewhere. He seemed to know about this and said the villagers were trying to stop her being buried in the churchyard. Finally a verdict came – 'Death by misadventure' – so they had to let her in.'

'And the kids?'

'They went to the parents, I think!'

Then Julie said:

'I reckon he killed the lover, as you said. There is a very deep love hidden here: some early bonding of the heart even back in childhood.'

At this moment there was a further hammering on the brass dolphin knocker on the front door. 'That'll be him!' I said. 'I'd better go. I expect he is going to ask for the gun again.' And with this I left the kitchen and walked along the narrow hallway toward the form I could just see against the frosted glass panel of the front door. I was gone some time. Julie sat with Annie in the kitchen sipping their drinks trying to hear what was going on. The whippet flimmered by her side and rested his head in her lap. When I got back they asked eagerly what had been said.

'WAS it him?' asked Julie, seeing my face was pale.

'No. It was a policeman.'

'What did he want?'

THE RELUCTANT ANGEL

'He came to ask if I had lent a twelve-bore gun to Gwydir this afternoon.'

'Well?'

'He must have got one soon after. He shot himself through the mouth by the cemetery lych gate this afternoon.' Julie was white in the silence that followed, her blue eyes full of tears, the silence which was only broken by Annie's cracked voice coming out of her as pitiless truth.

'There now. What did I say. I knowed 'en. It was 'ee raped the 'ol dumman up Hatchets Pond, and I shoul'nt be frightened if 'ee took't the maid in the woods 'an buried 'er up. Darft as a stoat 'ee were. No good, Feyther. No good to we. 'Ee were what we calls a Mazed Man, and 'ee done the best thing by shootin 'isself!'

Julie looked at me.

'Yes. Annie was right!' I said. 'The copper told me he had no wife or children: only a record of rape, embezzlement, horse-stealing, drinking and gambling and, they think, murder on at least three counts but they could never pin it on him. He was so quick.'

'The devil certainly 'ad 'im by the tail,' said Annie, cackling, for she had known pain and grief too long to upset her serenity. 'Didn't 'um, Feyther? The tail, in front and the tail behind, if you ar'st me!' She moved towards the door. 'Good-bye now. 'Appy Christmas. And don't forget to soak the pig's face in salt water overnight. Bye!'

We stood watching the frail old woman make her way down the pathway with the basket of food and wine: 'Don't get tiddly, Annie!' I shouted after her.

I did not carve the angel for Gwydir after all: like the black fox there was nothing left. If ever I do, it will be for a man who dared to live too much. As my friend Grant Watson had written to me in a letter: 'We invoke the angels to help us, but the pull in the other direction is too strong for us.'

WING'D FIGURE SVEN '94

Lone Woman Moor

The Admiral walked the village street with the Hussar who had a sabre cut across his face: both raised their hats to the Indian Lady riding by on her Grevy's zebra. In the pub, Blondie hugged her china doll stuffed with pound notes, while the General rode her like a Palomino horse and the Idiot Boy squeezed his pet Aylesbury duck under his arm to make it fart. . .

My dream was broken by the huntsman's horn and hounds giving voice. For once Julie was awake before me because she always got very excited when she heard hounds and the whole countryside woke to their sounds.

'Come on, Big Mush, let's drive 'orft to have a look at the sea before we get caught up with hounds!'

I was usually painting by this time, but the Creation Cycle was finished and I had not got going on stone. There was still some work to do, and the *Pietá* to finish; there were other smaller sculptures that were going on. The book at the time was still *The Cry of Merlin*, so I was about Forest life; Julie's suggestion fitted exactly. The energy of art seems to come from a deep place, separate from that used for other activities: especially with painting and sculpture. Painting draws one's life-force out through the eyes, but sculpture takes the spirit as well and one's physical connection, which is probably sexual, just as dancing demands the extra anguish of the body. But when I say spirit it is difficult, because I am only saying what it is not. But if I say sculpture removes a layer of spirit that can never be replaced, I get near to explaining what I mean. To be with Julie, giving out her terrific vitality, could not have been equalled. We snatched a cup of tea with a sandwich and were off.

I drove across Lone Woman Moor as I called it, from seeing a gypsy gathering snowdrops at dawn, on towards the sea. It was also where we took Julie's greyhound – she called him 'Gentleman' – to run over long stretches where the heather was short, at great speed: but it became dangerous because we realised that, being retired from the track, he sometimes mistook a distant car for a moving hare and coursed after it.

The landscape spread its brown wings under a sharp ice-blue sky with high cirrus clouds, reflected in the decoy duck ponds as Julie called them, formed by flood rain, in the scrub and gorse where wild ponies stood silent, as if outside consciousness, or grazed the spiked branches and chrome yellow pods that smelt of wild pineapple in summer. A hawk hovered over a terrified shrew. A heron, with his listening feathers, fished a stream for wild trout. And under the tumuli, ancient kings, like the one the Ice Queen owned, murmured in their sleep. Far south on the fringe, a ridge of pines hid the sea beyond. The little steam train cut the landscape and reappeared like a running dinosaur. Here and there we passed through small farmsteads and then into open country towards the oil refinery, so near that the tall chimneys with their waste flares were like eagles of fire hovering over the pattern of red, blue and yellow lights that formed the haunting automatic emptiness of that strange city where I carved the White Buck, sacred image of the Forest, a decade earlier. We could smell the oil, black blood of our Jaguar car driven by a Neanderthal hand. To the south and west remained part of the big feudal estates, but soon the moor broke up into fields, the fields into salt marshes fringing the Solent, where short oaks embroidered the hem of England with a strong stout stitch, giving way to water and the luminous hills of the Island. How beautiful the shore can be, unseen these days because so much pursued and looked for.

Pheasants were everywhere, grazing with tails down, running as if drawn on a wire with tails up. Pheasants fighting, attacking the groin of their opponent with the dew-claw and pecking fiercely at the olive green patch on top of the head, trying to penetrate the brain under the red oriental warrior's mask-bronze, green, gold and blue feathers flying. Even a single silvery white bird and one melanistic, ran like the spirits of good and evil among them. A covey of red-legged partridges whirred up from the road where they were gritting, as our car approached.

Along the lanes as we got near the shore, twisted oak and thorn grown away from the prevailing wind, led to the mudflats where the moorhens and seabirds nested. A pair of swans on a salt pool near, floated round each other in a spiral of love: not to be put asunder.

'They have the secret,' I said. 'They mate for life!'

'And don't you forget it,' replied Julie as we came out on the shore road to the tiny front of Lepe where there was nothing but a row of fishermen's cottages and a converted lifeboat house, near the mouth of a Forest river entering the sea, flashing over the rocks, salt and fresh water merging in a love affair never to be resolved. This was a place where salmon entered England: a place also, whence a French Dauphin escaped.

The tide was out, as on the day a man's two wives had been drowned and it seemed for a moment that the ghosts of Angie and Deirdre and, later to join them – Nyree – were floating on the mist. A few bait diggers laboured in cinnamon, black, orange and weed green oilskins, gathering ragworms which they put in red, yellow and white plastic buckets, in a ritual as ancient as the rock and sand where they dug, dreaming of the tug of fish. They are eternal images. I had painted them as had Turner, their sinister and silent occupation the same then with the same stance as they had now. On the marker posts at the mouth of the Beaulieu river, cormorants, like images in bronze cooling from the furnace, spread wings to dry. Shelduck, oystercatchers, curlew, turnstone, all made a moving decalcomania on the glass fringe of the sea, with horned eggcase of skate, chalky cuttlefish, rubbery weed, pellucid shell: minute crabs, like tiny green sculptures in jade, with equally small flat fish, in the wrist of golden sand bangled by a shaft of diamond. There was still some mist, but slowly the Solent, slippery as a huge mucous ray, slapped our feet with its wet fins.

'Listen!' said Julie, holding up her hand. 'The sea bell is tolling in the distance.' Her face was clear, her head on one side, body flamingo, in white suit with red boots. A marvellous moment which, like a coin falling under water, lasted till it reached the bottom of the mind, settling as part of that love, like an anchor bedding itself under a rock, is held by chains from which two people cannot get away, even though they are excoriated by the surge of reality beyond endurance.

'The sort of place,' I said, 'where you might find Ulysses, shield stuck in the sand like a boilerplate from a shipwreck. 'And his helmet!' added Julie. 'Think what a size that would be. He was a man if ever woman dreamed one up: tied to the mast with all them sirens trying to get in. That must 'ave sent 'im mad. Crumpet on the rocks and 'yer hands tied. And the only arms in the world that were strong enough to pull back that bow, remember. A chest as deep as the ocean and a face like Seaton cliff, after all them voyages. Eagle eyed. COR! What a bloke to meet.' I was feeling diminished and jealous by her eloquence. Under my influence Julie had read the Odyssey – we read it together, not as a classic, but as a wonderful adventure, which it is. It was, and is, precisely this and to other great writers like D. H. Lawrence, Lawrence Durrell, Hugh Walpole, Chuang Tzu and Hardy that she gave a unique interpretation when lit by her unpolluted country mind and a new magic to my own vision of life.'Yes, darling,' I interrupted. 'But look at that school of porpoise. They usually go south to the Island. Perhaps the salmon have come this way.' But Julie was looking down the coast to try and see her own cliffs near her home at Seaton – it was still too misty. 'Real fisherfolk down there, Mush in the West Country which 'oi come from. I AM IT. None of yer make believe AWrrr an ARRR-ig, like on telly. See, the mist is clearing. Sheltered under the cliff, protected by an arm of rock are people of the sea. My people they are.'

This outburst of simple unaffected pride in her origin was the very thing that made Julie what she was and she did not want to be anybody or anything else. An utterance that somehow made me feel homeless, having been born of two countries and reared in a great city with the brown river running through at that time too polluted to receive the salmon: the mudflats my beaches; its life a seething mass of humanity searching for food, reduced at times to hunting the alley cat and doing the dustbins. A time of great poverty was know by the Londoners and only the rich got through without harm or hunger.

In the country and with the fisherfolk – for the harvest was gleaned also from the sea – there was always enough even if it had sometimes to be stolen. One virtue of the feudals was their concern to see the serf was fed well enough to serve them, and at its best, the system worked well as one great happy family. But underneath the rule of the Big Houses, there was a secret Maquis of survival who handled the creatures and the harvest of land and sea. Although the penalties were severe, from cutting off the right hand, transportation to Australia or hanging, the natural sources were there and could be got one way or another: in the city they were not there, nor the natural surroundings. It was this simple truth that made Julie's utterance so meaningful. She still had roots: I had not. My father was from Sweden, my mother from Yorkshire and even the place where I was born in London was bombed out of existence. I had broken with all tradition and become a wandering artist and had come to look on the earth which I loved, as my home. I am a man on earth, as the gypsy I saw on Lone Woman Moor, gathering snowdrops: I belonged nowhere. The amazing thing is that my quest for beauty and to solve the mystery of life should be accepted into the harsh realism out of which Julie emerged as an eager intelligence with attractive and spontaneous humour. Could it have been that her ancestor, finding the first ichthyosaurus in the grey sarcophagus of blue lias at Lyme Regis had made her aware of an extended life, as the Tomb of Tutankhamun had done for me? What it is that makes two people of different origin come together through an identical search for enlightenment is not known.*

As I watched her sitting on the breakwater with her hair blown back I realised how much all this came together. Here were no compartments really, poetry and reality were one, as were truth and myth. How much she was from the sea and the legends of Aphrodite and Circe and Calypso became true because they are memories of what has happened set in the same hard realism of 3000 years ago. She told me of her tall ancestors, who were her uncles and aunts watching the sea for the shoals of fish to come in the bay and the miraculous draught of fishes – 30,000 herring in a single catch – when the whole town turned out to haul in the seine nets from the sea. The beach was silver with herring – the legend had become truth. Never again the excitement of such a miracle, now that the great trawlers worked the channel and the herring have changed their ground. The fish no longer came to their shore in the early days of winter, as in Cornwall. Visitors became their new summer industry – grockles as the Devons call them, when they take them out for fishing trips at £30 or £40 a day and no longer have to think back to the days when eating fish for every meal was an act of survival to the point of nausea.

In the winter they still paint and repair their boats; make a seine net for the river-mouth when the salmon return. A trawl for the nightfishing. It remains their life. And Freddie Newton on the front at Beer keeps his fish shop going. But the big thing is visitors, and fishing with Duggie Orley and others. They come in shoals and spend their money. Out of season the fishermen have plenty of time. They walk round Woolworths, have their hair cut and maybe deliver a new life-boat to France. Get drunk and talk of the past which, like a great white Cenotaph, stands silent on the cliff where their ancestors stood watching the sea and return to their graves at night.

'My Granfer Anning was a fisherman,' said Julie.

---

* What Julie learned from me was not part of a Pygmalion job: it was a delightful pinnacle of bringing to flower a plant that had already germinated in the deep earth of her people and was eager to grow into the unique person she has become.

LONE WOMAN MOOR

'Yes. You said. Was that the one who was a builder and got done?' 'Yea! He built half Seaton!'

'Would you like to go back?'

'Not now. I might one day. But it's so narrow down there and they drive each other hard – even to suicide. It's not easy to live there even if you are one of them. I love them. I love Devon. But once you 'bin away you realise there are other things. And they are always pinching each other's women. Running away. . . No. Not for me. Not yet: anyway I would be a stranger.' Her eyes were blue like the tolling of the seabell and her voice gentle, in some way strange. I could not enter. 'It all makes me wonder why you chose me!' I said. 'Grizzled, selfish, obsessed with work, isolated, rootless – not much more than a vagabond underneath, really. . .'

She put her hand on my sleeve.

'Dear soul! I chose you because you were lost when I found you. I don't think you would have lasted long. It didn't look like it to me. When you came to me I knew I could save you from whatever had hold of you and was destroying you. And now, as somebody said to somebody else, you are my husband, father and my brother, friend and guide; king and slave, teacher and priest, my university. What else could I ask for? With you I have the royal right of incest, the freedom of real love, joy of absolute trust which makes me your Queen: therefore the other half of your soul. Is that not enough? Do you remember what you read to me from the *I Ching* in the early days of our meeting? I have learned it by heart. In the same way I have learned how you look when you are angry; how lost you looked when I first saw you; how life returned as we came together and like those swans we mated for life. Simple things that bring simple answers to great problems need only a touch of truth to be solved.'

'What did the *I Ching* say?' I asked. 'Do you remember?'

> When they come together their sadness
> Shall change into joy.
> When two people are one in their inmost hearts
> They shall shatter even the strength
> Of iron and of bronze.
> When two people understand each other
> In their inmost hearts their words are sweet
> And strong like the fragrance of orchids.

LONE WOMAN MOOR

Her voice trailed away at the last fragrance with a slight burr and the whole beautifully spoken. Utterance without ego is from the spirit: in this case, innocence.

'Yes. I know. But I am not your young Conquistador, dear Julie, but a hardened old sod, with the experience of war, marriage and divorce, free living: everything that a young man has not. You make me feel soiled and terrible.'

'Young men make me want to spit!' she exclaimed, looking angry. 'I don't WANT a young man. I want YOU. So don't be so bloody stubborn. To look into your mind is enough.' She took my hands. 'Like a great sea, there is storm and sunset. You are obstinate, cruel, wise, kind, difficult and the toughest old bugger I've ever met. But you're TACHO – truthful, Mush – and that's everything.'

'And drunk!'

'Oh, THAT! If you think so. I don't. I come from folk who have always been hard drinkers, because they love life and work hard – so do you. Drink never hurts a man who works as hard as you do. You don't drink much. I don't care if you do. I can't turn back now. My people used to say you can't have the miraculous draught of fishes twice. And you are my miraculous draught of fishes, so that's that!'

It was my birthday. I felt happy for once on that day and now more so, by what she had said, and strangely unworthy of her words because, when I looked at her and listened in the enclosure of that moment it was difficult to believe that what I heard and saw was real. I let her go on.

'You are right: I am with you: the image you have been searching for years. That is why everything is working when everybody said it would not. Drinking, like you told me about Li Po – he also died drunk – is the key to your inner life as much as prayer. He fell in the Yangtse trying to embrace the image of the moon. Sitting here by the estuary together there is no difference – we are the river running back into the sea.'

'What a beautiful thing to say to me, Ju. I reckon you know more about it than I ever will. I was trying to work it all out in a poem yesterday. I know you say you don't like poetry but shall I see if I can remember it?' Standing together I told her the poem I had written. It went like this.

> Save for the estuary of death
> I have no watershed that bars

LONE WOMAN MOOR

My way, stills my heaving breath:
I have no country but the stars.

I have no field that grows my seed,
No quarry where the heart is stone,
No rivers where the salmon breed:
I walk the universe alone.

No law that holds the countryman
Strikes sunsets through my spinning brain,
No groundswell tears my sinewy land
Like flesh and stitches it again,
Making the heart swell and break
On beaches where a child ran wild:
No tree bows down to give and take
Its leaves until the soul's beguiled.

I am a man on earth, belong nowhere,
The centuries control my breath:
No minaret shall call my prayer –
None but the estuary of death.

I spoke the poem quietly and when it was over, the ends of time had come together and we stood beside each other in a timeless moment by the sea.
'A Complete Man!' said Julie, holding me. 'And I'm your Queen!' 'Let's go!' I shouted and we drove across Lone Woman Moor at nearly a hundred miles an hour in our great car. Julie was so excited she was singing at the top of her voice,

> Bring me my Bow of burning gold!
> Bring me my Arrows of desire!
> Bring me my Spear! O clouds unfold!
> Bring me my Chariot of fire!'

'Poetry!' I shouted. 'Wonderful, wonderful poetry! That's the real thing, my darling. It makes me stand on end! And I thought you didn't know anything about it? You are the best poem I have ever written.'

Kaleidoscope

Once I had finished the Creation Cycle of Paintings, it was uncanny how quickly the deeper patterns started to move, like a spring thaw on the lakes of Sweden when the trees, cut down during the winter and piled on the frozen lake, slowly start to float and plunge from the head of the river, downstream, while the snow is still on the early leaf. It is right that this collection of large paintings should have the same effect, for at such times the whole of life is involved: not only surface leaf and thorn but down to the deep rhizomes.

In painting a dream I had awakened a dream going back to childhood where the seeds were first sown – even to my mother and father who seemed to have transmigrated to the two great oaks in the field opposite my cottage with their heads among the stars and the universe beyond, through which I had travelled on the long train of racial memory to the beginning: forming, for me, the dome of glass which is my life: a place where inner and outer events had become one as in art. No distinction between body and soul, subjective and objective and all opposites that at present have only the vehicle of enantiodromia to make their change, one to the other, are seen as on a revolving stage to be the same – only at different points of duration.

All the meditations of this kind awakened by the two great oaks who were my mother and father, were made with the consciousness that they might soon be under the concrete of a council estate as the Forest loses its history, its territory and its ghost, which I had known for many years since I lived in its most secret depths with my dark friends who are now gone. It is to be believed there is even a cosmic protection going back to the sabre-toothed tiger, that will extinguish any who betrays its law with a false kiss.

Painting the Creation was the experience of many aeons of Time. The first green leaf caught in a fang of ice, as though a transparent spider had transfixed a new life, was no less a shock to Julie than when she realised I had to sell our home to pay our debts: as though a hedge-plucker was tearing it out of our hands, revealing an abyss.

During a long year of painting my imagined Genesis and behind that, cutting out the *Madonna* and the *Pietá*, my attention had become diverted from business matters, because I am no businessman. It is an occupation with its own priesthood, its own ethic and its own purpose, to make money, and since my Jewish friend in childhood had forever shaken my belief in its value, by making my first pound note vanish into thin air in a practice conjuring session, I had failed to meet its requirements.

The only sales at that time were from an occasional visitor or friend and from the activities of Liz Trehane who still promulgated my work in London, and through the Chelsea Arts Club kept me in touch with the art world. I had a show under her wing in the Strand at which the guest of honour was the boxer Henry Cooper with whom shaking hand was like gripping a bronze replica of himself. But I counted on his London humour and when I was introduced to him and his sweet little Italian wife, I said 'Honoured to meet you, Mush!' This surprised him and got a smile sharp enough to cut across the facade of being so famous. I meant it, too. It came out naturally. But the atmosphere was different from the gallery world of London and the provinces that I was used to. Except for meeting my old friend, the painter Bill Redgrave, who now seems to be overlooked and forgotten by the world. Afterwards Liz and Richard paid for a taxi across London to the Chelsea Arts Club where we met Alan Lowndes, the painter, and drank an enormous amount of brandy. We slept in the Augustus John Room with Julie keeping a naked watch on the late arrivals through the window, after kissing the waiter goodnight, and we got away in the early morning in a taxi across St. James' Park to Waterloo, after having breakfast with Alan, who was so fragile that he feared to tap the shell of his boiled egg with the spoon in case his head should crack open. A gifted man who died tragically early.

That is how it was. Julie was disorientated in London and completely bewildered by the whole operation, from which we thankfully made £600.

One work in the exhibition stays with me, by a Fijian I think, of a Broken Man, cast in bronze with an excess of copper, so that the dioptase had taken charge and he looked just as I had seen men, green and indifferent in death on the battlefield – chests excavated, faces half blown away: a reminder that in battle there was a negative horrifying beauty, but in peace all loveliness quivers under the threat of being smothered at any moment by the invisible hand of an offended Polyphemus.

During the winter the pressures increased, hardened by pulmonary troubles to which I was more subject in the Forest because of the trees and my use of chemicals in bronze castings which affected my lungs. In some ways it reminded me of the 1938 experience on the North Cliffs of Cornwall, though without the rigours of five days with no food. But likewise it was snowing and likewise it was Christmas again. Now there was food – but with debts so appalling each meal was like eating nuggets of gold and each drink like robbing a bank. Better the yawning drunkenness of starvation with the Woman with One Blind Eye who always says NO! with its mystical overtones of ecstasy. We were in bed as on the previous occasion, but no one knew the situation. In great danger, stay silent! Like Kusakov in Tolstoy's *War and Peace* I became recessive and waited to see if I had dealt a mortal blow to the enemy. The phone rang. It was Philip Ziegler from the publishers, Collins, asking if I would write a book on the gypsies. Liz Trehane had met him at a banquet in London and had told him about a manuscript of mine, which was a novel concerning gypsies set against the background of the Cerne Abbas Giant in Dorset, the great prehistoric image carved on the side of a hill where the local maidens sleep among his genitals to make them fertile. As I had said to her in a letter: 'It's the novel Hardy left out because he could not deal with the Giant!' Ziegler enjoyed it but wrote: 'How CAN I publish it? Ask Sven if he will do one on the gypsies?' Even in the sixties it would have been attacked as pornographic to use the image. Although it was owned by the Ministry of Works, it remained a silent symbol of our greatest and most important urge. I believe there is a move now to clean it up and research into its meaning, which will most likely mean castration or Y-Fronts in chalk. I still hope to publish *Under The Giant's Thigh* with his full image on the dust jacket, as a statement of universal truth.

The outcome of this was that Ziegler came down to see me and gave me a contract to write a book, as I insisted, on my *experience* of the gypsies, not another chronology with dates and places which are death to literature. He was a tall cultured man, an ex-diplomat, with a quick and shrewd mind, whom I got on with immediately. A respected historian and biographer which is quite a different matter from the modern documentary. The book was commissioned as *The Tents of Kedah* and finally became *Dromengro*, for which I got an advance generous enough to see us through till the Spring if we were careful. My bank manager, Mr Hayles, who knew my ways and trusted my integrity, would have found a way somehow, but he had retired and the new man, like a new Hoover, emptied me out with the old dust bags. Situations always depend on personality in the end. The shadow had taken over. The green hunger of the Forest was about to devour us. The advance from Philip Ziegler saved strangulation – but he did not know.

I had got out of bed to meet Philip Ziegler – he didn't know that either – and as soon as my mind was strong enough to grip the whole task of writing a book on the gypsies, I started making notes. Having been ill, the psyche was open for excavation and the impetus released all my experience and all that I had read and forgotten about that wandering tribe. It was already a decade since I lived with them and I was ready emotionally to write about them, and screen off the seemingly unreal aspects of art I had been involved with earlier. This was real. To carve the *White Buck* was real; cast the *Rain God*; cut out of the *Madonna*; finally, paint the *Creation*. All art of inner and outer reality which contains the whole truth.

Ten days later I started writing my book, following my personal method of handwriting the whole text first to a framework of notes, pursuing it with a second writing on the typewriter, so that every spurt of fire is digested into the main body of the text and every meaning made clear, every experience followed to its conclusion. I am wary of electronic writing as a threat to the imagination and spirit of the writer, which two things are the essence of literature. I would use them as I would use a JCB to lift great girders of prose from one point to another in stitching two manuscripts together and avoid overlapping, but shudder at being slave to their logic otherwise.

Writing about the gypsies demands freedom and spontaneity anyway; anything that gets in the way of the Duende is out. They themselves, at the time I knew them – except for Cliff Lee – could not read or write. I often wrote letters for them: or letter headings, such as:

>BENNY WELLS. TREE SPECIALIST.
>SHAVE GREEN WOODS.

I now get letters from their children written in fluent English: 40 years later.

They had all the powerful human emotions intact, yet were gentle, like children – even innocent at times: one reason that painters and musicians have always been drawn to them. I felt I had their whole psyche in my trust in writing about them, to preserve the truth of their nation. It was a special mission given me by the Gods and I did it well.

When Philip Ziegler had first asked for a history I told him about George Borrow, Walter Starkie, John Samson with his great English-Romany Dictionary which Augustus John found 'good bedside reading'; Dora Yates, Brian Vesey-Fitzgerald, Watts-Dunton, Croft-Cooke, Jean-Paul Clerbert, Dominic Reeve, Juliette de Baraclai Levy; he was content to leave me to write my experience of living with the gypsies in England and France in my own way.

It was as though the book was waiting to be unwound. How good of the scholars to have toiled away at the history and language of these wandering people, leaving me free to write about those who lived and died within the orbit of my own life. One by one they came back and spoke to me again like visiting spirits. Jesse who died under a tree after killing a great stag. Benny Wells with his whistling jacket. Sadie with her fierce attraction, so like Bloody Mary but not as violent. Luna, asleep in her open coffin on the Romsey Road, while the wailing women decorated her with roses.

As if to make a codicil, I added the tale of Takajo, the Japanese traveller I had invented, as I wove the story. He had walked into the sea when he was drunk and could not get out again; just where Nyree, Deirdre and Angie had died. Did another soul go unredeemed or did he turn into an osprey?

Out of the trees these golden people came to meet me, not with the stink of old clothes but smelling of wood smoke and evening, history and the perfume of hedgehogs and horses, just as they had done twenty years before when I entered the Forest with Ishtar and Jasper. The Forest with its animals and birds and wild men moved in a strange under-ocean light with the spirits of those who had been lost or murdered, devoured by the green trees and the hungry sea: suddenly they screamed on the wind!

There was Luvvie Cooper bent against the blizzard; and the Romanichals lighting a fire at the bus stop on the top road, opposite the Compton Arms, while they waited in the driving snow for Syd Saunders to march the children back from school to the huts weeping with cold. Microcephalic Jacko smoking his huge pipe and Dosha with her beautiful eyes. This was their personal story which no one but I would know, the clam that held their lives together – placed in my care, until they could write and speak for themselves.

I had not the dark anger of George Borrow carried like a cloak of madness on his broad shoulders. I met no Belle Berners to challenge my manhood. I wish I had. But to stop Parno Smith killing his wife with a hatchet, and burn down his tent, was something to be remembered. To see him watching an ichneumon fly in the evening light was something of equal importance. It was part of a trust in escrow put upon me to speak a pattern of life that had not been said and it is fitting that I should be asked to do it during my last days in the Forest.

I try for a thousand words a day to increase with stamina and viscosity of the life force, always governed by the quality of the writing. Sometimes it will write itself and then is always good: sometimes it is an immense struggle and comes out with a limp. But the thing of most value is to give continuity and growth to the deep underground work – like head-driving a tunnel by hand, or planting a tree and spreading the roots well. But a book is different from a sculpture, which you leave as an objective fact in the workshop. A book is like a nymphomaniac woman who is with you day and night drinking, eating, loving, dying – seeking an orgasm that never comes, yet you can't get away. Even in dream she has you by the queue. Alice and Julie steadily got the cottage ready for sale, making it look clean and well founded without too much show. Whatever you do the new tenant will alter it anyway. This saved me breaking the back of my story which would go slack like a thread if I left it.

But there was also the search for another place to live and the curious viewings by the curious, who walked about my house as though it was already theirs, and offered to buy it for a song. There was the strange entanglement with agents, who at once cast a net of fear and insecurity over my life; endless columns of advertisements to go through; journeys to places that are unsuitable and to other places you never find; searching all the time for the place that is right, that has a friendly ghost who says: 'Yes come here. You will love it if you do. It will be all right!' Then you are a fool if you don't.

Friends appear from abroad.

'But why live here, in this dump, my dear. You must be mad. Why not come to Majorca or Teneriffe, Corfu, Crete, La Somière where wine is so cheap. . .' – as if the idea was to spend the rest of life drinking oneself to death in the sun as a preconditioned alcoholic, screaming for grey skies, a month of rain and the sweet parsimony of an English winter.

Then the friendly solicitors, solicitous of your solutions being right, giving bridging loans, saving one's sanity by making the whole diabolical game look like a pleasant set of tennis between a society of gorillas – mending the fence over the abyss with a smile when the deeds are lost.

I learned to move through them each day, resisting phone calls with a surprise offer or an insistent request for a viewing even when business had been closed at least for the day. There were hours of bargaining with some sex-blocked idiot who wanted to take the property off my hands as a favour. The most vile of all being the late call announcing a severe cut in the agreed price at point of contract – GAZUMPING. The shoal of piranhas nibbling at the carcass of my home did not leave more than a skeleton of the valuation price, even though several skilled surveyors had poked the wainscott, scraped the paint, tested the damp course and roof, measured the field and made notes like oriental signs to say she was well founded.

But I still had to write my book, much of which I did at night. A book about the gypsies who were saints in comparison – my only comfort being that I could never become the same as those who surrounded my Lion-Sweet home like necrophonic flies.

In the end we sold the place to a genial couple who were horse-manic and paid an honest price, enough to ameliorate our troubles.

But the next day, when I went to sign the contract for a cottage we had viewed at Lepe and got the agent to hold for us until we had sold Home Farm, he told us that he had let it go to someone else the evening before. We had nowhere to go. Particularly sad because it was near the White Buck I had carved by the great waterways looking out to the Island, quite near also to where the spellbound sisters had been drowned.

The kaleidoscope of patterns had moved in a mysterious way. I was dreaming of men from the moon parachuting into the Solent again, and of lovers floating among the trees of the Forest like lost souls, and painting them – dreams that interpenetrated the floating world of everyday life for the coming weeks.

On the way back from Lepe we stopped at Lymington market to look through the stalls for an strange image or scarf of bright colour we might find, when I came upon a gypsy figure standing upright against a stone wall selling snowdrops. I had known her years earlier when she was fine and beautiful and had made some good drawings of her: now she was worn by a hard life. She and her man, Atty Smith, once took my greyhound. I talked a moment and then went on after buying flowers.

SONG FOR ROSIE

Rosie selling snowdrops
In the cold on market day
You stand against the grey stone wall
And stop one on the way –
   But none know you at all.

Remember Flaming Liza,
And her man was called Black Fred
And we wrecked the Village Drinking Hall
With those who are long dead –
   But they know you not all all.

Goliath and Nelson and Mighty Jim,
Son of Benny Wells, and me,
And the dear Deerman Jesse
Who died beneath a tree,
   Are the ghosts now watching thee.

The Bechstein Bat, Dosha and Pris,
Parno and Kaulo and Liberty Boy,
Born on a mound of Forest loam –
Trout in the stream and a duck decoy
   And a shooshi to take home.

The long dog by a bit a yog
Burning Forest ash,
Beer for the Mush and kushti mash
With carrot and rat and dog –
   But none had any cash.

O, Rosie selling snowdrops
Grown old on Market Day,
Smile against the grey stone wall

And stop one on the way.
Here's silver for the moonlight,
A sovereign for the sun!
All lie dead in Minstead Yard
And those that know thee now are none.

This was the last real link I had with the gypsies: a bunch of snowdrops picked on Lone Woman Moor.

*"Sophia" cast by the Artist, shown in TV programme on
New Forest 1958. Bronze 14"*

"Stag Beetle", bronze 1960 cast by the Artist.

Luvvie Cooper. Pencil drawing 1954.

IX. Arrival of Goliath. Beats up ~~Absolom~~ Lorenzo. Camilla comes to me.

X. Camilla calls sunny morning in Snow. Quarry walk to Carn. Snowed up. Commandos, police. Absolom + Shawn's Lilith waiting. She stays

XI. Give up children. Take Bhonska's Cot. Haemorrhage. Priest. Life + death. (~~Death of Lilith~~) Cut Iris DR

XII. Destruction of a Society

XIII. Build a new one. Quoit — Tigers Rage

XIV. Battle of the Tower CHRISTOF
Death by fire — Death of Lilith. PT II ENDS
Death of Lorenzo

XV. ~~Arrival~~ Dance of Defiance.
Poets Patella Death of Giantess
End of a season. Camp. Defiance. Death of child.

XVI. The hills to Giant's Madonna. Dark Monarch.

XVII. Journey to the Forest.

XVIII. Snow. The Critter.

XIX. Gypsies

XX. The Dark Monarch PT III ENDS

Chapter Synopsis in Author's Handwriting for "Dark Monarch" – Verso

Merry Tree

Good heavens, how it rained! My courtyard at the back of the cottage was a prison of water. Images stood still behind steel bars as if existence had been suspended, hiding from my eyes the clicking of my troubled brain. Forms emerged and stood in their own right, as before man saw them – dissolving into the rain. The blue of the aviary contained a block of space that had been flight cage for velvet monk sparrows with hazel-nut brown, black and white flashes; grey cardinals with bright scarlet heads – one with a leg missing, chopped off in anger by a toucan hiding from a murdering macaw. Gandayas who called down innocence and loved one another. Amhurst, Golden and Reeves' pheasants – all fragmented in the mind by Time's collisions and gone in a cloud of feathers like a painting by Kandinsky. Ghostly forms of flat rats left by a poisoner's hand. And a Mother and Child sculpture carved some years before in granite, dreamed in the rain, discoloured by algae and bird droppings, a male fern uncoiling between the breasts as the end thread of art's existence joined with our own psyche's kaleidoscope. A bantam hen outside the wire pecked the podgy ground – her glorious peacock lover gone also.

The chalet where I had painted the Creation was galvanized at the bottom of the paddock under some twisted ash trees that had the same *otherness* captured by Hokusai in rain. The Barbary ram and Caliban the swine were but ghosts that had been uncreated. No lion's bass timpani thundered here. None answered the ass's archetypal bray to disturb the retired gunner who had built his house on the hill I called Ararat, to save him being drowned in whisky; while I, as Noah, had put away my animals waiting for a sign. Like him I drank wine.

The fortuitous meeting of a Grevy's zebra with a mechanical muck-spreader would never again happen on Paradise Way. No more would lovers copulate under the Merry Tree or

> Stroll among the trees and stray
> Down Goosegog Lane on Donkey Down.

Such things had gone on since we came to be at Home Farm, mostly to do with animals, because when they are about the whole human soul is exposed and anything might, and, indeed, did happen.

The macaw that murdered the toucan and dive-bombed the Duke on his way to the pub for an early gin had been shot in mistake for a jay – or so they said – because jays were vermin. The armadillo, given to me by a unique person called Snakey Williams, dug up the floor of the colonel's potting shed, but after he was rescued seemed to live a good life and was an endless fascination to me when he rolled up in a ball – one more beautiful object I failed to draw, and only thought of making a bronze of after I had given him to Gerald Durrell for his zoo on Jersey. I flew him off on the aeroplane to his new life. The Barbary ram, given me by Desmond Morris, went to a zoo in the Isle of Wight. Sadly the llama who spat at the millionaire got pneumonia and died in the orchard where we buried him.

I remember all this as part of the *Ukiyoyi: Floating World*, as the Japanese colour print artists succinctly named it. And it seemed to be more so, as the small city I had built, fell into ruins. There was a corresponding weakening of the inner partitions enough to allow projection and illusion to increase, which I think had been going on much longer than I realised, so I entered into what modern psychologists and Americans call a 'fantasy area' – in truth another aspect of reality, seen from a new angle or without a certain curtain of invisibility: the creative imagination when transmuted by the artist, and made immortal.

The old countrywoman whom I called Auntie Rotter was an aunt of Julie's who stayed with Alice and Harry for a time and was often in my mind as an example of this state which increases with age. She was dying of a crumbling spine: broken and unable to walk well she clung to a bunch of violets and sang to herself the fragment of a song:

> Every morning I bring thee violets,
> Every evening I bring thee roses. . .

I wondered what lost love had awakened this in her heart. She said to me one day when I had taken her for a drive with Julie just after we were married:

'I had fifty years of married life and I wish you both all the joy in the world!'

Afterwards I remarked to Julie: 'Dear old thing. I wonder if she knows that if we do have fifty years of married life I shall be 102?' As I write this there are only eighteen years to go!

Yet how difficult to die, alone with herself. She made me think of

Annie Bright, who was the same age but a much harder woman, still allowing life to glance off her. I realised I was not only seeing the end of a decade in my own life, but the death of a whole centuries' old way of life among country people who belonged to the earth, the trees and the sea.

Years later, when relations were clearing up the bungalow in which Julie's parents had lived, they found, in the bottom of a wardrobe, an urn containing Auntie Rotter's ashes, and did not know what to do with them. One suggested putting them in the dustbin, but Julie said no, take them to the priest and ask his advice. Later under his own initiative her brother David took them and cast them in the ocean, which was intuitively right, as Julie said when she heard: 'Good – we came from centuries of fisherfolk, it is right she should go back to Mother Ocean!'

As I sat there drinking wine in the rain, sitting under a table umbrella, the earth began to give up a gentle smell because it was so mild and I remembered Da Vinci's observation that faces of people soften in the rain and looked more beautiful. Perhaps it was a virtue of Roman women in Roman rain, which I noticed in Julie's face as she came out to ask me something and watch the snails gallop up the stone wall in a silent cavalry charge.

'What about Annie Bright, Mush?'

'What about her?'

'She hasn't been yet and it's Saturday.'

'I expect it's the rain. She'll be here soon.'

Annie still came with the bits culled from the town bins and, of course, the pig's face at Christmas, or on special occasions, and Julie gave her a basket of goods. It was a happy way to celebrate life and we enjoyed her coming, but sometimes were anxious to be doing something else. She still wore the cuckoo brooch on her old coat, getting the perfect birdnote every time as she sang the song of the Merry Tree that had graced the corner of the field like a fallen angel where love had been sown and the years had cast their blossom.

She brought the inside news of the Forest and I wondered if she had heard about us leaving. I asked Julie.

'Do you think she knows? I haven't told her. Perhaps we ought to. It'll be quite a shock if she does not know.'

'This bloody rain!' said Julie suddenly. 'Its running down my 'air into me ear 'oles. Why we're sitting out here, I don't know! You mad ol 'bugger. We'll catch our death!'

She got up to go in and I followed, carrying the wine and glasses and listening to most of my city of clocks strike at the same time. 'All but one!' I shouted as they became silent. The telly stared at us with a blank face and only needed a touch to set its mad brain going, but we left it alone, both being a bit anxious about Annie. 'What do you think?' I said.

'I've got a feeling we ought to go and see. Going off down the lane last week she didn't look too good.' As she spoke, Julie opened the front door. 'Listen!' In a while we heard a faint cry. We ran up the lane and found Annie fallen forward in the hedge unable to get up. It looked like a slight stroke. Her basket was upset and the rain washed round her. It was as though she had been struck by a claw. She had a look of dismay but her blue eyes smiled sweetly when she saw us. In one, I saw a tiny tear and I remembered her saying she had not cried since she were a cheil. I wondered what had hit her – from inside?

We helped her to the cottage where her sister Lily was waiting by the gate quite truculent and aggressive. 'I told 'er not to go out to you. I knew this would happen if she did, but she wouldn't listen. Now come on in by the fire Annie, and git dry.'

Lily was dressed in long skirt and apron. The skirt had been given her by Lady Gurney-Dixon, who lived on the plain. She was a small stout person, so it was wound twice round Lily's frail body and kept her warm.

'Better if you put my skirt on, Annie.' But Annie would hear none of it, and Lily stomped off with her walking stick she used for her broken foot and cracked glasses askew on her face, while Annie pushed her felt hat back where the crimson dye was running down her face.

We got her to the back door where tins, pails and boxes were piled high and gear hung on the low wall of the cottage. But they would not let us enter the dark interior, which was stacked with faggots of wood, newspapers, china oil lamps, tins of food years old and pictures among which could easily be hidden a Morland, who used to travel these roads to the Isle of Wight in 1799. But I never broke the unspoken rule, forbidding even me, their chosen 'Feyther', to enter the temple; nor would I touch one fragment of their treasure, as though it were holy silver. I noticed the thatch was in bad nick in the scullery where the beams had rotted, probably owing to woodworm, which was everywhere in the Forest: only Julie was allowed in – for she was 'country'.

MERRY TREE

We could just see Lily making up the fire which must have been burning for the best part of a century all the year round, making perfect central heating and place to cook, costing nothing at all. Annie walked in saying she didn't want no doctor or no vicar or anybody else. She could manage if Feyther would draw some water from the well before he went because Lily couldn't do it with her bad foot — which I did. Then Julie and I left them and walked back to our own cottage. On the way we saw the pig's face in the rain laughing at us from the hedge. 'Got it!' I said.

'Got what?' Julie asked.

'The pig's face. She never brings one except on Christmas or a special occasion, like my birthday or our wedding.'

'Whats special about today?' 'Nothing. But it means she knows we are going. That's what's upset her!'

We were both feeling sad and instead of watching telly we opened a bottle of brandy and sat talking. The first draught of the golden spirit was followed by a deep drag inhaled from a woodbine. This, inhaled like diamond boart dust into the terraced hangers of the lungs, seemed to asphyxiate the brain and send the medulla oblongata floating to the ceiling like a Zeppelin, where it exploded in flames.

We talked of Annie and Lily Bright who, of all people in the Forest, had brought enchantment to our lives and bewitched our history.

While this was going on we heard a wild crowing in the distance. We listened. It was repeated, only on a higher note.

'That's not a cockerel,' said Julie. 'That's Ally Slope crowing'. She gave an imitation nearly as good as Annie Bright could do it. We listened again and the boy crowed back from his cottage, which was nearly opposite Annie and Lily, and he was most likely at the window with his pyjamas on his head and his pet Aylesbury duck under his arm.

'I worry about him sometimes, when he comes to the gate!' said Julie. 'When I'm alone. Annie say he's all right — sweet natured but it's his madness I fear. What's locked up in 'en?'

'You should know,' I said, tormenting her. "Yume a country girl. A Breughel 'ead!'

'Don't take the piss, my Mush!' she replied, shaming me. 'I'm serious. I expect it's all right. Yes I should know, I suppose. Annie said that. "Don't 'ee be so silly young dumman. Yume be a country lass same as us. So don't put on yer airs an' graces. Ally Slope be all right!"

'Well there you are, my Ju. I think so too. It's them that hides their madness that are dangerous. Ally Slope is a charmer really. He is the Poet's Idiot. Shakespeare knew him: 'full of sound and fury signifying nothing'. John Clare knew him and Yeats: Tom the Lunatic:

> Whatever stands in field or flood,
> Bird, beast, fish or man
> Mare or stallion, cock or hen,
> Stands in God's unchanging eye
> In all the vigour of his blood:
> In that faith I live or die.

It is the madness of the poet of whom Plato said:

> There is no invention in him
> Until he has been inspired
> And is out of his mind.'

'That's right,' Julie exclaimed. 'I understand that.' And she loved the song to which poetry is joined because she had a beautiful contralto voice, trained from singing in the church choir. She remembered Annie's song – or one of them:

> Sing, sing, what shall I sing,
> The cat ran away with the pudd'n string!

'That's what I sings to 'en,' Julie went on, imitating Annie. 'An she goes into a song that 'ud kill 'ee laughing.'

I remembered some of the verses and recited a couple to make her laugh more:

> The boys are up Wood Fiddley
> Climbing in the trees,
> An Mother's got a butterfly
> Caught between her knees.
> She told me what the dustman did
> An what the milkman said
> The night the nightjar spun a song
> That Mr Buckle died.
> Cock-a-doodle-doo!
> The cockerel's comb is red.

'An such a silly darft song taz.' We finished up both of us almost crying with laughter then we heard Ally Slope answer the crowing in the song. 'There he goes again!'

After a little while we heard Annie crowing to the mad boy. She must be feeling better. What a good thing. We lifted our glasses:

'To Annie and Lily!' we said and emptied them, then went on talking into the night, which was one of the great delights of knowing Julie. Sex, she said, was an over-rated pastime, but talking about ancient times could go on forever. Once it lasted two days and nights.

In this case she set me off by saying: 'When did you come to this place for the first time?'

'Oh years ago, Ju. When I was about eighteen or younger. I walked from London to Bournemouth to see a girl, and on the way I came through the Forest – that is, from Sydenham where I was born, which is really north Kent and I came this way to look for the gypsies. There were many of them in those days. And I stayed here for one night sleeping rough. I always think you visit the places of your future long before it comes around, and this was it. It gave me a very strange feeling even then.'

'Come on then, get on with it, Mush,' said Julie sitting by my legs on the carpet with her head on my knee by the fire. 'How was it strange?' and poured me another brandy to get me going.

'It was getting dark so I rested on the roadside by the stream and I remember saying to myself, "This place is enchanted. Here the goat's foot has danced while men are sleeping!" I could hear the curlew on the meadows and just see their shadowy forms, but even stranger, I could also hear the sea, which is fifteen miles away to the southern edge of the Forest.'

'Sure it wasn't the trees?' put in Julie.

'It could have been except it was still with no wind. I could have fallen asleep or simply been in vision, which is something that happened from an early age. At those times the mind is paper-thin like a Japanese wall recording shadows and sounds without actually seeing them. The silence of the Forest was quite frightening. The Delius Bird kept fluting near the brook and lilies shone at my feet. The thing about it is the sea sound increased until it was dominating the landscape, as if it was an outside power spreading through immensity. Then I looked at the hill at the back behind our place, the low hill where the black fox used to cross and I saw a figure crouched on the summit holding something to his head, swaying and chanting. This was the source of the sea sounds. It was like an opium dream to me. Who holds the evening in the palm of his hand? I wondered. Who has touched everything with mystery? Who is it on the hill? Out of whom runs the music of the sea? No answers came to my questions and when the evening light gathered into the corner of the sky, the crouching figure went down the side of the hill out of sight.

'Lights were lit in the village: mostly oil lamps and candles in that time and the stars swarmed over the sky just like flat bees making for the flower in the west. I felt very lonely. The moon rose, making the stream look like a wide silver track left by a snail dragging the hill on its back. The gravel road crunched as I walked through the village – this village – that was the first time I came here. It is still crystal clear in my mind.'

'Yea, but what happened? Tell me what happened, Mushter!' put in Julie. 'You always go all round the houses!

'I remember a pair of lovers gliding by, as if enclosed in tomorrow, but not strange any more. The world had opened and I could see the souls of others. Who knows at such times that the universe itself might be split in half like a blade of grass.'

'Go on then. Tell me what happened next!'

'I was confronted by a man in the moonlight. A lanky person with long hair who looked like Ally Slope, but with a wilder look in his eye: both sweet and magnetic. Can't explain really. He gave me a timeless feeling – older than the hill under which he lived: older than the snowdrops on Lone Woman Moor, or the Spring itself even. His face was a flower I had never seen before. The sounds of the sea were still breaking in my mind when I heard him begin to chant one of those ridiculous songs we've been reciting:

>   Bees on the sun,
>   Moths on the moon,
>   Fungus grows on lonely trees
>   Life is never done.
>
>   Give me a needle,
>   Give me a thread
>   Sew death together
>   Lying down in bed.

> I had a loved one
> Who took my copper horn:
> Moth on the moon
> Fox in the corn.
>
> Give me a needle,
> Give me the sun,
> Sew the two together
> Death is never done.

"Christ!" I shouted out loud, "That is the maddest song I've ever heard!" He smiled at what I had said and swung round suddenly only because a Forest pony took fright at my voice and ran between us leaving me in a cloud of dust. When it cleared he was gone, but on the road was a huge conch shell rocking to and fro which he must have let go of. I put it to my ear and could hear the crash and thunder of the sea. . .'

Julie looked at me in amazement. 'When I told Annie Bright years later she said: "And that would have been Tommy Slope, Feyther to this one, Ally. And he was the same". He always went to the hill when the moon was rising, especially a harvest moon, and he'd sing. An' we girls would say: "Tom's on the hill and we can hear the sea!" She remembered the song too:

> Tom's on the 'ill
> An we can hear the say;
> Curlew is calling
> Call away! Call away! Call away!

'And she would get the exact curlew note as she did the cuckoo.'

Julie said that what I told her was beautiful but she thought I got it mixed up with my own dream. I agreed it was not always possible to tell.

The life of the village was lived over and above these two old sisters who might almost have invented themselves. They were custodians of the inner life of the Forest and the creatures and people who lived there. It will be called myth or legend by scholars in later times, but in truth it was really a record of life and experience right on the frontier of the human mind.

Julie and I then played *Le Sacre Du Printemps* by Stravinsky, which seemed to fit in with and even extend the feelings of this curious village in which we lived yet belonged to no more.

A few nights later there was a great storm, bringing down many trees, and the thatched roof of Annie and Lily's cottage fell in. A Colonel Sangster, who lived on the plain, had been to see them and called at our cottage to ask if we could let them go into our chalet while their roof was repaired, but our whole property was already sold and contract signed. We ourselves had nowhere to go. They managed to carry on in their one main room where the great fire still burned, until news came that the Lord of the Manor who owned the estate was unwilling to repair the roof. This refusal brought about an insoluble crisis and they were forced to agree to go into the old people's home, severed forever from the Forest where they were written on the green tablet of the years. Annie Bright's cottage went up for auction almost at once: it fetched £6,700. Subject to demolition.

Annie retired to her bed and died soon after. We went to see her but she scarcely knew us and, save for her gentle smile, we would not have known her. Lily had sat staring in the fire for a long time, and suddenly emerged as a dominating person, bossing everyone about. Then she disappeared and was found poking about the ruins of the cottage where she had walked alone. They took her back and she died also.

I wondered if Arthur Cockerel, who loved Annie so dearly, and was killed in the first world war, ever returned to her again?

'Oi love thee Annie Broight. I wisht I 'ad tookt 'en in Wood Fiddley before I went to war. Now I am hung on barbed woire with a hole in my head and a gas mask on moi face. My face is gone now. Rubber lasts longer than flesh because the floies don't eat 'en. No chillun come out of war, Annie, only death!'

> Merry tree! Merry tree!
> Lover come back to me.
> Cuckoo! Cuckoo! Cuckoo!

SONG FOR ANNIE BRIGHT

MERRY TREE

Each time you note your timeless time
                           CUCKOO CUCKOO
And the Merry tree makes a symphony
                           Who Who Cuckoo
And into the tower of Springtime climb,
                           Who Who with me Cuckoo?

My Spirit flies her hawk at the dawn dove,
Bursts the sun in a sea of air
And breaks the back of the future there
As I watch the flowing years of love.
There is no way to hold the sound
Of the miracle made in the Merry Tree
Turning round like a merry-go-round
And Beauty is wed in three.

When I hear you give your timeless call
                           CUCKOO CUCKOO
In the secrecy of the Merry tree
                           CUCKOO CUCKOO
Calling till the blossoms fall
Merry Tree! Merry Tree! Merry Tree!
Lover come back to me
                           CUCKOO CUCKOO
                           CUCKOO
                               Cuckoo
                                   Cuckoo
                                       Cuckoo

Annie Bright
I sing for thee

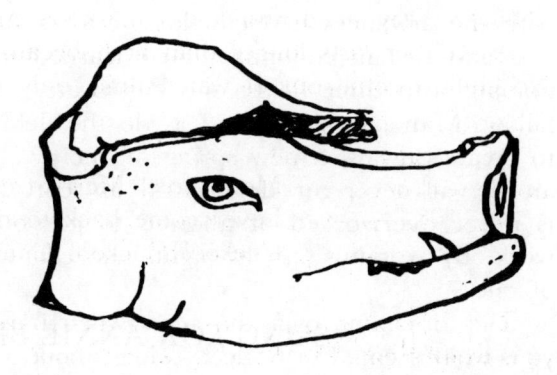

Pharoah's Tomb

Quite early in life I saw that the main business was self-realisation in every way that could be considered possible for any one particular person.

Development of the body by the skills of the body, so that one did each thing as well or better than anybody else: even to riding a bicycle or climbing a tree. So when my destiny in trying to be a painter led me into dancing it was not a diversion but a widening of consciousness that took me finally to sculpture. My obsession with the meaning and beauty of words took me to poetry. My love of light and colour took me into painting. My insight and experience of natural forms took me into the cosmic task of drawing the whole of creation. In the end I saw that each was an aspect of a single thing – understanding life: that took me to the quest of the spirit and the inventive imagination to interpret what I had discovered. So it was not a frittering away of energy on several things, as the specialist world into which I was born thought it was, but a growing awareness of every aspect of existence, and indeed, experience, with attendant emotions. As I grow like a tree as I die I notice that those specialists are themselves constricted in what they do because they are hooded, and resistant to the things which I am able to express in several ways without any change of attitude – unique because they are my own and will therefore persist as creation.

During this time of which I write, my fortunes were changing with the advances in technology, and it was particularly difficult to find and sustain continuity. So I learned to treat myself as a smallholding with three fields: one I cultivate, one I sow and one I leave fallow. Man has his seasons as do the fields: there is always a place to create, always a new spring of energy: 'draw upon it as you will and it will never run dry,' as the ancient Chinese knew. The ground is never overworked or allowed to go sour. One need never stop work. By working also at night, one can have two lifetimes, instead of one.

This discipline over the years when hardship in isolation is upon you, what seems like neglect, brings about a *habit of work* that makes it possible to continue all the time under any conditions – shellfire or starvation. An artist is not someone who stops his processes during times of neglect, when there is no stipend but a bare bone – any more than the stars change their courses because the world is evil. The only real sin an artist can commit is to neglect, ignore or – worst of all – pretend his talents. He continues by following long periods of painting, then of sculpture, and again of writing, each complementing the other in being part of a *whole psyche* expressing itself, thus advancing towards the azimuth, adding a millimetre to the human spirit to shine in the darkness of tomorrow.

I worked often at night on the furnaces after being at my desk writing from dawn. I worked from fact to fantasy, poetic instance to the hard reality of stone, packing case to packing case, the whole landscape of my floating dream and, like William Blake:

O how I dreamed of things impossible!

It became the daily dream of life, because understanding the behaviour of the whole psyche is the only chance we have of touching fingertips with the Original Creator – if he is there: I think he is, sweeping the skies of Time. If he is not there he is being recharged with our own effort to give the eagle his flight and the gypsy his tear as he weeps over his dead child, so that creative evolution cannot die out, but be a prayer to the recreation of God by being his antennae of consciousness of what he has created so far, including ourselves with this extended gift. . . no longer separate.

Packing was all part of it. Though I was sad, I saw it as the next fall of Time's huge foot. The house became a shell. Every room full of silent furniture and boxes, on one of which I worked, with my books of reference and dictionaries piled around me, at the manuscript of the book on the gypsies.

Julie, with her mother Alice, working hour after hour with a fag hanging out of her mouth, were both women of great devotion and saw things as they were without all my prismatic explanation, brought the task to a slow conclusion of desolate rooms while I kept on writing. But I had not realised how hard it was for Julie, losing her first real home after a childhood travelling from one job to another as the daughter of a hunt servant, county to county over the years. Now the stability of her own home, which she had grown to trust, was dissolving. She was tough enough to take it, as was I, because we had both had a difficult passage, but the truth is that Home Farm in the Forest could have been the lasting answer if I had handled it properly and not been obsessed with my hydra-headed soul and its demands. That is probably why we never had children although I wanted them. Julie said no and was quite emphatic, but she turned out to be pure gold.

'It is not a disease, it is a way of life: that's how it is.'

Meantime the Creation Cycle was in the lecture hall at the college, as my Sistine Chapel for their future – which was a great comfort to me. But there were hundreds of paintings and drawings to be packed and taken to another studio by the big workshop, which I could then use if I was able to commute from wherever we were going. The contents of the workshop itself went to the college engineering department, with the furnaces and foundry equipment, along with the Madonna, on permanent loan. My carrier Derek Reeves took them with special care as he had moved my work for some years. I had hoped in some way all these tools and equipment and raw metals would be absorbed for use by the students, but never had confirmation of this. Julie's and my main concern was to see the works of art safe. She dedicated herself to placing each of the important pieces in its proper place, so that even our apparent failure at this point was a mission: one far more difficult and long lasting than either of us could have foretold.

Jasper, my son by Ishtar, whom she left with me when she abandoned ship, and who Julie helped me to bring up from the time we met, now appeared from nowhere – as he had the night he helped me pour the metal for the stag beetle. But now he was a tall short-bearded young man of fine looks and a whip in body and wit: quick, sharp to sting, alive: full of spontaneous comedy which I had only found among professional comedians when I was an adagio dancer on the music halls. My task was made easier by this demon with his sword of humour. I got a laugh, apart from the joy to have him near for a short while. Together we moved the gear to the lower studio and set up a small hut as temporary living quarters in case Julie and I had not found a place by the time Home Farm was taken over.

The final bonfires were lit where once we had celebrated weddings in the open and millionaires had danced with gypsies; where the llama had eaten the General's rose and I had married my Julie. Animals were gone, fields empty, recovering in the first flush of spring, an area of life over; one turn of the Big Wheel, one more click of Destiny.

'Starvation is better!' I said to Julie. 'You have only to deal with the knot in your belly and hallucinations – it is pure, like being with the angels. But to sell out and pay all that money away, yet find a place to live and work, is a problem for a saint. We will come out with little enough – but not bankrupt, thank God!' I had experienced the harsh mercies of that as a child. We really did not know what to do at this point.

At last inspiration came to us through an advertisement Julie found in the *Southern Echo*: a disused pub on the Isle of Wight. We crossed the mysterious water to the mist-shrouded hills and were driven to the site by an agent, but it was damp, smelt of stale beer and had a hostile ghost. A bramble tore my face as I came out, which I took as a positive command to fuck off. We were driven to the office and introduced to a senior man who in turn drove us to a small place down a long road in a little wood behind Cowes, running down from the prison. We knew at once it was to be our home before we went in. A long two-storey building with roses and wisteria, a garage and an acre of ground completely on its own. No other cottage on the road. There was a woman inside who looked haunted: later we found she was ill. 'This is it!' we said simultaneously, looking at one another. We were right. After a short talk with the man we returned to the mainland, across the long fjord of the Solent, soon to be so familiar and even more mysterious, planning our move. But what about the workshops?

'Commute!' Julie answered at once, her hair blowing and sea-blue eyes alight.

The seagulls called overhead and the mainland was like barracuda laying in wait. We both knew we must live within the sound of the gulls crying. For Julie it was home: for me it was St. Ives without the Great God Pan. It was the need of two grown into the law of the sea, though neither of us cared about sailing on it: we had too much respect – as we would not ride a friendly dragon. Now we could see all the premonitions that had pointed to this solution to our problem: the figures floating in pyjamas over the Solent with the hills of the Island in the background, and other paintings of dream figures hovering near the shores of setting suns – even the Creation Cycle was a prophesy. Strange dreams. Meeting a Fijian who told us how to ride a turtle and not get drowned. The experience of Tom Slope listening to the sea, and Annie Bright. Every day I drove to the sea, painting it at dawn and moonrise. The involvement with those three beautiful women who were drowned, as though a triple soul had gone before me: about which I have written elsewhere. The violent death of Takajo. All these events now emerged as a complete pattern of precognition and we could no more help crossing that narrow neck of water than my wild ancestor Brody-Berlin could help crossing from Helsinger to Halsingborg in south Sweden two centuries before.

Now the vital piece in the pattern had been found we could synchronise the practical details with precision – and had to do so – quite quickly.

Dismantling a sculptor's workshop was a more complicated matter – in a way more distressing – so I got to my improvised desk at five a.m, wrote my book till lunch, then turned to the stone.

There was a block of green Irish marble from Connemara out of which I had half carved a Sleeping King. It might as well have been an emblem of the Forest as of Ireland; or of Hermes Trismagistus who carved his wisdom on a green tablet before he died. It was a hard brittle piece from the serpentine area of the seam and had been difficult to work. I had ordered a block from the softer yellow-green section which cuts better with a chisel, but there he was, and did not wake when I blocked him up on the edge of the pit so that I could work him from underneath: I had to make sure he was safe, and I well shod in case he should move and crush me to death under his 2½ ton weight. I loved the mechanics of all this and even tempered my own chisels in the forge. It might have been good to have had an assistant in this case – a mature man who understood the behaviour of heavy masses of stone, but years before, when I saw John Wells, Terry Frost and Denis Mitchell working on the British Festival sculptures for Barbara Hepworth, and refused her request to join them, I vowed my work in stone should be from my hand alone, with my spirit going into it. Although I have done less because of this and mostly smaller things, each is a unique creation by one man. That is my way.

I spent several hours hoisting him to a safe position to leave. There was only one dicey moment when I nearly broke a leg, but my dancing skills saved me because I look upon the mechanics of the human figure as a masterpiece of engineering that responds to exact laws.

Next thing was to lift the Madonna back on the sunken pedestal on which I had carved her with lifting gear. Being in alabaster she radiated light which was beautiful – and her gift to others. The same sculpture that had been chosen for the Christchurch Priory, the sacred building between two rivers, that holds the Presence of Him for whom it was built and who might walk out of the stones and say: 'I that speakest unto thee am he!' But modern alchemy active in the church saw to it that my sculpture did not get there – for fear she was the Woman from Samaria.

This was a serious blow in that it broke a set of forces built for a single quest – my own – and shattered the crystal.

I moved the *Pietá* on its mobile scaffold to the centre and all the sculpture round it for safety. Benches cleared, furnaces cleaned, moulds stacked. I greased the vices and tools, save for a small hand set of hammers and chisels packed into an eighteenth century toolbag called a cunt, for use in the next world. Swept the floors clean, fixed the doors against storm, tempest and robber. All was ready if they had to go to the College, which in the end they did.

Jasper had gone to be near his mother and complete his "O" levels at Salisbury. Quite sad because he had been brought up here all his young life and helped me pour the molten metal in the greatest transfusion of all – making a bronze, of which I never became master but was a willing neophyte. Paul was away working on an estate near Salisbury as a carpenter.

The great blue steel building which I had always thought of as a Mississippi Steam Boat, stood in the spring sunlight bright against the fields and trees of the Forest. But inside it was like the Tomb of an Ancient Pharoah, in which all the images were stored for future use after the metamorphic change into the Eternal Life. I felt like the young King with whom I had started as a boy, Tutankhamun, now growing old and withered into the skin within the sarcophagus of Time, but without the mask of eternal life because the metal to make it was unobtainable. The tomb that carried the images of the other world, the Unconscious Mind, I had divined so early; the sacred images of the spirit of poetry without which the process of evolution and deliverance would end. This was my contribution. This was my final defeat in which I was to end the present stage of my life in the bright dragonfly flight into a fierce old age.

I had forgotten to die.

The work was done so far. Now I must follow the golden thread that must never be broken but lead into the next era, and the means to do more. I knew in my heart I could never commute, nor did I. Once you leave a place, you no longer belong in the same way: only as an outsider. So ended one chapter, so began another.

When we got to the Island we sat in the empty cottage with our things around and wept. We were £77 down, but our debts were paid. The bank closed on us now its maw was full. Fortunately I had set aside the advance on the book in another place, without telling anyone.

Next morning Julie started to build the new home and I set up my desk on a packing case and continued to write my book about the gypsies: *Dromengro*. I had lost one day. The thread was not broken.

Otherwise we left only our doves, flying round Donkey Down like the souls of those we loved and who had also gone away.

Before I left the Forest I wrote this *Epitaph* and wanted to carve it on the back of a stone but there was no time:

EPITAPH

I STAYED ON TO WATCH OVER THE SPIRITS
OF THE UNREDEEMED. I HAD LEARNED TO SPEAK
WITH THE VOICE OF FISH AND OF OCEANS AND
I LOOKED OUT OF THE TREES WITH THE EYE OF
THE WHITE STAG. ALSO FROM THE MALE FERN
AND THE PROSCENIUM OF MOON AND STARS – FOR
I HAVE ENTERED THE WILD PLACES AND BECOME
THE LIFE WITHIN: THE ENCHANTER WHO BRINGS
THE DAWN, THE GREEN ONE WHO PUTS OUT THE
SUN IN THE FOREST. I CAN SEE ALL THINGS
THAT HAPPEN IN THIS PLACE: I AM A VOICE
CRYING FROM THE GREAT RIVER: THE SALMON
WHO ENTERS ENGLAND. I HAVE TOLD YOU OF
THE CREATURES WHO HAVE COME AND GONE; OF
THEIR ACTS OF LOVE AND CRUELTY TO ONE
ANOTHER AND OF THEIR DREAMS. I AM THE
POET WHO SANG FOR A BARE BONE AND HEARD
THE ROAR OF THE LAST DRAGONFLY IN THE
GREEN CATHEDRAL OF TREES AT THE END OF
TIME.

MERLIN

Circe under the Clock

> Now dropped our anchors in the Aegean Bay
> Where Circe dwelt, daughter of the day.

This quotation from Homer might well have been true for us also – and indeed partly it was, for every poetic statement has its casing of reality and can yet contain a poetic instance. When I first saw this Island I was convinced it was Paradise lying on the sea in a golden mist: but for the harsh reality of our entrance it could well have remained so. We called our new home Merlin Cottage and settled in.

A piggery just a little way down the long road to the sea reminded me that I must have an antidote or, like the crew of Ulysses' ship, the beautiful but invisible Goddess Circe could turn us into swine. Ulysses had the white moly flower given him by Hermes to protect him from the spell of the Goddess. I had nothing: my moly flower must be the continued act of creation. But even this did not ameliorate an insane depression that had fallen upon both of us: claustrophobia and the feeling we had been trapped. We did find what I think was the moly flower near Shorwell: on the steep banks there was a form of wild garlic with a white flower and a black root.

One of the first things was to get to know the ferry times and we crossed to Lymington whenever we could. Being strangers, they played us up and often kept us waiting several hours to get aboard. But we went back and forth all we could until it was a journey that could not be concluded and we found ourselves asking 'Which is the other side?' And when the thread was broken by mist or storm there was only the isolation as it would be on Circe's Island and we were reduced to hog-level depression and swine-chopping brandy, until we got to know people. Otherwise, when we went into Cowes it was like St Ives without Priapus. All the women were pregnant, and all the men were like Cliff Michelmore: a very curious illusion after having been on telly with him in his programme *In Town Tonight* when *I Am Lazarus* was published.

The ferry we found to be the determining factor and the more we used it the less we needed to do so. Still having the Mk 10 Jaguar we sometimes went across to drive to Salisbury and look at the Sleeping Knights of the Wars of the Roses and Crusaders in the

Cathedral; also Henry Moore's bronze of a warrior, which was the ultimate human agony enshrined in art. Or else go to Kimmeridge: the rock-strewn bay where the cliffs catch fire because of the oil, and the stones are black and smooth for the same reason. I took many of these home and did carvings, but after a period of time the oil left them and they became ordinary sandstone heads or whatever. But the place was still quite prehistoric and gave out energy which we took back also to the Island where there was no art and therefore no generating life force – only great beauty waiting to be opened up by some fierce painter of the future: like Ophelia with her flowers, it was still floating on the water, had not yet died.

We drove everywhere on the Island also, as though driving over and through a great sculpture left by primitive man: crags and haunting downs where the ghost of Tennyson still strode in wide-awake hat and cloak of black; silted harbours, quiet villages, busy market town at the centre, and a dead railway where the station at Ventnor was still open, but wrecked and empty with the signs upside down, giving a strange feeling to the place where trains no longer arrived, and corrugated iron sheets like strips of sticking plaster, stuck on the mouth of the tunnel prevented them ever departing, and the platforms settled for the violet buddleia that grew through the stone, visited by the Lady Glanville Fritillary butterfly unique to Boniface Down; below this, on the very day the young Churchill saw the wrecking of the *Eurydice* from this station nearly a century before, Swinburne wrote in prophetic anapaests:

> In a coign of the cliff between highland and lowland
> The ghost of a garden confronts the sea.

None spoke at the silent terminus and indeed none spoke to us for quite a while.

Mighty oceans surrounded us and above all there was the prison so near to our cottage, where men waited, as on Devil's Island or Alcatraz, for unholy redemption for unholy deeds. The souls of lost men gathered together: the Kray Brothers. the Ripper and others who, twenty years before, would have been used as images of sacrifice to the crimes of the nation and, as with Ruth Ellis, the wrongs against women committed by most men. The place gave out a silent negative distress note, except when later on there was a prison revolt and the men climbed on the roof throwing slates at the 'screws', who walked about in dark blue uniforms with long key chains hanging at the side. I made a drawing of the men. In fact my first real release was to be drawing all the time, wherever I might be.

Once I had finished my book, Philip Ziegler came over at a point of change in his own life, bringing with him his children and his new wife-to-be. A memorable day with wine and lettuce, contact with literature and the lifeline of intelligent publication I so needed. He gave me a further contract for a second book: *Pride of the Peacock, The Evolution of an Artist*. Which meant another advance. Also the Arts Council gave me a small grant to tide me over the writing period.

Julie's parents came for a visit and took over the cottage while we went to Cornwall to stay near Johnny Wells and see old companions like Bryan Wynter, Denis Mitchell, Patrick Heron, Hyman Segal and others with whom I had scooped the husk of Cornwall and fled, which also gave end threads to weave into our new fabric. About this time my old friend Grant Watson had chosen to die and being away I did not see any news bulletins or receive letters. It was a note from Katherine waiting my return that told me. It caused me considerable distress, not so much that he had died, because that's what he wanted – to get to his beloved Ida and shed the shell of Brother Body – but because on our last meeting I had promised to go to his funeral. Now I could not do so. He who wrote: 'May the open wounds speak honestly, little else does.'

VALE. Peter! Rest well!

I started to paint and carve stone. In the first I made immediate contact through my drawing and did many of long shores and sad sunsets over ships at anchor. In stone I found difficulties. There was no striking surface in Vectis stone. Perhaps it was too deep for me to understand, like the ocean. There was no connection with the immediate present. I found the Island soft with no bite. I still do. The shape of the Island is female with her cunt pointing north towards England, the great luminous, intractable Solent a serpent swimming into her and retracting, the interminable ferry plying between birth and death:

> The ferry moves, slides away,
> Creeps toward evening,

> Curves always toward those
> With a penny in the hand
> On the other side:
> Or that obolus under the tongue
> To pay for the journey
> On the boat of death.
> Green and tough, O Charon, tell us,
> Which is life and − death?
> Which is the other side?

I was able to work between periods of black hatred, which I associated with Queen Victoria's forty years grief for her dead Consort in that ugly ochre house stuffed with bad art, sapping England's strength − and with the sadness of Charles I, the sorrow-laden Tennyson in memoriam for A.H.H.

I have always thought the Islanders in the north side − the entrance to the Medina, which divides Cowes like a split peach − must have been members of the staff at Osborne House: servants, gardeners, footmen, butlers, cooks, huntsmen, stable lads, clerks, matrons, equerries − all of whom lived in the same hive as the Queen Bee and served her: also shared her grief, her status and, to some extent her riches, and are therefore still unconsciously holding allegiance to her ghost − or were until George V and Sir Thomas Lipton revived the yachting, the Schneider Trophy was flown round the Solent and later the Duke of Edinburgh started to bring *Britannia*, the royal yacht into the Solent for Cowes Week. So among the upper areas of West Cowes population, who are mostly shopkeepers, there is an unwritten snobbery which makes one feel they might even have VR embroidered on their 'serviettes'. And likewise, in East Cowes, there is a curious legacy of happy, reserved but very human workers from the same hive with whom it was more easy to make friends. Together these two natural sections of defence form a formidable fortress against the invader, the *Oberer*, from across the water who are now the main source of survival as in St. Ives or Beer and Seaton, in fact all seaside towns around our shores.

No painter had ripped the landscape open where it bleeds into the sea at evening with a miraculous transfusion of colour, nor torn her rocks with a fierce brush, wrecked her little towns with an eruption of hot lava. It is hard to tell why. What would have happened if Van Gogh had chanced to cross the Solent when he was teaching at

Ramsgate or Gauguin had gone there instead of Tahiti? Probably nothing because the Virago was not there to strike their flame: in the Camargue and the Pacific – she was there – likewise in Cornwall. It is the cosmic genius hidden in certain places at certain times in history that causes the volcano to erupt and the human soul to pour its molten metal into new forms as surely as bronze. No sculptor had dug into the uterus of Circe's womb. It was a Writer's Island, as Keats, Swinburne (himself a Wighter) and Tennyson knew. This I wrote up on my desk. The other arts must follow when the soul of this strange place – this Enigmatic Woman – entered into me: or, more properly, I entered into her. She was dressed in a secrecy more beguiling than Circe in her mist-shrouded beauty, her timeless shores: hills, valleys and enchanted ports: vast oceans that are her robe and estuary lights her friendly warnings. She was a woman that refused to have it, and the Great God Pan had died – or slept on till a new awakening.

I had to remind myself that from the Island you had to travel north to get south and that all roads lead to the sea. There was no beginning, no end and no other side as in the maritime sense. This helped me to understand the paradox of the people in that they did everything separately to use up the time; they would not serve you in a shop if they didn't think they would, and they did things the other way round, not dishonestly, but to bewilder and tie up the outsider as they must have done the French when they invaded in the thirteenth century. They let them in to nearly the centre then cut them to pieces. I often think of this recessive opposition in the mind of Charles I, when he was imprisoned there in Carisbrooke Castle. The Island is a prison: I have heard it called Alcatraz even by the Islanders, and that is its greatest defence. Prison is its dominant feature, mentally as well as physically. The House of the Shadow behind the sunlight. The Chokie Hole. The Dungeon of Ugalino and his children.

The stone is like the people: outwardly soft with a hard centre you can't shape into anything else. If you strike it, it flakes into laminations and steps: a dirty white melancholy stone. It is in the fluidity and endless moods of the sea that the Islanders awaken to completeness. These outwardly soft, truthful and obdurate people have absorbed invasion for centuries, from Roman ships sailing up the Solent to the incongruity of the Pop Festival in 1970.

At first the festival seemed harmless enough as they came in ferry loads over several days and nights: and on the radio all you could hear was 'they say the roads are jammed as far as the Midlands!'

'They are coming down England' said the car park man as though hoards of Vikings from the north were advancing towards us. They swarmed over the Island in their way-out clothes. Men in ponchos and bearskins, women in kaftans and bare feet, miniskirts and high boots, fur hats and dark glasses like those in sculptures of ancient Sumar and modern Frink. Probably she was watching too. Hell's angels with a swastika flag and smoking pot.

I remember the first evening, because it was also as though a big sunset operation was going on in the sky when God's belly was opened in a miracle of crimson and blue, with yellow lining, under pink lung and silver bone, pouring torrents of blood and puss into the holy waters of evening under which the olive eel searched with small ultramarine eyes in the shades of a Marine City to mug an octopus for a stolen meal. Everything was predatory, even the tiger sun slouching behind the Hill of Desolation as the invaders had already named it.

Soon the moon was there like a sharp knife and a white blackbird flew to safety unnoticed by the crowds as they walked with their packs and bundles to build their new city under the shelter of the hill in two great fields. Thousands of tents grew like mushrooms and, climbing up the Hill of Desolation, hundreds of tiny fires were being lit like those of Asian hordes waiting to do battle under the command of Ghengis Khan or gypsy processions crossing the plains of Persia from northern India, on their journey a thousand miles long in the fourteenth century.

At its best the Pop Festival was like a religious event without a Christ. It had no centre and no apostles, but those who played the music and the music itself, which was the beginning of a great creative happening among the young people, might even have been an extension of what happened to us in the forties in Cornwall with sculpture and painting; the wave had moved on. And likewise there was sacrifice, as all Gods demand. In this case Jimmy Hendrix was crucified by drugs and died, his guitar forming his cross. And yet another unknown whom we watched, screaming in an ambulance tent.

At night the crowds roared and surged with the music in the arena and it was difficult to stand on two feet while the artists sang and played their instruments on the lime-lit stage. Barricades were broken, police were called in: it was at riot pitch, releasing all human emotion. The Beatles dropped in by helicopter, Dylan and The Who. Stravinsky would have given balance. But No!

Then they slept like frog-spawn under the stars. Dawn made them cold, their blankets furry with dew, like ghosts in fog under the flags of many nations. 'Men like trees walking.' This was a pilgrimage with only one meaning: the expression of the human soul in music and the need and the right for youth to prove itself and stamp its face upon the clock of its own generation. They would spill their dream across the hills, break the barriers of iron, free the arena from limits, because of too much learning, too much knowledge, too much mortgage, too much ambition to be what they did not want to be, locked in chains by their fathers till the *duende* dies. This was, more than anything, a rebellion of the *duende*; the spirit of creation that rises through the soles of the feet and transforms life.

The next day they appeared one by one or in little groups as out of one tent with a notice 'Girls wanted: no experience necessary', or out of rows of long bundles like Henry Moore drawings of 'Sleepers in the Underground' during the war. The Grey Sleeper, The Red Sleeper, The Blue Sleeper suddenly became men and women naked and wandering in the morning mist like the crew of the Ancient Mariner. Then an extraordinary thing happened. Instead of getting dressed, as if by a tacit understanding, they moved up Desolation Hill towards the sea. Thousands of naked men and women against the morning light. We drove round to the Military Road, built during the war, and met them coming down the other side passing our car parked on the verge and down the rest of the slope to the sands, which they crossed slowly and entered the sea as though to return from the journey of evolution and go back to their origins. One, who had probably taken one of the more powerful drugs like LSD, ran down the high hill and leapt into space.

> He died wanting to fly
> From white cliff to blue ocean
> Where his naked friends swam
> Like souls of dead sailors
> Come from the sea
> With sirens and mermaids
> Who pulled them down
> Long ago with love to drown.

CIRCE UNDER THE CLOCK

O, how he died!
Thinking he could fly
From Desolation Hill
Where the angels were singing,
To join the beautiful people
Bathing in a silent High
In the long waves near the shore,
Unheeding his poor bloody head
Bleeding where the policeman stood,
The press cameras clicked
And another history was read.

He died on the shore
Flying from Desolation Hill
To the blue sea:
His young head split open on a stone,
Like a sculpture by Henry Moore.

The Islanders watched through the week of the invasion until all the energy was used up and by its own exhaustion the festival came to an end. The people started to recede across the Solent, all vigour, sexually, spiritually and financially extinct, not knowing the Island had ever been successfully invaded, or hear the real music of the original Lotophagi,

that gentlier on the spirit falls
Than tired eyelids on tired eyes.

They left in their bearskins and bare feet, with silver faces and gold bodies: leaving 300 tons of tin cans to clear away with piles of old clothes and bottles, broken fences and broken hearts from one mighty orgasm that wrecked the Island but demonstrated to everybody the need for music, freedom and love. As one Island woman said in the village shop: 'O well, it was better than war! Is there any butter left?'

During the first night of the Festival a journalist I knew stopped me and suddenly said: 'Jesus — I've just seen £10,000 in notes! A pop group from America refused to perform unless they were first paid in cash. The counting is still going on in the press enclosure. They have been at it about two hours now, terrified someone will crash the tent as the money is sent in from all the entrances. Come and look!'

We went over to a corrugated iron fence covered by an awning, and looked in turn through a hole to the inside: under a single arc lamp, like soldiers dicing for Christ's clothes, four men counted feverishly while two men packed the notes into hessian sacks, with a look of fever and guilt. The rest looked on from the shadows like men in a painting by Rembrandt.

This momentary glimpse into the financial background of the Festival somehow signified the violence and destruction released by the music and drugs in an enormous expression of the religious need and spiritual fervour of a generation who would be the generals, bank managers, the artists, politicians and scientists of the future. I realised later that by spring, the wounds of Desolation Hill would be healed and the autumn would yield another corn harvest with bales of straw strewn like stones left there by prehistoric man.

Summer brings millionaires, politicians and tycoons to the Island with their yachts. They are more welcome than the lost children of the globe seeking unity and love. They advance up the Solent with coloured spinnakers like an earlier Viking invasion answering to the brass cannon that marks tomorrow's victory. Later the power-boats with small helicopters and Austercraft flying low over them, straight from Mars it would seem. There is one more big race and the season is over and the Royal Yacht leaves for Bermuda, after fireworks and fights.

Winter brings stillness, emptiness, storms and being alone. The Islanders don't talk to strangers until Christmas, after which they are silent till the season starts again and all is magical, seen through an alcoholic haze. We were safe enough if the moly flower had been plucked.

Although these experiences completed the process of transition for us, we were not settled. The Festival had been like a spontaneous celebration of the youth in which I could no longer participate and which Julie had not yet completed, which made it more difficult to bear. To arrange the hanks of thread for the next session with the loom was not so easy. The Happening of the Soul had signified also my allegiance to the arts I followed always with devotion, to my peril, and not yet with certainty of their final flowering. But as long as the magic shuttle continued to work properly, with truthful invention as a result, I was committed to go on. It was simply the finances I could not bring to fruition or induce some shadowy figure to pay out in notes at the right time to save disaster. 'Yet Continue', was my colophon for each day. There was one gigantic upheaval when we almost packed up and sold out, but we were handcuffed by a financial sum that would not go the other way north to get south. We thought of moving my workshop over the Solent, with its Silent Madonna and Sleeping King, to store and work in an empty church, but this was too expensive.

When I am blocked like this I always do the opposite thing. On one of my many trips across on the ferry, where one could see things from both sides, I realised the Island wouldn't work for us unless the metamorphosis was complete. The workshop could not be shipped over — nor could I commute: I tried but it was no good. I was a stranger in the Forest and the spirit had died. Sell the workshop: that was the answer — to a man named Tess who sold me my Jaguar Mk 10 — for converting more Jaguars.

'Yes. He keeps on about it!' said Julie. 'Sell it to him and take Roy Hall's offer to store the Madonna and other gear at the College in Poole.'

'Of course. It all fits together. What a fool I am! And your mother moving back to Devon says she will take all the paintings. Perfect!'

When we docked at Lymington we drove straight to the Waterloo Arms in Lyndhurst and there was Tess having a pint and talking to the landlord, Joe Wateridge. 'Look who's here!' they said with some delight, and stood us drinks.

I always thought Tess was of Irish extraction, with the black hair and blue eyes. Joe was a man of great vitality, quick as a razor in business and spending his life buying and refurbishing Jaguar cars. After kissing Julie and being told by me not to make a meal of it, he said: 'Blood bruvver! 'Ow you get'n on? When are you going to sell me that workshop. I ain't got no place to work.'

Lunchtime drinking is the best of all pub-time pleasures, but not recommended to the weak of head: it is likely to split it open later. But this time it was worth it. Before the session was out we had done a deal, which included the wooden studio at the side and a row of stables at the back. He eventually used the studio for sleeping quarters where he had a large self portrait of me by the door and every night when they went to bed after considerable heavy drinking, they each in turn saluted the portrait and said 'Good night, Mush!'

CIRCE UNDER THE CLOCK

I got in touch with Alan Hutchinson, Principal of the College, and his colleague, Roy Hall and the arrangements were made to move the contents of the workshop to Poole, with the *Madonna.* The *Pietá*, weighing 2½ tons had to be left in the centre of the workshop which Tess said would not be in his way, but on no condition would he move it outside because, being alabaster, it would erode.

Contracts were signed, the money paid and we were able to carry on and complete our transplantation to the Island. The paintings went to Devon. I kept a cunt of tools to work with in the garage at my new home.

The conflict over the Island was over and the people accepted us now we had come to live there. We made friends among whom were a few Islanders and some otherwise individuals who had come for sanctuary like ourselves. Among them there was a good-looking antique dealer whose name was Nimrod Light, with whom we traded a few of our objets d'art and became friends. He was very attracted to Julie but not intrusively so. Julie likewise! He shared our liking for the pubs, but at first we were rather inclined to be reticent in that respect. The Island was not like St. Ives where you became famous overnight and a genius by the morrow; drawn the next day and quartered at the weekend by experts. To begin with, the art did not matter here and it was a relief to behave as an ordinary human. I wore a sailor's peaked cap as I had in Cornwall. It was the best head-gear to keep stone dust out of one's hair, but people took me for a retired admiral and I had only to make a remark like 'There's a good following wind today!' and it was proven, though I knew nothing about the sea. Nimrod had a friend named Lynn whose daughter had been blinded by a bullet in Beirut and was the more beautiful because of it. I called her Butterfly and used to say to her when we met 'Remember your soul, Butterfly. Remember your soul!' In the end it became a short poem. Such fragments of the experience with new people started to cling to our lives like goose-grass. One would turn and say something like 'The Island is a trap!' – perhaps in response to some complaint made by one of us about how difficult it was to settle. This became an expanding pattern when we went shopping in the stretch I called Rotten Row, where some of the snoots were, till we began to feel more at home. The Cowes girls were friendly when they served you in the superstore and shops, but were expert at passing the shadow if they were out of sorts or – if you were familiar – would suddenly make a pass – that extra interlocking of the psyche that sends a shooting pain through the sacrum. In the end we were part of the scene and no one knew about our precarious situation. Everybody collected antiques, so we were able to exchange and sell quite a few until later when they did know. Thereafter we got ripped off once or twice.

Below our cottage was a field containing another cottage in which lived a family of Islanders who were quite unique, helpful and friendly, named White. Norman was probably of travelling stock. He had a huge bull which he called Grenadier, which his sons used to take for a walk along the long wooded road every morning and evening. I used to stop work and watch the majesty of his slow walk and his mighty strength. There was a man and wife called John and Frances who worked at the prison and an old man living alone who stood on the road most of the day, shouting to any passer-by. If it was a woman wearing trousers it was always: 'I like yer knickers, lady. I like yer knickers!' Girls who worked in the prison had to walk from Cowes and went by early in the morning arm-in-arm, singing together, laughing.

I have stitched these few people into the cloth of my new daytimes to show the background and moving film against which I started to work again, when the bruised psyche was able to become pliant enough to look inward as well as about me. I had not the gift of spontaneous union of the two worlds but the warning systems were working again and impulses were beginning to come. No nonsense about being in the mood, but learning again to walk in that strange country between the eye and the inner mind which is the birthplace of all good art. The ghost of the Forest had let us go: the Green Hunger no longer devoured us. Although we thought it was a time in the desert and were recessive, it was an entry into Paradise, if we could see it that way, perhaps to mature into a wiser syzygy in a different Eden.

I did several small stone sculptures using different materials I had with me. I remember particularly a horse's head in pale green Connemara marble, the eyes inset with turquoise. The closeness of the colours in the two stones gave it an almost ethereal look as though it were a horse of the spirit. Beautiful! When this happens in its own way, after years of experience, it gives me a secret thrill for a moment, then like a Zen monk, I move on unless I can't let go of it, or wish to imitate what I have done, which is the unforgivable sin.

The larger and more ambitious work, if you can call it that, came to me as a consequence of my 'Creation Cycle' of paintings. Almost directly after their conclusion in the Forest I had quite an urgent desire to paint the Stations of the Cross. Partly I suppose because I was nearer the Bible, which is for me the most profound collection of early poetry, and partly because Genesis of the Old Testament triggered the Gospels of the New Testament. Thirdly because for many years I have had the feeling, and later the conviction, that there is always a Presence at my shoulder guiding me to sanctuary: particularly for the lone artist on his quest for Beauty and Truth as fundamental verities and the third, Goodness, before which I have faltered so long.

I couldn't start this work in the Forest because of the breakdown of structures that made it possible for me to stay there, but I did tell Tom McArdle of Lyndhurst and it was enough to make him sweep through the town with extra spiritual zest for some time. Although he knew, and as I explained earlier, I am a poor churchman, he knew also what I was about and the quality of my intention. The impulse recurred as soon as I was settled, like a returning wave, and I got started first with a host of large and small drawings, but getting the place ready to paint them. It was a shed only 6ft high and the larger paintings were to be 8ft high × 4ft wide. Almost dark inside with one tiny window. So it was a question of working, like Michelangelo on the Sistine Ceiling, in every possible position.

I always say that in difficult situations the right person appears at the exact moment or is already there. It turned out to be an Islander named Colin Baker who ran a D.I.Y. shop in Cowes on Rotten Row. A quiet man with red hair and the pale skin of the Wighters. I had gone in for some undercoat and asked if he had Swedish hardboard in stock. The standard sizes were OK, but needed support and he offered to fit them to a pine framework at the back, soaking each together so that they would not go out of shape with damp, which on the Island was a present from the sea mist. It was quite a task to take on single-handed but he did not let me down and turned up with each panel as it was needed, while at my end I got into the task of painting a sequence in the life and death of an Invisible Man making his visibility only an explanation of his being there. I am convinced he moved among the revellers at the Festival and the naked men and women on Desolation Hill, and when they were on the sand returning from the sea they slowly formed a circle of over a thousand people standing silently as though an invisible Presence was at their centre

CIRCE UNDER THE CLOCK

INSCRIPTION

WORDS CUT IN THE BACK OF THE STONE

Though you are my breath and mind,
I leave you now,
Not as a broken man,
But stronger than the wind.

In the event of my continuing through the universe I would venture to say: Let each man and woman be concerned with completeness in what they do, because, within the sacred shrines of the eye and of the mind will then exist truth and Beauty in their natural residence and are themselves concerned with total vision and peace of mankind, having been excoriated of evil by the chain's of love reaching like a spread hand into the darkness of tomorrow – and then there will be goodness.

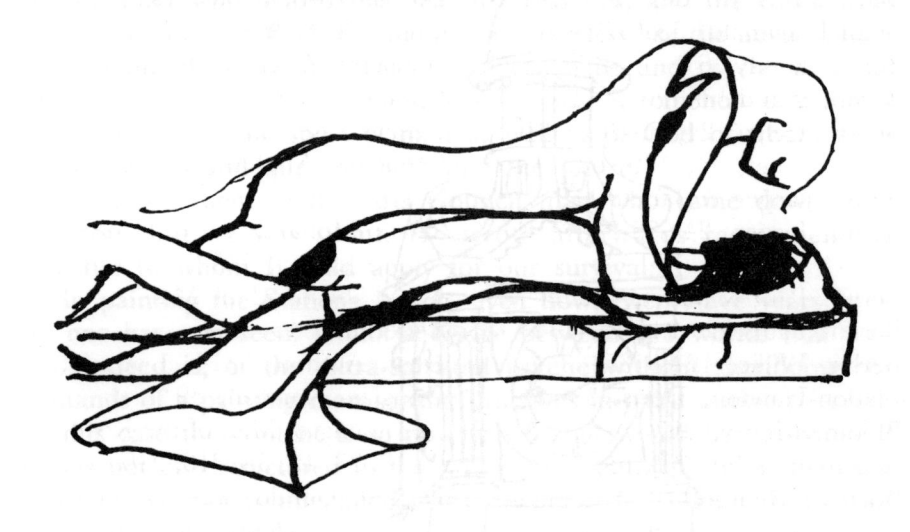

Index

"Alfred Wallis, Primitive" 113-4
Amergin, 9
Anning, Mary, 34
Arts Council, the, 156, 159, 254

Bacon, Francis, 62
Baines, Keith, 97-99
Baker, Denys Val, 22, 40, 47, 61-3
Baker, Ida, 64, 67
Baraclai Levy, Juliette de, 58
Barrett, Max, 19
Bassett, Lords of, 25
BBC documentary, 146
BBC production, 70
BBC, broadcast on, 163
Beer Quarry, 56
Beer, Sir Gavin de, 35, 47, 120
Bennet, Donald, 55, 57
Berlin, family, 61
Berlin, grandchildren, 132
Berlin, Helga, 24, 35-36
Berlin, Janet, 24, 130, 97
Berlin, Jasper & Janet, 119
Berlin, Jasper, 24, 35-37, 40-41, 144 et seq.
Berlin, Paul & Janet, 123 et seq
Berlin, Paul, 22, 24, 35, 172
Berlin, Willie, 124, 135
Bladon-Hawton, Doris, 58
Bloom, Monty, 157
Boorman, John, 71, 133
Borrow, George, 17
Bournemouth & Poole College, 194 et seq

Bright, Annie & Lily, 59
Bright, Annie, 8
British Council, 159
Brode, Anthony, 47, 57, 70, 81
Brody, David A, 20
bronzes, casting of, 146 et seq.

Caddick, Arthur, 116
Callot, Jacques, 17
Carroll, Terence, 132-3
Chaplin, Charlie, 86
Charon, 22
Chartres, visit to, 77
Cheeko the Bum, 97-99
Christchurch Priory, 160 et seq.
"Coat of Many Colours", 157
Constantine, Eddie, 80
Cooper, Luvvie, 42, 55
Corpus Christi Fair, 15
Craze, John, 22
"Creation Cycle", 58, 189 et seq
Cripplesease, 22
Croucher, Michael, 70-72, 133

"Dark Monarch", 156, 159, 113 et seq, 165
David (husband of Mai Zetterling), 43
Dent, Anthony, 114 et seq
Douglas, Norman, 39
"Dromengro, Man of the Road", 18, 33, 42, 58, 216, 240,
Durrell, Gerald, 224
Durrell, Lawrence, 38, 78, 121 et seq

257

INDEX

Ede, H S, 162
Elmhirsts, at Dartington, 55
Emery Down, home at, 57-58
Epstein, Jacob, 55

Fawley, oil refinery, 51, 55
Fergus (Irish groom), 86 et seq, 98 et seq, 107
Festival, Isle of Wight, 245 et seq.
Finlayson, Graham, 47
Fleming, Amaryllis, 55
Forestry Commission, the, 46
Frink, Elizabeth, 54
Fritham Moor, 52
Froshaug, 47
Frost, Terry, 151 et seq, 238

Gabo, Naum, 157
Gailor, Edie, 47, 57, 189
galleries, Bladon, 58
galleries, Lefevre, 55, 158
galleries, Leicester, 54
galleries, St Georges, 158
galleries, Tooth's, 54, 158
Gosse, Sir Edmund, 104
Graham, Sydney, 116
Graves, Beryl, 87 et seq.
Graves, Juan, 47
Graves, Robert, 9, 47, 86 et seq, 93 et seq, 104, 121 et seq
Grose, Irving, 157
Gwydir, 183 et seq, 197 et seq.

Hambly, Arthur, 29, 157
Hayle Towans, 18
Hedin, Sven, 30
Hepworth, Barbara, 238
Heron, Patrick, 243

Hilton, Roger, 151 et seq
Hitler, 20
Home Farm, 58-59, 64
Home Farm, sale of, 220
Hughes, David, 70-71

"I am Lazarus" 59, 65, 113 et seq.
Isle of Wight, 237 et seq.

Jacko, Microcephalic, 8
Jackson, Peter, 42, 54
John, Augustus, 9, 17, 20, 43, 45-47, 55, 58, 88, 105
"Jonah's Dream", 72, 122, 145, 155
Juanita, 20
Julie, 117 et seq.

Lanyon, Peter, 116 et seq, 184-185
Lapp hat, 73
Lascaux, visit to, 77
Lawrence, D H, 21, 39
Leach, Bernard, 55, 157
Lee, Cliff, 43-44, 81
Lee, Cliff & family, 135
Lee, family, 44-45
Lee, Ken, 44
Lemco, Tutti, 74
libel, action for, 120
Lorca, Garcia, 17
Lowndes, Alan, 215

Madonna, sculpture, 54
McArdle, Rev'd Tom, 194, 253
Milligan, Spike, 95
Minton, John, 73
Mitchell, Denis, 238, 243
Morris, Desmond, 224

INDEX

Morris, Guido, 47
Mousehole, 20
Moyne, Lord, 58
Muncaster, Martin (BBC), 60
Musselwhite Alan, 42

Nicholson, Ben, 55, 157
Nicholson, Sir William, 67

Otaka, 180 et seq

"Pieta" sculpture, 170
"Pride of the Peacock", 243

Radnor, Lord, 46
Redgrave, Bill, 215
Riding, Laura, 105
Ryan, Adrian, 54, 62

Saintes Maries, Les, 70
Salmon, Tom, 70
Segal, Hyman, 243
Shave Green, 47
Smith, Rosie, 8
St Eia, 15, 16
Starkie, Walter, 17
Stokes, Adrian, 39, 157
suicide, Helga's attempted, 117

Tambimuttu, 81
Tarka the Otter, 39
Tate Gallery, 157
Tehidy Woods, 25
Thomas, Dylan, 104
Trehane, Lady Elizabeth, 164, 215
Trehane, Richard & Elizabeth, 157 et seq.
Turk, Dr Frank, 29, 157

Vaughan Williams, R, 9, 17, 47, 102-103
Veal, Brixy, 47
Vesey-Fitzgerald, Brian, 43, 47

Walker, Polly, 62
Wallis, Alfred, 26, 29, 34, 118
Wallis, Susan, 56
Watson, Grant, 9, 38, 40, 61, 64-67, 73, 88, 181, 243
Watson, Katherine, 66-67
Wedding, Sven & Julie Berlin, 45, 138
Wells, Benny, 52
Wells, John, 19, 170, 238
West, Anthony, 94
West, Rebecca & family, 94
"White Goddess", 95
Williamson, Henry, 9, 39, 40, 61-64, 69
Wilson, Jack, 157
Winter, Bryan, 243
Wood, Manfri, 43
Wormleighton, Austin, 63-64
Wright, Bill, 22
Wynter, Bryan, 47, 116

Yeats, and Fanny Brawne, 105
Yorke, Rev'd Leslie, 160 et seq, 194

Zec, Donald, 21
Zennor Moor, 9
Zetterling, family, 74-75
Zetterling, Mai, 9, 15, 43, 70 et seq, 89-90, 115, 121, 135
Ziegler, Philip, 216 et seq.
Zoo, Children's, 115

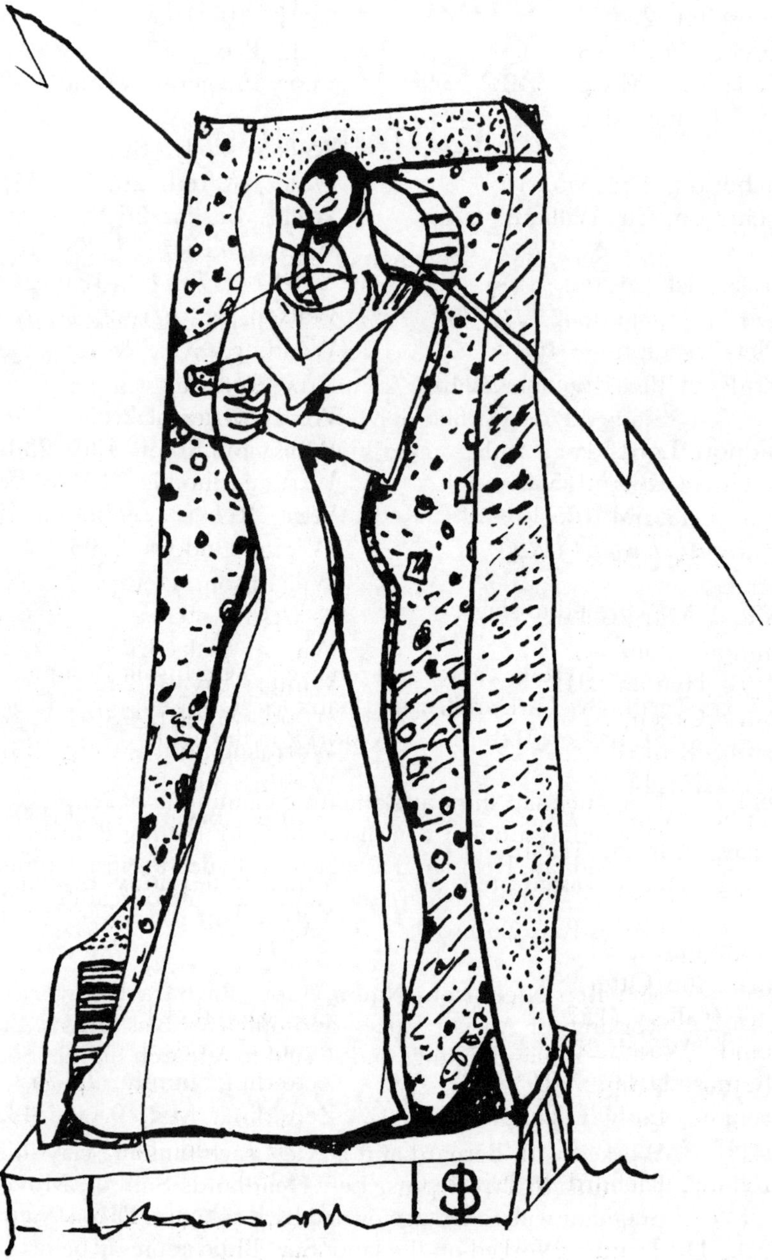

Publisher's Appendix 1
Sven Berlin –
A Chronology

1911   14th Sept. Born Sydenham, London.

1929   Published *"The Adagio Dancer"* Article in *"Dancing Times"*

1934   June–Dec. Stayed near Camborne, Cornwall with Dr. F. A. Turk, Studied Poetry, Philosophy, Biology, Oriental Art and Literature, Psychology and Comparative Religion. Studied at Camborne – Redruth Schools of Art under Arthur Hambley R.W.S. Lectured at Murdoch House, Redruth on *"The Sex Life in the Work of Thomas Hardy."*

1935   Returned to stage.

1938   Gave up stage career and returned to Cornwall. Resumed studies with Dr. Turk and Arthur Hambley. First sculptures. First visit to St. Ives on 16th March. Worked on the fields.

1939   First one man show at Camborne Community Centre, Cornwall. Worked as a boilerman in the Milk Marketing Board factory at Treswithian. Registered as a pacifist. Joined pacifist community in Devon. Worked as gardener and teacher at Headlands School, Carbis Bay, Cornwall.

1940   Met Ben Nicholson, Naum Gabo, Barbara Hepworth, when working for Adrian Stokes, and other St. Ives' artists. First saw Alfred Wallis paintings and started to research his life. Son born: Paul.

1941   Worked with Bernard and David Leach building clay driers and learning to throw pots. Left Headlands School. Moved with pregnant wife to cottage owned by Robin and Dicon Nance, near Zennor. Worked on the land. Saw British convoy being attacked by German planes and decided to join the army.

PUBLISHER'S APPENDIX 1 – A CHRONOLOGY

1942   Joined the St. Ives Society of Artists on the invitation of Borlase Smart. Death of Alfred Wallis, Moved into St. Peter's Studio, St. Ives. Wrote article on Wallis, Joined armed forces, leaving wife and family in St. Ives. Daughter born: Janet.

1943   Wallis article published in *"Horizon, a review of literature and art"* Vol. Vll, No. 37, Jan. 1943 pp 41–50, Military training in various parts of U. K. during which the book on Wallis was written.

1944   Signed contract for Wallis book with Poetry London on D-Day. Took part in the invasion of France as Forward Observer for the Royal Artillery and in Normandy, Belgium and Holland. During this time of continuous action I took notes and made drawings for book *"I am Lazarus"*. Poem "Hill 312" published in *"Modern Reading"* Moore, R (ed).

1945   Discharged from the army on V. E. Day. Returned to St. Ives. Took up residence in *"The Tower"* on the island. Met John Wells, Peter Lanyon, W.S. Graham, Bryan Wynter, Guido Morris and Denis and Endell Mitchell. Designed dust jacket for Henry Miller *"Sunday after the War"* Editions Poetry, London. Exhibited at Redfern Gallery, London in mixed shows.

1946   Terry Frost appeared in St. Ives whom he helped and advised. Many new arrivals in St. Ives. Formed the Crypt Group with Lanyon, Wells, Wynter and Guido Morris and had first show. First one man London show at Lefevre Gallery. Published Manifesto for this show (printed by Guido Morris).

1947   Second Crypt Show. First one man show at Downing's Bookshop, St. Ives. and Mid-Day Studio, Manchester. Exhibited in mixed show *"Artists of Fame and Promise"* Leicester Gallery, London, BBC broadcast, Plymouth *"My Spectre Around Me"*. Illustrated Pollard, Peggy *"Cornwall"* Paul Elek. Met Adrian Ryan, Mary Jewels and Augustus John,

1948   One man show at St. George's Gallery, London and Downing's Bookshop. Third and last Crypt Show. Published *"Some aspects of Creative Art in Cornwall"* Facet Magazine, Bristol. Designed dust jacket for Gogol "Overcoat" Eyre and Spottiswode, London. Met Henry Moore, and Epstein.

PUBLISHER'S APPENDIX – A CHRONOLOGY

1949   Publication of book *"Alfred Wallis, Primitive"* Nicholson and Watson, London and articles in *"Cornish Review"* (ed. Denys Val Baker) *"My World as a Sculptor"* No. 1. Spring. pp 55–61. *"Books of the Quarter"* a review of *"The White Threshold"* by W. S. Graham, No. 2. Summer. pp 95–96. Founder member of The Penwith Society of Arts.

1950   Tower compulsorily purchased by local council. Moved to Cripplesease, near St Ives. Learned to cut granite. Produced first granite sculpture and entered it in Festival of Britain Competition for Sculpture in Cornwall. Awarded second prize. Hepworth first esigned membership of Penwith Society. One man show at Castle Inn Gallery, St. Ives. Article published in *"Cornish Review"* entitled *"Death by Fire"* No. 6. Winter, pp 38–42 plus front cover illustration. Frontispiece drawing for Levine, Norman *"The Tight-Rope Walker"* Totem Press, London. During this period took part in the Arts Council and British Council travelling exhibition of contemporary art.

1951–52   One man show at Downing's Bookshop. House burnt down.

1953   Son born: Jasper. Left Cornwall with second wife; travelled by horse-drawn caravan to New Forest. Exhibited in mixed show *"Important Contemporaries"* Tooths Gallery, London. Moved from a field owned by Edie Gailor, at Brickiln, near Robins Bush, to Home Farm (see text) Emery Down, near Lyndhurst.

1954   Exhibited in "Important Contemporaries" Tooths Gallery (with Epstein).

1955   Tooths Gallery (with Epstein and Frink). One man show at the Fox and Hounds Gallery, Lyndhurst, Hants. Augustus John bought a painting.

1956   Exhibited at the Bladon Gallery, Hurstbourne Tarrant. Show opened by Augustus John and Lord Moyne.

1958   One man show at Mailman's Gallery, Lyndhurst. White Buck sculpture carved on site at Hythe, near Southampton. BBC T. V. documentary *"Casting a Bronze"* produced by Michael Croucher. Made film with Mai Zetterling the Gypsies.

PUBLISHER'S APPENDIX 1 – A CHRONOLOGY

1959   The Ovar Museum, Portugal acquired painting of Gypsy Woman.

1960   A drawing for article published in *"The New Forest"* entitled *"The Gypsies of the New Forest"* pp 38–52. Galley Press, London. BBC T. V. Documentary *"A Portrait in Time"* Produced and Directed by John Boorman.

1961   Book *"I am Lazarus"* published. The Galley Press. One man show at Aldine House, London. Rain God cast for Wright Rains, Ringwood, Hants.

1962   Publication of *"The Dark Monarch; a Portrait from within"* Galley Press. London Published on 7th Sept. and withdrawn on 16th Sept. (see additional note). Cartoon in *"Southern Evening Echo"* 16th May. *"!Sven's Back!"*.

1963   One man show at Maye's Gallery, Southampton.

1964   Publication of *"Jonah's Dream, a Meditation on Fishing"* Phoenix House, London. BBC broadcast on *"Jonah's Dream"* with Maurice Wiggin. Four poems and one article published Aug–Dec, in Western Mail Literary Supplement.

1965   One man show at Creative Art Patrons, London. Mother and Child acquired by Bowring Building, London. Six poems and four articles published March–Dec. in Western Mail Literary Supplement. Two extracts from *"Jonah's Dream"* published in; Moore J C; *"Best Fishing Stories"* Faber. London. *"Granite Mother and Child"* acquired by Spastics Centre, Chertsey.

1966   One man shows at Bladon Gallery, Hants. Bronzes and drawings at Emery Down Workshops and Studios. Five articles published Feb–Oct. in Western Mail Literary Supplement. Illustrated Davis P. D. C. and Dent A. A. *"Animals that changed the World"* Phoenix House, London.

1967   Illustrated Grant Watson, E. L. *"Animals in Splendour"* John Baker, London. Poem *"Boy with a Kite"* published in Parker, D. *"Poetry Review"* London, BBC T. V. documentary *"New Forest"* written and narrated by S. B. Produced by Michael Croucher. One man show at Ogilvy and Mathers, London. Sponsored by Sir Richard and Lady Trehane.

1968   One man shows at Ross-Lawson Gallery, Mayfair and Pace Gallery, Houston Texas.

1969   Painted the Creation Cycle of paintings. One man show at Hamwic Gallery, Southampton and mixed show at Beaulieu Gallery, Beaulieu, Hants.

1970   One man show at Poole College Festival of Arts, Article entitled *"The Lotus Eaters"* published in *"Hampshire, The County Magazine"*. Vol. 10. No. 12. Oct. pp 46-47, BBC TV Omnibus production. *"Shapes in the Wilderness"* produced by Tristram Powell. Moved to Isle of Wight, Merlin Cottage, Parkhurst Forest, near Cowes.

1971   Publication of *"Dromengro: Man of the Road"* Collins, London. Article entitled *"The Silent Terminus"* Hampshire County Magazine Vol. 11. No. 8. June pp 24-25.

1972   Publication of *"Pride of the Peacock: The Evolution of an Artist"* Collins. London.

1973   Contribution of *"Tree Full of Stars"* (from Dromengo) to Baker, Denys Val (ed) *"Stories of Country Life"* William Kimber, London. Poole College acquired *"The Creation"* cycle of paintings. Painted Stations of the Cross cycle of large paintings.

1974   Poole College acquired "Falcon" sculpture in porphyry.

1977   Article entitled *"The Stone that would be King"* published in *"Irish Post"* 8th Oct. Poole College acquired *"Madonna and Child"* sculpture in alabaster. Exhibited at New Art Centre, London *"Cornwall 1945-55"*. Sculpture *"Horses from the Sea"* for Milk Marketing Board (commissioned by Sir Richard Trehane).

1978   Publication of *"Amergin: an Enigma of the Forest"* David and Charles, Newton Abbot. BBC TV film *"Augustus John"* with Holdry, D. Produced by Tom Coleany.

PUBLISHER'S APPENDIX 1 – A CHRONOLOGY

1979   Lord Weymouth paintings acquired for Wessex Collection.

1980   One man show at Higher Gaunt's House, Wimborne, Dorset. Sir Richard Glyn Collection acquired *"Irish King"* sculpture. Bernard Leach: A Memory, for Takashi Tanahashi, Japan. Original manuscript of *"Jonah's Dream"* and letter to Alfred Wallis and S. B. from Ben Nicholson acquired by the Victoria and Albert Museum, London.

1981   Publication of *"Sven Berlin: An Artist and his Work"* Wimborne Bookshop, Hoade. One man show at Wimborne Bookshop. Opened by Lady Trehane and Elizabeth ????

1982   Tate Archives acquire drawing of Guido Morris 1945. One man show at Wills Lane Gallery, St. Ives September Festival. Also produced drawing for poster *"Sven's back"*. Readings from books and poems and talk on sculpting a swan at St. Ives School of Painting.

1983   Shows at New Art Centre, London. Drawings acquired by the British Museum and Victoria and Albert Museum.

1984   Exhibited at Liverpool Garden and Sculpture Festival. Madonna Vandalised at Poole.

1985   Exhibited at Tate Gallery exhibition "St. Ives 1939-64" February-April. Exhibited at Parkin Gallery, London. Publication of extract from *"Jonah's Dream"* in *"Magic Wheel"* by Profumo, David and Swift, Graham, Heineman Picador.

1986   Exhibited at Yorkshire Sculpture Garden, Wakefield. Poem *"Joke Grim"* published in *"Cornish Scene"* April–May.

1989   Exhibited at Belgrave Gallery, London and wrote introduction.

1991   Exhibited *"Garden Sculpture"* Dean's Court, Wimborne.

1992   Exhibited at Belgrave Gallery (wrote introduction) and Royal West of England Academy (wrote introduction). Alfred Wallis book reprinted (Redcliffe Press), Article in St. Ives Times *"Man in Sackcloth"* and a poem. *"Notes on Drawing"* Book Gallery, St. Ives.

PUBLISHER'S APPENDIX – A CHRONOLOGY

1993   Exhibited at Dean's Court, Wimborne *"Garden Sculpture"*. Publication of poem "Death of a sculptor" in St. Ives Times.

1994   Publication of autosvenography *"Coat of Many Colours"* Redcliffe Press, Bristol. Exhibition of sculpture *"Golden Girl"* and *"Man with Children"* Tate Gallery, St. Ives.

1995   Exhibited at Dean's Court *"Garden Sculpture"* and Russell-Cotes Museum, Bournemouth Festival *"Creation cycle of paintings and sculptures"*. Published article on Alfred Wallis in Arts Review, article V E and V J Day in St. Ives Times, drawings for *"The Ancient Mariner"* Odyssey Press and VIRGO IN EXILE.

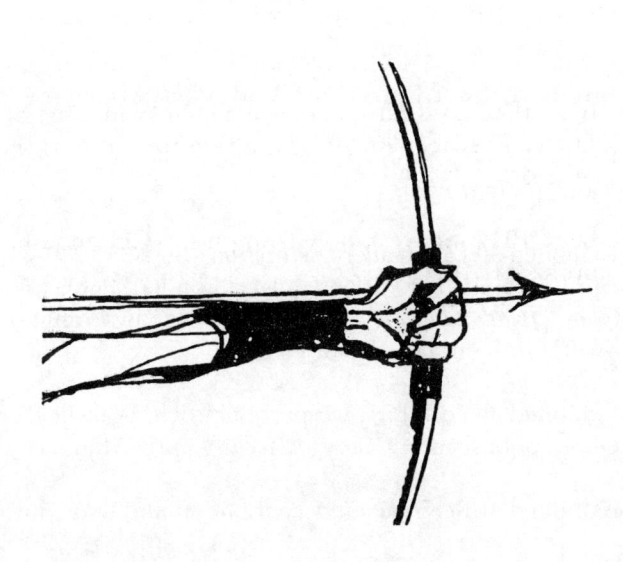

PUBLISHER'S APPENDIX 1 – A CHRONOLOGY

PERSONALIA

Married: i)   Helga (dec'd)
          ii) Juanita ("Ishtar")
          iii) Julie

Juanita (born 1925), first married at age 16, was herself both artist and author, (as Juanita Casey), her most recent book being *"The Horse of Selene"* (1986). Currently living in Okehampton, Devon (UK).

CHILDREN

Jasper born 1953 (in St Ives), now an artist in New Zealand, with family.

Paul   born 1940 (in Redruth), now living in Wimborne St Giles, U. K. Lecturer on philosophy and comparative religion. m. 2d.

Janet   born 1942 (St Ives), now living near. Charmouth, sculptor in bronze. 1s,1d.

Publisher's Appendix 2
The Dark Monarch

The author himself describes in the text, the saga which followed publication of "The Dark Monarch". Certain additional comments are offered here. In the first place, though the publishers of that book doubtless did the best they could, the exercise of recalling all printed copies as ordered by the Courts, was far from successful. Twenty years later, a number of Public Libraries around the UK still listed the title among their holdings and perhaps still do. Numerous copies are still held privately, and are occasionally offered for sale, mainly by specialist dealers such as the St Ives Book Gallery. The publishers of this volume are in possession of an original typescript and the St Ives Book Gallery have or had other material relating to the work.

Most of Sven Berlin's many friends would readily testify to the enormous damage, both financial and psychological, the episode inflicted on him. Even today, the scars are apparent. A lesser man would have been felled by the multiple blows. Sven's survival and the continuing virtuosity and astonishing breadth of his output are a testimony to his many great inner strengths. A speculation as to what might otherwise have been, is almost irresistible. Those who so petulantly wrought such damage, some of them now dead, must live with their consciences as to what they did. The moral climate in which we live, changes over time. Read today, "Dark Monarch" comes across mainly as boisterous good humour, coupled with a mordant insight into the characters of those (see below) it is said to describe. It is the opinion not only of the writer (as a layman) but also of those legally qualified, that its content would not jeopardise its publication today. One has to read it very closely indeed to discern the allegedly offensive passages.

There are those in the "Art World" who believe that the Establishment continues to this day, to exact its revenge for the irreverent comments in *"Dark Monarch"* describing some of the best-known artists in St Ives. The writer makes no comment beyond saying that, in the end, History will have its way.

PUBLISHER'S APPENDIX 2

Finally, let it be quite clear that Sven Berlin, ever since the legal proceedings, has stoutly refused to admit that *Dark Monarch* is in any way a *"roman a clef"*, for all that the success of the legal action argues to the contrary. In and around St Ives, however, there are various written and oral "lists" and annotated copies of "Dark Monarch". It was judged that, with passage of time, there was a danger that some of this material might be lost and the decision was made to set something on record. There follows below what is believed to be the first ever published "key", based on recent research. In some cases, more than one identity has been suggested, in others it is felt the character in question is a composite of more than one person. Clues to some identities are found in Vol. 1 "Coat of Many Colours".

Those who took legal action are believed to have been Arthur Caddick, a bibulous barrister, notoriously litigious by nature who alleged the book portrayed him as a heroin addict (which no-one suggested he was). Also his wife Peggy, Mabel Lethbridge and Ms Vivien Morris (previously Thomas).

After so much pain, it would have been invidious for the publishers to seek to involve Sven Berlin himself in this exercise and it was felt right to insulate him from it. The list is therefore a distillation from St Ives "folk-lore" and in no way does it carry an "imprimatur". At a time of his own choosing, Sven Berlin may or may not decide to comment, as indeed may others.

A.T.K.

PEOPLE

Name in D.M.	S.B's description	IDENTIFIED AS
MARK ABBEY	Ex doctor and friend lives on Scilly Isles. and paints.	JOHN WELLS b.1907 left Scillies 1945 founded Anchor Studio in Newlyn. Artist.
ROGER MOSS	Friend of S.B. Tall, elegant, charming, takes benzedrine. Cottage on Penbeagle Carn = CARN COTTAGE near Zennor	BRYAN WYNTER 1915–1975 Artist.

PUBLISHER'S APPENDIX 2

Name in D.M.	S.B's description	IDENTIFIED AS
LIONEL & LINDSAY STRAUSS	Twins collect early cinema equipment.	THE BARNES FAMILY Founders of Barnes Museum of Photography, St. Ives now closed.
CAMILLA GOLD-STRAUSS	Their sister blonde, petite, lively, and attractive. Lives in cottage on Wharf. Separated from husband.	Joan, married to a Mr Sachi (Saki) (Solly Gold in (D M)).
HARRY GUMTREE	Cartoonist	HARRY ROUNTREE 1878–1950
PETROUCHKA	Toymaker, white face, large heifers' eyes.	SUSAN LETHBRIDGE ex-wife of Bryan Wynter. Toyshop called "The Toy Trumpet in the Digey. (now the "Old Bakehouse".)
ALBERT MANTIS	White hair, walrus moustache also called "praying mantis" because of his religious turn of mind.	BERNARD LEACH 1887–1979 Potter.
HYWEL THOMAS	Publican of the "Fort" = CASTLE INN Tall man with black and red colouring (looks like S.B)	ENDELL MITCHELL 1906–1991?

PUBLISHER'S APPENDIX 2

Name in D.M.	S.B's description	IDENTIFIED AS
DAI THOMAS	Brother of Hywel. Friends of Dylan Thomas. Enormous man, curly hair, looks like Harpo Marx	DENIS MITCHELL 1912–1993 Sculptor (worked with Barbara Hepworth)
CHRISTOPHER WOOD	Painter on Scillies. Friend of Mark Abbey (John Wells).	CHRISTOPHER WOOD 1901–1930, Artist Also known as "Kit", committed suicide. Went on walking tour with Ben Nicholson & "discovered" Alfred Wallis
LORENZO SMITH	Printer of Hebrew books, small.	GUIDO MORRIS 1910–1980 Owner of Latin Press. Worked as London Underground guard from 1956–1975.
GRETA		Mrs Helga Berlin (dec'd). Her daughter was Greta
JULIAN & JILL	S.B.'s children	Paul and Janet.
DAVID QUOIT	Miner's son, public school, artist, rich Cornishman.	PETER LANYON 1918–1964 artist. Killed in gliding accident. n.b. – ill feeling towards S.B. over his biography of Alfred Wallis – felt a local Cornishman should have written it.

PUBLISHER'S APPENDIX 2

Name in D.M.	S.B's description	IDENTIFIED AS
DIANA CORACLE	Sculptress	BARBARA HEPWORTH 1903–1975
SIR STANISLAS ROBINSON	Abstract painter, divorced from Diana ("Delphic") Coracle	BEN NICHOLSON 1894–1982 Artist (ex husband Barbara Hepworth)
BINGHAM-HART		BORLASE SMART 1881–1947 Artist. Leader of the "traditionalist" school at time of schism
MAGGIE BENDIX	harsh, foul-mouthed black eye patch, hooked arm, pet spider called Charlie	MABEL LETHBRIDGE MBE, (award for gallantry in London munitions factory)
EDWARD BROWN	Ex art teacher from Dulwich	LEONARD FULLER 1891–1973 Founded St. Ives school of Painting 1938.
PAT RAWLINGS	Dressed in male clothes. Friend of S.B.	MISS PAT CHAMBERS Patron and Friend of S.B. (this attrib. contested)
DADDY LONGLEGS	Owner of cafe "Brass Warming Pan" Very small and rich. Big pipe and baggy beret.	'Pop' IVOR SHORT owner of "Copper Kettle".
TOM	Landlord of the Sloop	PHIL ROGERS (19??–19??)
VI GANNET	Cornish, divorced. Lived in Gaza Flats.	Identity not disclosed for legal reasons

PUBLISHER'S APPENDIX 2

Name in D.M.	S.B's description	IDENTIFIED AS
LILITH MORGAN	Irish girlfriend ill with TB in Tehidy hospital.	MS JACKIE MORAN Married but separated from Victor Bramley (artist). Lives in Nancledra
ELDRED HADDOCK	Poet, popeyes, large man, drinks.	ARTHUR CADDICK poet born Yorks. Lived near St. Ives at Nancledra from 1945–1981
CHARON	Ferryman called John.	TOM TUCKER – see "Coat" potman had stable next to S.B's studio now public toilets. (this character thought to be a composite)
JAMIE GREENOCK	Deaf poet	JOHN FAIRFAX - deaf and dumb poet. or: W S GRAHAM, good friend to S B.

OTHER CHARACTERS (SOME UNCERTAIN)

Name in D.M.	S.B's description	IDENTIFIED AS
John Hoskin and Arabella his wife	Landlord of Cuckoo Inn	LANDLORD OF HALSETOWN INN Engine Inn = Tom Humphreys??
Skaparios (Octopus) Cassio	Cretan, Jewish, works in Copper Kettle. Bad painter. Wife in London. Friend of Brian Wynter.	"AIR-FORCE TEXAS" waiter at Porthminster Hotel

PUBLISHER'S APPENDIX 2

Name in D.M.	S.B's description	IDENTIFIED AS
Clarrisa Harlow	???	???
Ffrederika Ffirth-Fforth	Underwater painter. Lives with Fuschia Chimes in Gaza Flats.	WILHEMINA BARNS-GRAHAM 1912–
Sarah Barclay	Old lady – once kept pub in Islington. Lives in Gaza Flats.	MRS LLOYD
Tessa Arbroath	Blue Eyes	NESSIE GRAHAM wife of. W.S.G
Mrs Pequod	Manageress of Leviathan looked like Aga Khan, large cod's-fish mouth, dark glasses silver hair. Buys SB's painting for hotel lounge.	MRS MABEL PERKIN
Christof Frazer	Painter, shiny face, bulbous forehead, jutting lower lip, thick neck – madman?	CHRISTOPHER FOSTER? FROSHAUG?
Fuschia Chimes	Spinster painter – Secured Chapel on Island for nation. Painter	MISOME PEILE 1907–1989
Paddy	Barman of Sloop (red beard)	
Fred Canute	Regulars at the sloop	FRED BOTTOMLEY
Wee Willie Wilner	Regulars at the sloop	WILLIE STEVENS
Micky the Admiral	Regulars at the sloop	MICKY FARRELL
Count of Wong Fu		"WINKLES" RICHARDS

275

PUBLISHER'S APPENDIX 2

Name in D.M.	S.B's description	IDENTIFIED AS
Ada Polkinghorn	Evacuee from Portsmouth has epileptic, cross-eyed son – Ephraim	
Jonathan Lovelace	Reaches out for imaginary objects.	
Polly Mountain (Fat Pol)	Homosexual husband – Simon	
Dr Krishna Jones	Fake doctor	
Castellano	Wears Japanese armour Cornish boy of PortuguesE Descent.	RICHARD CARE co-worker in local hardware shop.
Father Flannigan	R C priest	FATHER AUSTIN DELANEY
Brandy Twist	Tall, vermillion head.	
Annabella Moorland	Hairy tweeds, brogue shoes.	ISOBEL HEATH? 1908–1989 SHEARER ARMSTRONG? 1894–1984 MISS MOORSHEAD (Lady Gerrity)?
Mr & Mrs Mountain		MOLLY & DICK TREVORROW
Morgan Fountain		MAURICE HILL *or:* GEORGE MANNING-SAUNDERS

PUBLISHER'S APPENDIX 2

PLACES

Name in D.M.	S.B's description	IDENTIFIED AS
HILL OF CUCKOOS	View of St. Michaels Mt. to South.	TRENCROM HILL? VORVAS HILL? TRINK HILL?
PENZION (Marazion)		PENZANCE
CUCKOO		ST. IVES
MACKEREL ST		FISH ST, ST IVES
POOP	Corner of Mackerel St (FISH ST) haunt of artists.	SLOOP INN
CUCKOO INN		ENGINE INN, NANCLEDRA
MANTIS POTS	Built by Oriental friend	BERNARD LEACH POTTERY (Shojii Hamada instructed B-L)
WOOD-WORKSHOP (HARRY FINCH)		ROBIN & DICON NANCE – Woodworkers & Cornish Bards
LEVIATHAN HOTEL		TREGENNA CASTLE HOTEL
TOWER	S.B's studio on the Island behind Porthgwidden beach	Public lavatory built on site of yard. Tower still stands.
HYPERION LIGHT		LIGHTHOUSE ON GODREVY ISLAND

277

PUBLISHER'S APPENDIX 2

Name in D.M.	S.B's description	IDENTIFIED AS
FORT	Pub in High St.	CASTLE INN
MERLIN BEACH	Cemetery above	PORTHMEOR BEACH
HALF MOON BEACH		PORTHGWIDDEN BEACH
LINOLEUM CITY	Old fishermens huts etc on southside of Porthgwidden beach So called by Bryan Wynter	
SEBASTOPOL		THE MALAKOFF
SMITHSON'S PIER		SMEATON'S PIER
FOXHOLE		MOUSEHOLE
ST. THERESA'S ISLAND		ST. MARYS (Scillies)
ST. ELMO'S	Pension run by Lewis Carroll's White Rabbit. Free meals in exchange for sculpture.	ST CHRISTOPHER'S Run by Phillip & Sally Keeley. Facing Porthmeor Beach. Later owned by Denys Val Baker
CROW'S NEST	First point on mainland from the Island	CARNCROWS – netloft overlooking Porthgwidden beach. (Studio of Guido Morris) On the Wastrel
CARTHARSIS BAY	Home of Quoit	CARBIS BAY
ST. JUSTIN		ST JUST

Name in D.M.	S.B's description	IDENTIFIED AS
MOWHAY	Street in St Ives run from fields at back of town to harbour	BACK ROAD, WEST & EAST or Area above Tate Gallery, "The Meadow"
BOX FACTORY		Actual place. Was sited just below the Island. Bought in 1954 by local firm of builders and seven studios built.
KINGS HEAD/ ARMS	Pub	QUEENS HOTEL (NOW TAVERN) In High St opposite Lanham's (main suppliers of artists' materials).
GIRLON WEAVERS	Run by two ladies	OWNED BY FLORENCE L WELCH? Weaving shop on Wharf. Three looms. Employed young Cornish girls to help.
GIANT'S HEAD	At end of Merlin Beach	MAN'S HEAD
GAZA FLATS	Built 1930's	SUNNYSIDE FLATS above Commando Garage – (now shop).
BRASS WARMING PAN		COPPER KETTLE St Ives Restaurant.
PENBEAGLE CARN		ZENNOR CARN Eagle's Nest?
THE CASTLE – ISLAND		ST MICHAEL'S MOUNT

PUBLISHER'S APPENDIX 2

Name in D.M.	S.B's description	IDENTIFIED AS
THE EYRIE		EAGLE'S NEST, ZENNOR?
LAPP RESTAURANT		GAY VIKING, ST IVES
CIVET HILL COTTAGE		SKIDDEN HILL?

"Mother and Child"
height 12", Granite, 1947
(One of the Author's first sculptures)

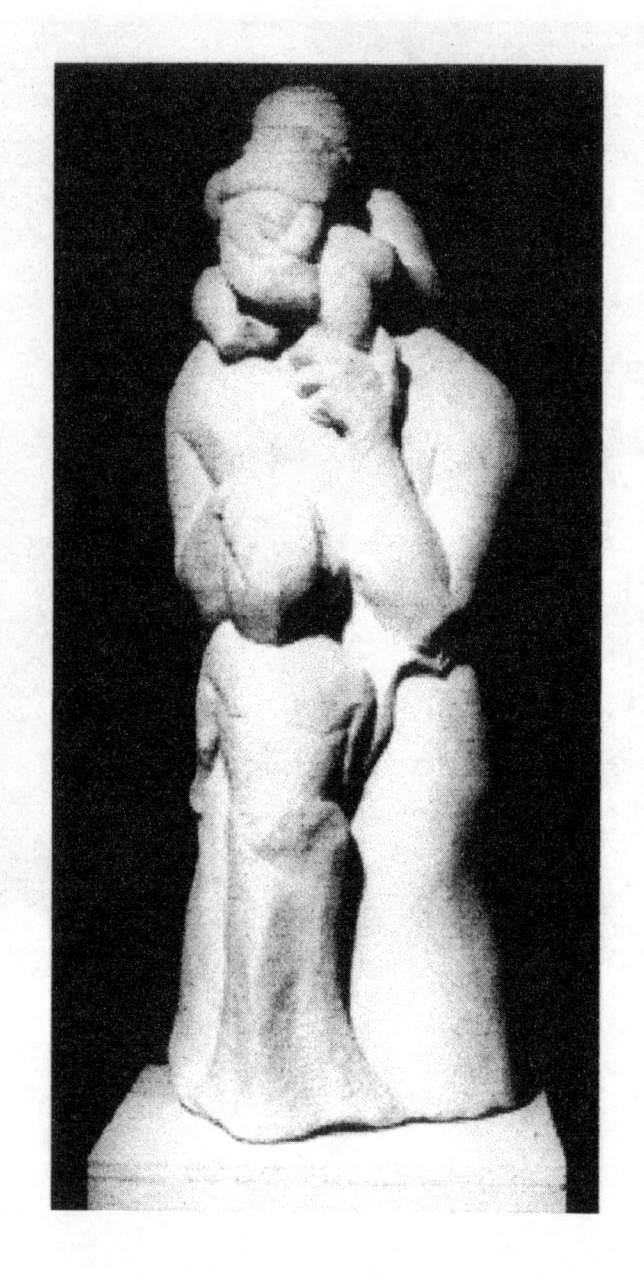

"Man with Children"
height 12", Carrara marble 1948

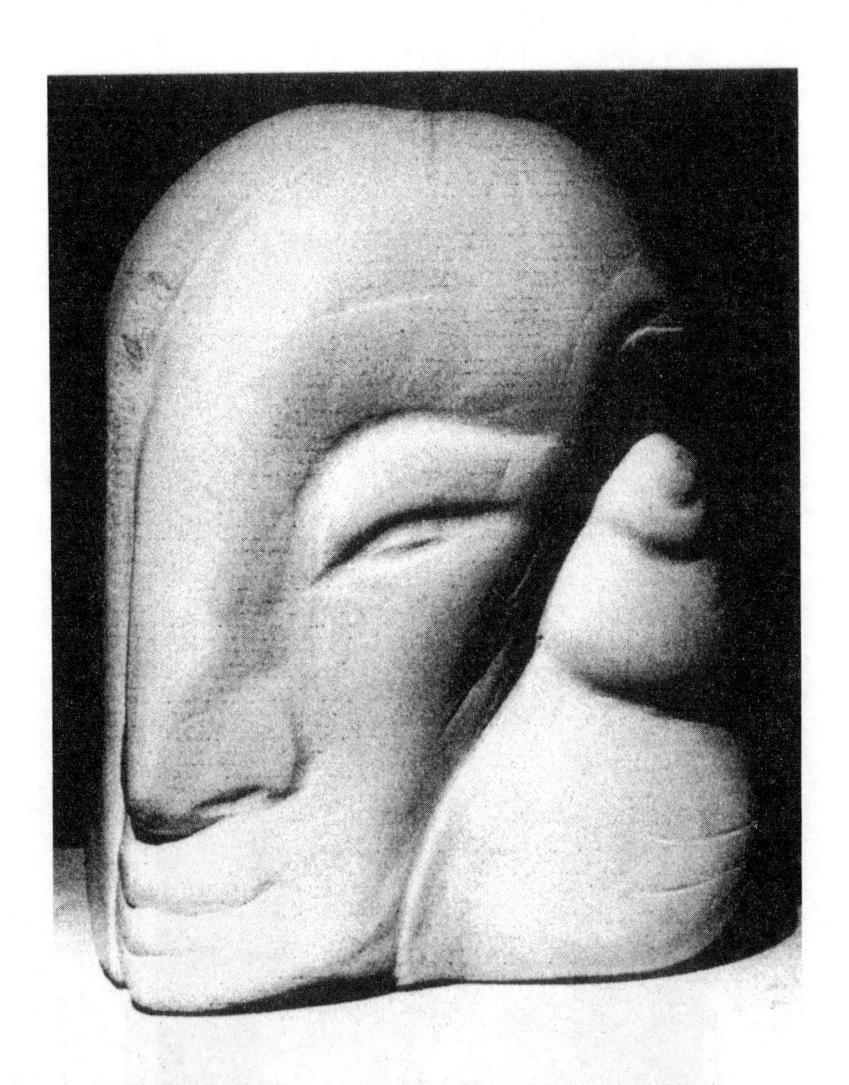

"Woman with a Shell"
height 12", Greek marble 1982

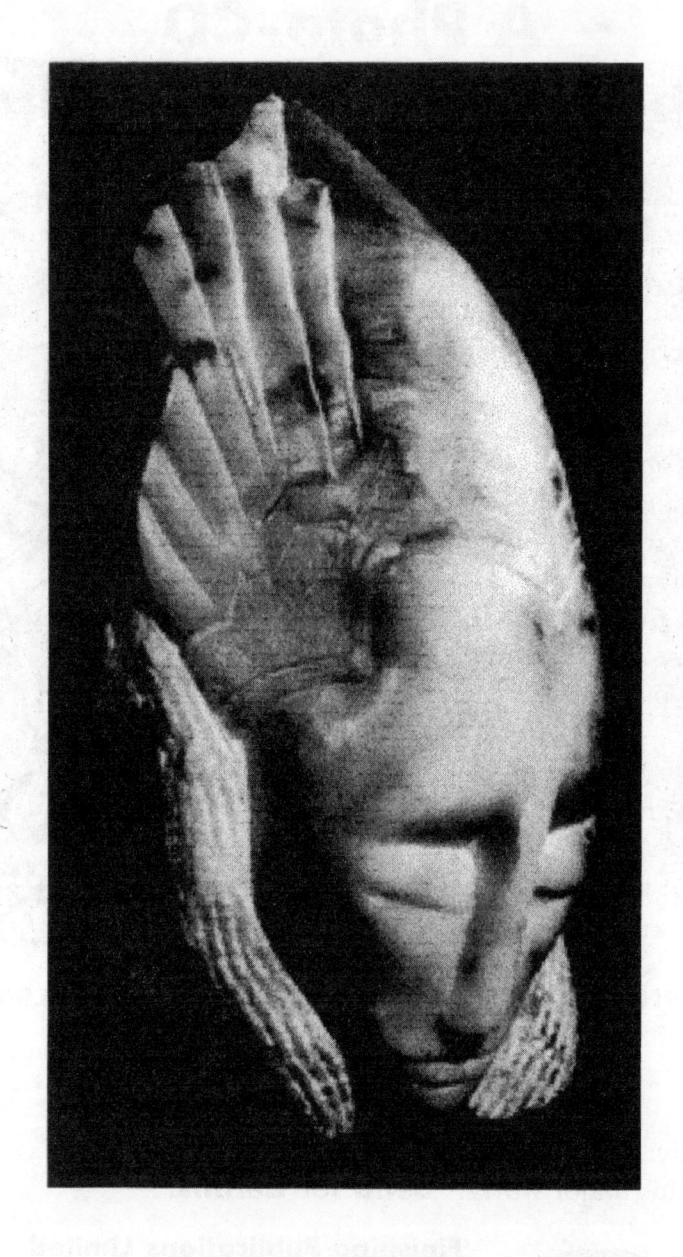

"Woman with feathered Headdress"
Egyptian Greenstone, 13". Carved in St. Ives, 1950

A Photo-CD
"The Best of Sven Berlin"

A Photo-CD with 100 images of the paintings, drawings and sculpture of this most versatile artist, ranging from his early period in St Ives where he was associated with famous artists, including Barbara Hepworth, Bernard Leach, Peter Lanyon through to his later New Forest period and his memorable religious and gypsy portrayals.

"The Best of Sven Berlin" Photo-CD runs on IBM PCs or Apple Macs. It comes complete with viewing software which allows images to be studied at any magnification. Images can be printed on most colour printers, and exported to other graphics packages for manipulation.

This unique collection is recommended for all with an interest in 20th century sculpture and graphic arts, not least for those with an interest in natural history.

PRICE: £65.00 + VAT (£76.38) – US $110.00

And ALSO AVAILABLE

An archival collection of the artist's work on 4 Photo-CD's covering most of his major works. **Send for details.**

Finishing Publications Limited,
PO Box 70, Stevenage, Herts SG1 4BL, UK
Tel: (01438) 745115. Telefax: (01438) 364536

email: 101554,303 (Compuserve)   *or:*   101554.303@compuserve.com